"If you have ever been a few seconds too late with a comeback, buy Reiss."

- *Playboy Magazine*

Have someone read this to you while you color in it, thanks,

Ted Reiss

No type described in this book is a specific person.

But, any relationship between the characters in this book and losers who are living or dead is purely intentional.

This book is only designed for an individual's private amusement.

Cover design by Frank Doyle, illustration by Ron Winnick, and lettering by Larry Puppo.

Copyright 1993 By Fred Reiss

All rights reserved, including the right to reproduce this book or portions thereof in any form whatsoever.

For information address Fred Reiss Comedy Productions, P.O. Box 3523, Santa Cruz, Ca. 95062

ISBN: 0-9623869-9-5

First semi-historic printing, August 1994

Insult And *Live!*

The ultimate abuser-friendly guide.

by

Fred Reiss

lavishly illustrated* with the wondrously sick pen of Ron Winnick

*With a few appearances by thirty-year old cartoonist Dan "Thag" Wedeking.

William Randolph Hearst said, "If you have one friend consider yourself a rich man." The following people are my friends, but I feel if Hearst knew them, he'd still rather keep his castle on San Simeon, his money, art collection, and his B-movie girl mistress. So, if you want to blame someone for this book, blame this list of people, because without their friendship I wouldn't exist.

My Dad
Who has taught me more about life than anyone.

My mother, Nana, two sisters, and brother
Who pray I succeed so I can pay them back the money I owe them.

Laurie Roberts
Who has given me complete devotion in exchange for sexual favors.

Ron Winnick
Who generously donated his art in a desperate effort to live through me.

Santa Cruz'n Soul Surfers
The 38th parallellers under the illusion their lifestyle has a meaning: Wayne "the Fader" Kenny, Pat "Pumpkinhead" Farley, Randi "Big Red Express" Fishel, Hal Stanger, George "Mr. Moto" Dumas, Al Baggett, Mike "Sea Hunt" Eaton, Hap Jacobs, Denny Aaberg, Mike "use The Club" Medina, Jeff Maldonado, Ranger, Frances "da Champ" Farley, Brandee Allen, surf shop rats Garrett and Josh.

Those who haven't aged well and can only hope their children will overshadow their accomplishments
Bob Moseley, Ken "Makes me laugh makes me cry" Dixon, Lee Yarosh, Joe Militano, Dave Dunleavy, John "Why leave there's beer here?" Kosowatz, Mikel and Janet Herington, Jack "Tooze" Berg, Steve Ide, Frank "Blind Lemon" Hadley, William "Omoo" Brown, David Feldman, Bill Mann, Tree, Larry "Bubbles" Brown, Mike Rivera, Dan Wedeking, Bob "Hillbilly From Space" Rubin, Dana Jang, Frank "White men can dunk" Doyle, Ted Kopulus, Stretch "Surf Drums" Reidle, Candy Chamberlin, Marty Wright, Frank Szivos, Dan "The Bed and Breakfast Titan" Floyd and family, Dr. Louis Filler, Bill "19th Hole" Nastri, Bobby "Binghead" Ackerly, Jennifer "Buns" Schraeder, Lamont and Tenelli, Billy Vega, Kit Lee, Constance "Ialsoam" Harrigan, Dennis Erectus, Richard Orr, Freehold N.J. high school teacher Leonard Alpert, and even Alex Bennett.

Insult And *Live!*
Table of Contents

Introduction To The World Of Fred..............1

Top One Hundred Losers Who *Must* Be Insulted......17

Loser Basics................35

Loser Review................85

Basic Losers................95

Pile-driving Stud Muffins
and Macho Nerds................155

Giving it Hard to Hostile Femmos................225

Blowing out Superior Snotheads................269

Cutting off Blitzed Boozers
and Substance Abusers................345

Cutting Down Vanity Heads
and Ugly Dinks................373

Heckling Hack Comedians................405

Losers You should *Never* Insult................433

The Final Solution................439

How Losers will Deny their Similarity
to the Jerks Described in this Book................447

If you can read this, you're too close.

Introduction to
The World Of Fred

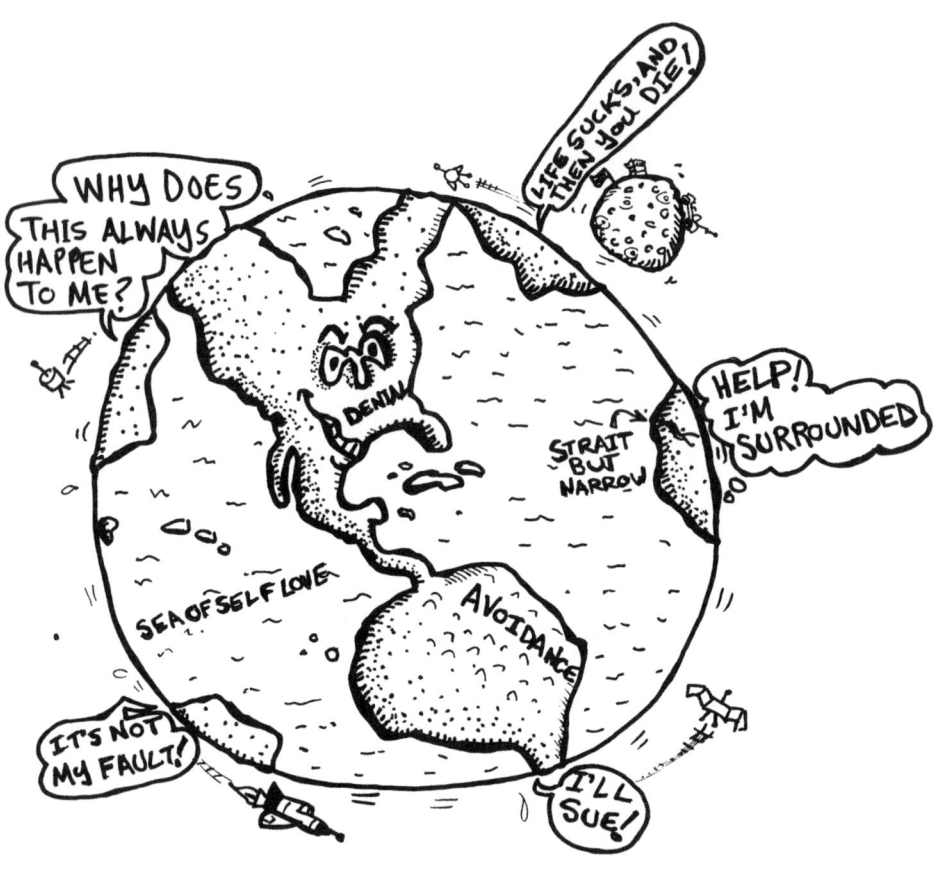

The World Of Fred is filled with losers who choose to ruin your life rather than face responsibility for their problems.

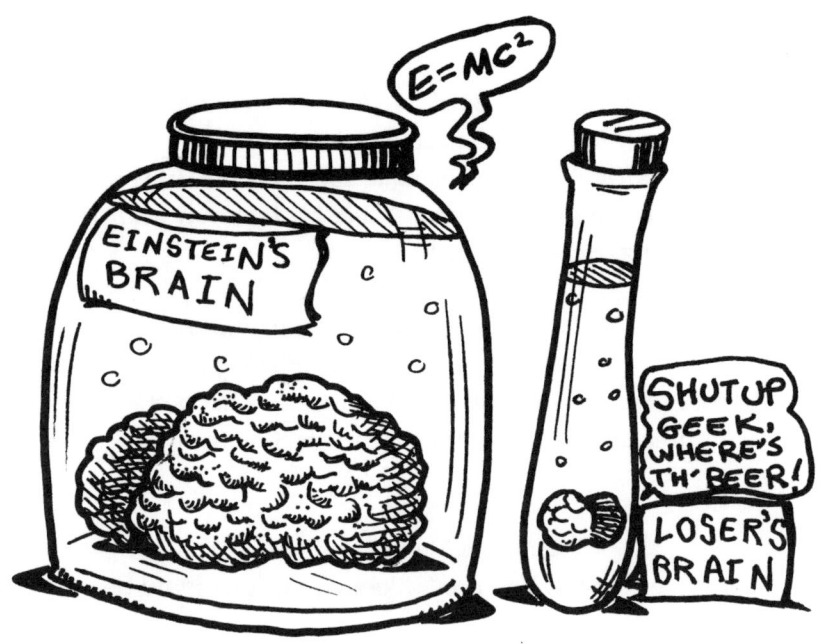

Why you need this book to survive in the World of Fred

You're annoyed by a total loser, but can't think of an insult to say to them. Hours later, when you finally concoct a perfect cut down, your opportunity is gone.

Now, wouldn't you give anything to change what you didn't say into what you should have said? Of course you would.

That's why *Insult And Live!* is the solution to your first-strike capability problem. It teaches you to spot and insult the self-centered morons who intentionally make your life miserable. Once you've mastered this abuser-friendly art, a loser won't be able to ruin your day, and you'll be able to ruin theirs.

The following is a before-and-after example of how this book will help you...

Situation:
The Slob On The Beach

*(Scene: Summertime. The Beach. A **Slob** has just finished his lunch. He gets up and leaves a drained bottle of beer, a sandwich bag, and an empty potato chip wrapper in the sand. **You Without The Power Of Insult and Live!** see this behavior and try to correct your fellow man's inconsiderate and unjustified act.)*

You Without The Power Of *Insult And Live!*
(Shouting to the departing litterbug.)
Excuse me, you forgot to pack your trash. That bottle could break. Someone could cut their feet on the glass.

Slob
(Trudging away from his garbage.)
It's a free country. You don't like it, go to a private beach.

You Without The Power Of *Insult And Live!*
Why should someone pick up your mess?

Slob
I pay my taxes for people to clean up this beach. Fuck you!

You Without The Power Of *Insult And Live!*
(Furious.)
Asshole!

Slob
(Exultant and smiling.)
Ha! *(Pause.)* Have a nice day!

Post-insult Outcome: You lost. Why? Because you fell into the loser trap. Instead of attacking a loser's character and pride, you went after their unrepentant social behavior. Big mistake! You see, losers are proud of their "attitude problem." Do you think you're the first to call any loser an asshole? No way. They've been called it before! They even like the sound of the word. It means they've gratified their needs and ruined someone's day.

You lost your first battle because The World Of Fred hasn't entered your life until this very moment. Here's how the teachings of *Insult And Live!* can reverse the confrontation so you can triumphantly hurl the perfect insult, turning the slob into a total loser.

Let's just pick up where your verbal joust with the loser began...

Take Two:
The Slob Meets Someone Who Has Learned
How To *Insult And Live!*

You With The Power Of *Insult And Live!*
Why should someone pick up your mess?

Slob
I pay my taxes for people to clean up this beach.
(Flips his middle finger.) Fuck you!

You With The Power of *Insult And Live!*
You're proof you can have children through anal sex.

Slob
(Reflexively.)
Asshole!

Post-insult Outcome: You won. You defeated the defective loser because he called you an "asshole." How did you win? Well, when you insulted the loser, you caught him off balance with a surprise attack. The loser expected you to belittle his behavior. Instead, you got *personal.* The loser got mad at you for your attitude! You tweaked him and prevailed. But, why is the rebuked loser furious? Because he resentfully realizes you did what all losers live to do to others: ruined his day.

Let Fred show you the way to improve your insult-to-loser capability...

How To Make *Insult And Live!* Work For You

Insult And Live! is an indispensable field guide that positively identifies the markings of various losers from both sexes in all levels of society and gives you a playbook approach to effectively slam every single one of them.

Each chapter lists the particular loser's irritating qualities in a variety of categories, such as...
- Loser habits
- Phrases losers use
- Jobs losers hold
- Loser jokes
- Philosophy of losers
- Loser tip offs

Then, once you've identified the loser you want to waste, just consult the specifically designed insults listed at the end of each chapter, chose a choice line, and grease your pest.

Why does an insult work?

The insult is the ultimate form of substance abuse. It solidly hits the only thing losers truly value and love: their narcissistic self-conception. An insult gets under a loser's insensitive skin and guts them out from the inside. Losers have no moral guidance system. They're out for themselves. They have no concern for anyone else's feelings or well being. But, just because these repeat offenders don't have a conscience doesn't mean you can't make them feel bad. Even a sociopathic loser is vain. All losers love themselves. It's their fatal weakness. They worship their problems. Losers are obsessed with gratifying their desires, and cleave to the psychological crevices of their unique misery. That's why a loser's pride is their greatest source of strength and weakness. It's their only vulnerable area. Defeat doesn't change them. If the loser succeeds it's because they beat the odds, but when a loser fails they blame the morons who undermined them. The loser's love of self remains intact and unwavering. So what does an insult do? It breaks up the romance between the loser and their pride. An insult exposes the loser for *what* they really are, not how the loser wants people to see them, or how the loser likes to see themselves. They're forced to publicly say hello to themselves. They hate that.

Remember, insulting losers...

- accelerates their growth process, giving the jerk a chance to see what who they really are.
- helps you filter out undesirables from your life.
- defines your turf.
- prevents the loser from getting what they want.
- enables you to meet productive and nicer people who admire you for putting the loser in their place.
- allows you to make comments behind a loser's back to impress people who also dislike the jerk.
- gives you a way to retaliate against a loser without stooping to their level.

How come some insults are more effective against losers than others?

Some insults in this book are more effective against one strain of jerk, while other losers are immune to them.

For example...

Anatomy Of An Insult:
High-grade Vs. Low-grade Slams

High-grade Intelligent Loser
(Dismissing your point of view.)
How does it feel to be sitting next to someone who makes more in a day than you will make your whole life?

You With The Power Of *Insult And Live!*
When Stephen King stops typing, do you disappear?

High-grade Intelligent Loser
(Miffed.)
Touche.

Here's why the High-grade insult worked on the High-grade loser...

High-grade insult autopsy: An intelligent loser interpreted your insult through the following thought process:

> 1.) They're aware Stephen King writes horror novels that deal with the supernatural.
>
> 2.) The High grader also knows King is a prolific writer.

So, the intelligent loser puts those two thoughts together and concludes: "You're saying when Stephen King stops typing I'd disappear because I'm a creation of the author's mind. And since this mind gave us *Cujo, Carrie, The Shining*, and various rotting zombies who returned from the dead to eat the living, you're implying I'm a monster too."

Post-insult Outcome: The intelligent person deduces they've been insulted by someone who is literate and perceptive.

Now, let's see how the a High-grade insult line works against a Low-grade loser.

For example...

Part Two
Anatomy of an Insult :
Low-grade vs. High-grade slams

Low-grade Ignorant Loser
(Explaining why it should complain.)
Hey, if I don't do it nobody else will. It's the squeaky wheel that gets the grease. Nice guys finish last.

You With The Power Of *Insult And Live!*
When Stephen King stops typing, do you disappear?

Low-grade Ignorant Loser
(Flatly staring at you.)
Huh?

Now, here's the reason the High-grade insult failed on the Low-grade loser...

Low-grade loser autopsy: The ignorant loser doesn't realize they were insulted for these reasons:

> **1.)** The Low-grade ignorant loser slightly associates Stephen King with TV or movies.

> **2.)** However, the Low-grade loser doesn't know King is a prolific writer in subjects centered on the paranormal.

Post-insult Outcome: You've lost. The murky-minded loser puts one and two together and concludes: "Why should I disappear if Stephen King stops typing?" *(Pause.)* "You're an asshole." Why didn't it work? Simple. Low-grade losers don't abstract from their biological needs, so, they never connect to anything beyond themselves. Therefore, low-grader insults must be self-explanatory or depict graphic crudities that don't require any outside reading.

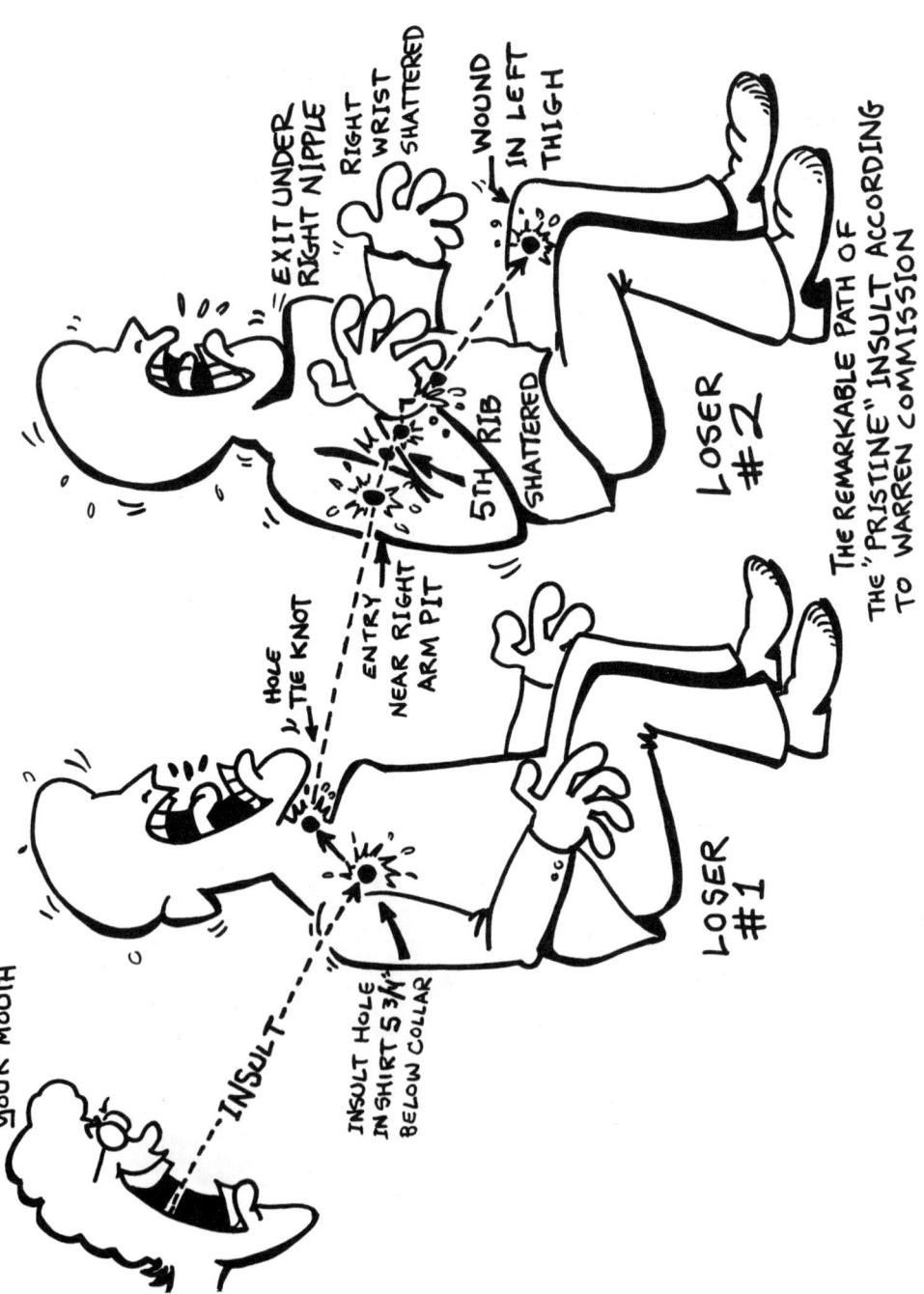

The safest way to insult any loser:
Ricochet shot to the ego

Sometimes you don't want to directly insult a loser because it creates a confrontation that can lead to shoving or yelling. There is a way to avoid this.

Insult technique: One of the best times to slam the loser is by embarrassing the loser in front of people the jerk is trying to impress, such as a date.

For example...

Situation:
Slamming A Male Loser In Front Of His date
(Scene Male Loser enters a gathering with an attractive woman. You With The Power Of Insult And Live! approach them.)

Male Loser
(Introducing his date to you.)
Hey, honey, this is the guy I always beat.

You With The Power Of Insult And Live!
(To the date.)
Hey, you're lucky to be dating such a great guy. Did you know when it comes to love he's a sixty-minute man? Yeah, I bet it's thirty seconds of love and fifty-nine-and-a-half minutes of apologizing.

Post-insult Outcome: You won! The loser's gotta take the hit. When you razz a loser in front of their companion, a loser is expected by their pal or date to handle friendly abuse. But, if the loser gets mad by taking an insult personally, it reflects badly upon them for not having a sense of humor; or, the loser looks mentally deficient because they couldn't think of a comeback.

World Of Fred insult rules

• Only insult someone if they've attacked you first.

• When you insult a person, preface the line with a compliment. For example, "Nice haircut," then slam their hair. Or, "You're brilliant," and then insult them for being stupid.

• Never assume an aggressive physical position as you say an insult, always lean back—it takes the confrontational edge off a line.

• When insulting a co-ed couple...
   1.) Men should insult the male not the female.*
   2.) Women have the option to insult either.
   3.) But both sexes can insult a couple as a unit.

• Never insult a person based on their race--it's far more effective to attack the personality under the skin.

• When you say an insult: smile.

---

* **World Of Fred Note:** We're talking risk management here. You see, if a guy insults the female in the couple, the line provokes a protective instinct in the male, which often leads to violence. But, women who insult other women don't have to worry about any physical threat, unless the female they insulted is from East Texas.

The most important reason to insult a loser

A loser's self-infatuation conceals an even more intense self-hatred. Losers are miserable people, have horrific personal lives, and pursue dead-end ambitions. They only enjoy the things they have and do if it takes enjoyment away from you. But, you are what you are, and you carry it wherever you go. Losers can't escape the bastard that's inside them. This submerged conflict causes their own body to rebel against them! Losers inflict themselves with ulcers, weird rashes, canker sores, hair loss, premature wrinkles, impotence, high-blood pressure, shingles, migraines, an aneurysm, hemorrhoids, tumors, sharp rectal pains, constipation, pinched nerves, gallstones, a heart attack, spontaneous combustion, or a nervous breakdown.

So, you ask, why even bother insulting losers? Let these preoccupied repeat offenders destroy themselves!

But, what if you go first? What happens when the loser's self-destructive behavior pulls you down with them? What if the loser gives you a stroke, and you die before they do?

An insult can save you and bury the loser. You feel an invigorating rush of ennobling endorphonic energy that improves your cardio-vascular system, burns calories, flattens your tummy, reduces stress, and helps you lose weight. And what is that euphoric feeling? It's called victory! Look deeply into the vanquished loser and see the defeat in their eyes. Savor it. Let them know you're enjoying it. And through this winning force you will attain a heightened state of self-awareness, self-confidence, and increase your self-esteem, which will lead you to create a better world. You no longer have to take a called strike. Swing away. Launch them out of the park. It's a new ballgame. They're history, and you're the future.

The main reason to insult a loser is quite simple: it will make you a happier person.

A moral fire exit:
What to do if you think you made a mistake
by insulting someone.

Perhaps you're humanely thinking a person might deserve an insult, but maybe they're entitled be cut some slack. After all, we all occasionally behave rudely to a stranger, talk too much about ourselves, execute a stupid driving maneuver, or get drunk and say a remark we regret later. We might have good reasons to justify our inappropriate behavior, but, if that holds true for us, than it also holds true for those other people. The loser annoying you could be a nice person just having a rough day. Maybe someone just broke up with them, or a person close to them died. Perhaps, they were recently diagnosed with a fatal illness or fired from their job. Who knows? So, taking all this into account, let's assume you might have made a mistake by insulting a jerk. There is a simple way of atonement: apologize. If the slighted stranger accepts it, they usually unburden themselves of their troubles, and you can make a friend, but sometimes they don't.

For example...

Situation:
Way To Apologize For Unjustly Insulting A Loser.

You
(*Walking over to the seething loser.*)
I'm sorry for snapping at you, I had a rough day, you had a rough day. No offense, I could have made the same mistake too—

Potential Loser
(*Snarls.*)
You're an asshole!

Okay, the verdict has been read by the foreman of the jury. The accused has gone from "alleged" to "convicted" loser status. You can't talk them down. It's useless.

So, what should you do now?

Go for it! Insult them without mercy. It's crunch time, brah. Fire up your World of Fred training to brutally waste the confirmed loser with every cutting line in this book. Take no prisoners! Go for the jugular. Turn them into a chalk outline. Put them on the road to Basrah. Use the choke hold. Tag their big toe and slide them into a body bag. Burn them beyond recognition. Try them as an adult! Pin their other shoulder to the mat. Read them their last rites! Impose the death sentence. Call in an air strike. Pull the plug on their life-support system. Loot! Blast them with an explosive insult at close range from a flat, low trajectory and make them do a JFK head snap!

And, what does Fred ask in exchange for this knowledge? All He asks is that you love Him.

Top One Hundred Losers who *Must* be Insulted

There are all types of losers who put their own needs above the welfare of others.

Why you must insult people to survive

It's nearly impossible to live in this zoo-ed world without insulting your fellow man. Look around you. It isn't a group of aliens fouling up this world. It's humans! We're surrounded by millions of geekazoids, dillweeds, flailing kooks, squid lips, assorted pond scum, gleeps, buttheads, dwids, scroats, clueless Daryls, lunkheads, Gomers, weiners, punks, doofuses, bozos, twinks, dickheads, asswipes, nerds, back-stabbing slimeballs, dorks, gagging wingnuts, yabos, scuzzballs, gimps, squids, hosers, Barneys, dinks, numbnuts, scumbags, boobs, twerps, gimpos, slapdicks, flakes, whack jobs, knuckleheads, whining wussies, goons, weasel dealers, straight-off Adolphs, sleazebags, tweaks, dirtbags, shitheads, wheazers, dweebs, control freaks, ginks, dickweeds, wonks, dipshits, boneheads, turkeys, corndogs, twits, butterbrains, yahoos, putzes, and yutzes.

And, they're out to get us!

And here is proof, here are one-hundred types of losers who make a conscious effort to make our lives miserable...

Losers don't see the big picture. They're only interested in their self portrait.

Top One Hundred Losers Who Must Be Insulted

1. Lovers who want to break up but remain "just friends."

2. Pedestrians who delay motorists by intentionally walking slowly in crosswalks, driveways, and parking lot entrances.

3. First acquaintances who constantly touch you throughout a conversation or speak too close.

4. Power-mad meter maids who instantly ticket your car.

5. Sketchy roommates who...
    - never do their dishes or take out the garbage.
    - "accidentally" eat your food.
    - use your razor blades and toilet paper but don't replace them.
    - stick you with an unpaid rent, phone, or utility bill.
    - help themselves to your detergent, bleach, or tools.
    - leave their clothes in the dryer or washer.
    - never refill the ice tray before they put it back in the freezer.
    - without asking, move in their lover but don't pay a higher share of bills

6. Schized panhandlers who get angry after you refuse to give them money.

7. Drunk nurses who care for the elderly.

8. Highly dense morons who...
    - blankly stare through you when you say "Hello."
    - rudely walk away while you're still talking to them.

9. Heartless bus drivers or lamebrains in elevators who see you coming but won't wait for you.

10. Opportunists who cut in line.

11. Pushy lawyers who know you can't punch them out because they'll sue you for it.

Top One Hundred Losers Who Must Be Insulted (cont.)...

12. Arrogant bicyclists who take up too much space on the highway and refuse to allow your motor vehicle to pass them.

13. Inattentive teenage cashiers who are so busy talking to each other about their oh-so-meaningful personal lives that they...
   - overcharge you.
   - forget to put an item in your bag.
   - make you wait too long.
   - inaccurately run your credit card and embarrass you by loudly saying, "You've been *declined.*"
   - get your order wrong.
   - place a breakable item in the bottom of your shopping bag, and then put a heavy item on top of it.

14. Spongeheads who believe you should "accept" them for the way they are, but insist on changing you.

15. Reformed drug/alcohol abusers who blame their addiction on the substance instead of their defective personality trait, so, they fanatically preach to you that casual use of drugs or alcohol will destroy your life the same way it ruined theirs.

16. Sleazy private investigators who approach you while your home is still burning and offer to represent you against your insurance company.

17. Oblivious motorists who park next to you, and without looking, fling their car door open and dent your vehicle.

18. Soulless romantics who insincerely overuse the word "love," and try to make you feel bad for not saying it.

19. Sickoids who graphically describe their infections, bowel movements, painful physical examinations, or the contents of their vomit.

Top One Hundred Losers Who Must Be Insulted (cont.)...

20. Theater patrons who talk or eat too loudly during the show.

21. Tattoo artists who misspell.

22. Etiquette haughty-taunties who...
    - give you a gift or assistance, but before you can say, "Thank you," they sarcastically snap, "You're *welcome.*"
    - intentionally say something hostile to you, but defend it by adding, "Only kidding."
    - get indignant when you refuse to accept their insincere apology and snarl, "Well, I said I was *sorry!*"

23. Insensitive people who sell or give away possessions you stored in their house while you were in the armed services or a trip.

24. Irritants who strategically wait until you're comfortable, and then ask you to get up and do something for them.

25. First dates who whine about former lovers, or are nasty to you because they can't take it out on their "Ex."

26. Overly motivated sales clerks who pounce on you when you enter the store, or follow you around.

27. Indignant people who unjustly accuse you of cutting in line because they didn't notice you were returning to your previous spot in the line.

28. Gruff job interviewers who heartlessly reject you for a position because "you're overqualified."

29. Low-rent heads who have ludicrously long messages or songs on their answering machines.

30. Nattering nibblers in denial who say they're not hungry but throughout the meal irritatingly pick off your plate.

Top One Hundred Losers Who Must Be Insulted (cont.)...

31. Sloppy smokers who...
    - furtively tap cigarette ashes on your rug.
    - throw down lit cigarettes in areas where people walk barefoot.
    - leave a burning cigarette on your window sill.
    - drop the cigarette on a tiled floor and put it out.
    - light up in your car, then ask, "Mind if I smoke?"
    - blow smoke in your face (or exhale it where you're eating).
    - leave butts in flowerpots.

32. Next-door neighbors who...
    - don't maintain their property, lowering your house's resale value.
    - add another story to their building that either blocks your scenic view, or overlooks your yard and ends your privacy.

33. Alleged problem solvers who see you looking for a misplaced item and try to help by asking, "Well, where was the last place you left it?"

34. Self-involved friends who never return your calls, or call to say they'll be late.

35. Meddlers who come over to your date and bluntly ask, "So, when are you two going to get married?"

36. Pinheads who play their radios too loud in public places.

37. Self-centered emotional cripples who tell you more about their lives and psychological hang-ups than you care to know.

38. Celebrities who contemptuously treat fans that politely ask for an autograph.

39. Disorganized depositors who take too long to use an automatic teller machine.

40. Uncooperative phone operators or ticket agents.

Top One Hundred Losers Who Must Be Insulted (cont.)...

41. Irresponsible pet owners who...
- have vicious dogs in their yards that they refuse to chain or properly enclose within a security fence.
- let their animals poop on your property.
- allow their dogs to run freely in public parks or beaches, so they spray you with sand, and eat your unguarded food, or attack your leashed pet. (This same petowner gets mad at "careless" motorists who cruelly run over their "helpless" animal.)

42. Unthinking browsers who pick up the book or magazine you were reading and lose your place.

43. Sun worshippers who sit near a pool's edge and complain about getting wet from splashing swimmers.

44. Long-time "local" residents who don't speak to new residents of *their* area.

45. Falsely optimistic people who cavalierly dismiss your hard times by spouting look-on-the-bright-side phrases like...
- "If it didn't rain, we wouldn't have rainbows."
- "When life gives you lemons, make lemonade."
- "You can yell horseshit, or you can look for the pony."
- "Let your smile be your umbrella."
- "Can't make an omelet without breaking an egg."
- *(After your lover dumped you.)* "You're better off."
- "Hey, one day you'll look back on this and laugh."
- *(After a tragedy.)* "At least you've got your health."
- "It takes fewer muscles to smile than to frown."
- "It's always darkest before the dawn."
- *(When you lose your job.)* "Hey, it'll turn out to be the *best* thing that ever happened to you." or "Well, everything happens for a *reason*."

46. Out-to-lunch creeps who bump into you without saying "excuse me."

Top One Hundred Losers Who Must Be Insulted (cont.)...

47. Unhelpful bystanders who...
 • impassively watch you struggle with a cumbersome object as you try to get through an entrance or exit.
 • stand or sit at an entrance, exit, or stairway, and make no effort to move or let you pass.
 • leave their personal belongings in your way and don't move them.
 • voyeuristically witnesses a crime against you or your car accident, but when you ask for their help they ignore you or say, "I didn't see nothing."

48. Life-force sapping customers who...
 • spend hours trying to chew you down in price.
 • impatiently demand immediate service.
 • complain you're not checking people out quickly enough through the line by saying, "Faster!" or sarcastically groaning, "Can you move a little *slower?*"
 • ignore "please wait to be seated" signs.
 • say they can't find an item because they want you to find it for them.
 • suspect you might cheat them so they come with a friend who is an alleged expert on what they want to buy.
 • haggle for a unjustified refund.
 • try to shortchange you by insisting they gave you a large bill, not a small one.
 • find ridiculous flaws in the merchandise; or, damage goods by testing its durability.
 • just come into the store to intentionally make your life miserable and storm out saying, "If you don't want my business I'll go somewhere that does."
 • demand you be subservient to their abusive behavior because they "paid good money" and the "customer is always right."
 • think because they spent a lot of money they're entitled to call you anytime at home and demand repairs or ask about problems.

49. Cruel scumbuckets who enjoy "telling people what they don't want to hear" and arrogantly defend hurting someone's feelings by rigidly saying, "Hey, I'm just being honest."

Top One Hundred Losers Who Must Be Insulted (cont.)...

50. Supposed friends who never stay in touch with you, never write, never phone, never visit, but when they see you ask, "Where have you been hiding yourself?" or "I've been trying to get in touch with you."

51. Indulgers in some odd sexual preference who try to seduce you by insisting you're *that way* too.

52. Unapologetic cable guys, repairmen, or contractors, who show up late; or block your car from getting out of the driveway.

53. Arrogant sinkhole brains who believe being a perfectionist means doing things *their* way.

54. Losers who travel without any regard for other people's comfort...
- the territorial hog who sits next to you on a long air flight and keeps their beefy elbow on the armrest that they're suppose to share.
- fellow travelers who take your seat so they can sit next to each other; and get indignant when you insist you want to sit in the seat you reserved and *paid* for.
- the inconsiderate recliners in coach, who sit in front of you and lean back in their chair until it presses against your knees.
- the preoccupied passengers who block aisles on airplanes, trains, or buses, until all of their belongings are stowed into overhead compartments. (Their luggage usually takes up your compartment space, or crushes the fragile contents in your bags.)
- the bodily-odorific clueless who take their shoes off so you have to smell their feet.
- the oblivious with shoulder bags who walk down the aisles, hit seated people with them, and don't apologize.
- unsympathetic jerks who show their discomfort during a parent's difficulties in trying to keep an infant from crying.

55. Coworkers who boast about their perfect attendance record, but come to work sick and give other employees a cold or flu.

Top One Hundred Losers Who Must Be Insulted (cont.)...

56. Unearned-Income gekos who have a Dutch-treat lunch with you, but without asking, grab the receipt to use it as a business deduction for their tax purposes.

57. Greedheads who conceal their financial motives in the pursuance of a lawsuit by saying, "It's not the money, it's the *principle* of the thing."

58. Emergency room nurses who take down your medical-care benefit number before they take your pulse.

59. Ballistic buttholes who yell at you for accidently dialing their phone number.

60. Careless parking lot valets who damage your car but don't tell you.

61. Puberty-engorged teenagers who feel no one older than them can understand the passion of their emotional depths, so they respond to any advice or criticism by snarling...
   - "I didn't ask to be born."
   - "All right, I'm stupid, I'll die."
   - "Yeah, yeah, you know *everything.* "

62. Pot-hole brained perfunctoroids who neglect to hold your reservation for a seat, a rental, restaurant table, hotel room, etc.

63. Warpos who attach a higher value to an animal's life than a human being's.

64. Bonehead construction workers or landscapers who get paid just before they nearly finish their job, but don't show up to do the final touches or clean up their mess.

65. The last guest at your house party who just won't leave.

Top One Hundred Losers Who Must Be Insulted (cont.)...

66. Way-out-of-tuners who whistle an unrecognizable song or melody for hours.

67. Tall people who could sit anywhere at an event, but maliciously sit in front of you to obscure your view.

68. Business associates who burn you on a professional promise and say, "I'll make it up to you."

69. Persistent office jesters who try to pin you down by the copier or coffee machine to "tell you this great joke."

70. Immigrants who run convenience stores or gas stations, act like they don't speak English, are unhelpful, never give you directions, and try to cheat you.

71. Disruptive tourists who justify being rude and destructive by saying, "Why should I care? I'm not ever coming back here."

72. Proud parents who sit in the bleachers at sporting events and point out how weak your child is compared to their little star.

73. Cheapskates who embarrass you in a restaurant by taking out a calculator and trying to figure out the bill's fifty-cent difference in the tax and the tip.

74. Devious bartenders who think you're drunk and try to shortchange you.

75. Amateur reviewers who ruin a movie by telling you the ending; or, say "I don't want to ruin the movie for you, but just want to tell you this one part."

76. Alleged friends who invite you to a party and then try to sell you cosmetics, insurance, vitamins, a diet plan, an investment pyramid scheme, Tupperware, or negligees.

Top One Hundred Losers Who Must Be Insulted (cont.)...

77. Oblivious shoppers who...
- block your passage by standing in front of you and read the label of a product.
- leave their shopping cart in the middle of the aisle while they look for an item.
- are in the check-out line with 30 items, and you have three items, but they won't let you go in front of them.
- get hot food from the deli, then sloppily and loudly eat their purchase in the grocery check-out line.
- stand in the shorter "cash only" line, and then, take out their checkbook, act surprised and say, "I didn't see the sign."
- go in the "check only" line, wait until the merchandise is rung up, and suddenly realize they should have their checkbook and driver's license ready.

78. Claims adjusters who lowball your damage estimates.

79. Snotty multi-lingual foreigners who know you're a tourist and can speak your language, but refuse.

80. Devious vehicular rear-enders and side-swipers who hit your car and admit its their fault, but afterward, when they talk to the police or an insurance company say you caused the crash.

81. Permissive parents who let their bratty but "gifted" child run unattended in public places.

82. Ridiculous indignant anti-smokers who...
- screech "Put that out, this is a non-smoking section!" or "Thanks for *not* smoking!"
- point to a "No smoking" sign and yell, "Can't you *read?*"
- reach over and actually pull the cigarette from between your lips.

83. Weasel dealers who call your answering machine when they know you're not home and cancel out at the last minute.

Top One Hundred Losers Who Must Be Insulted (cont.)...

84. Gossips who betray your most intimate confidences.

85. Pretentious sybarites who are brutally cutthroat business dealings so they can maintain an obscenely high income, indulge themselves in a luxurious life, yet describe themselves as a "survivor."

86. Noisy people who wake you up too early...
- Loud construction crews.
- Garbage-can clanging sanitation engineers.
- Loudmouths in front of your motel door at 6 am.
- Crack-of-dawners who mow the lawn.
- Motorists who honk their horn in front of a nearby building to announce they've arrived or are impatiently waiting for someone.
- Neighbors who play their stereos full blast.

87. Cowardly chickenhawks who use their privileges, connections, and wealth to avoid military service during wartime, but, when they're beyond draft age, pontificate there are "causes worth fighting and dying for" (with the exception of their own children.).

88. *(During a rainstorm, when you are briskly moving on the sidewalk.)* Unrepentant passing strangers who slash you with the prongs of their open umbrellas.

89. Sentimentalists who cry at the movies but are cruel and indifferent to the plights of people in their life.

90. Fix-upper homeowners who invite you to their house and then bore you with a twenty-minute video of how the place looked before they improved it.

91. Prating ignoramuses who finally read one book and suddenly know everything about a subject.

92. Hitchhikers who flip you off for not picking them up.

Top One Hundred Losers Who Must Be Insulted (cont.)...

93. Hustling cabdrivers who take you out of the way, to run up the cost of your trip.

94. Want-to-be-everything-to-everybody types who...
   • agrees to everything you ask them at work, but never does any of it.
   • says they're coming to your party, makes you give them detailed directions to it, and doesn't show.
   • *(Answers every invite with.)* "It's a definite maybe."
   • is late but adds, "I just wanted to put in an appearance." (Translation: "I have better places to be.")
   • says "we've got to get together" and never makes any effort to follow it up by calling or writing you.
   • offers things but fades on coming across with them.

95. Atonal aria-heads who wear earphones to listen to music, but loudly and poorly sing along with it.

96. Groping couples who sexually maul and deep-throat French kiss each other in public places.

97. Grumpy shop owners who lock the store's door just as you arrive, refuse to let you in, and snarl, "Closed!" (Variation: restaurant managers who won't serve you a breakfast or a lunch special because you arrived a few minutes past the meal deadline.)

98. Ungrateful swimmers who yell at you for saving them from drowning (They do this after you've helped them.).

99. Hose monkeys who criticize any skeptical observation you make by dismissing you as "cynical."

100. Jealous, willfully ignorant, self-centered, and dreamless people who don't find this book funny.

Loser Basics

Insult and Live! by Fred Reiss

Losers enjoy breaking rules and irritating people.

Purpose of this section: Shows you the blueprint to the unstable foundation that supports the loser's shaky philosophy of life.

Loser: 1.) Misguided victimizers who constantly blame "other people" for all the emotional problems the loser inflicts upon themselves and their victims.

The Loser

Losers are only concerned about the fluids and solids entering and exiting their bodies. They never appreciate anything they get for free. Losers believe the successful gratification of their immediate needs defines them as rebels, mavericks, and outlaws. They *live* to ruin a good thing for other people. These at-large desperadoes have no sense of discretion, refuse to respect protocol, and arrogantly lack the proper tact for an emotionally sensitive occasion. They are dull people who find themselves interesting. They like sniffing what's under their fingernails.*

*****World Of Fred Note:** Ironically, the losers who represent everything you hate, wind up becoming relatives who get drunk on your booze, stuff themselves with a holiday meal, fall asleep on your couch, snore, and intermittently pass gas.

These incident-prone losers don't expend a watered-down ounce of effort to accept responsibility, which is why losers commit rebellious acts that never take the form of progressive actions to improve society.* But, they arduously devote an astounding amount of energy to evade authority and rules. They take pride in doing the opposite of what someone tells them, even if it's in the loser's own best interest. Why? Because "no one tells me what to do with my life." Or, the loser reasons, "So I made a mistake, at least it's *my* mistake not someone else's."

Chronic losers don't care about anyone's feelings. These self-centered imbeciliacs instinctively hurt people's feelings and take advantage of others for personal gain. Then, these losers defend their offense by saying they "didn't realize" what they were doing. That's the great loser lie. Losers do realize what they're doing. Have you noticed a loser only apologizes for their allegedly unintentional screw-up when they want something from their victim? For example, a loser will smoothly say, "Remember that time three years ago when I said I'd pick you up at the airport on New Year's Eve and didn't show up? Well, I'm sorry. Can I borrow your car, tonight? Mine is in the shop." Losers do think. These losers just think about what they want first. That's why these allegedly clueless units consistently make mistakes that benefit them but shortchange others. You never hear a loser lament, "I can't get drunk tonight because I paid my phone bill today."

---

*World Of Fred Note: Losers never obey signs. Typical example: Loser is driving. Loser sees a sign that says, "Slow Gravel." Loser accelerates to peel out, spraying parked cars with gravel, scratching their finish. If you don't like their behavior, tough. After all, the loser "isn't here to please you."

Congenital limitations all Total Losers share

A total loser.....

- Is insecure.
- Has an enormous ego.
- Doesn't have a sense of humor.
- Talks about themselves; never asks about you.
- Hates to be alone.
- If yelled at for rude behavior, concludes the person who yelled at them is the jerk.
- Feels a vindictive world is unjustly persecuting them.
- Believes no one appreciates their "true" qualities.
- Hates being treated the same inconsiderate way they treat other people.
- Reflexively denies responsibility, it's always someone else's fault.
- Never loves anyone, they only love what the person can do for them. (Also, they don't love life, they only love their own life.)
- Is unable to be happy for someone else's success.
- Doesn't vote (Why? Because they erroneously think it will help them avoid jury duty.).
- Doesn't give blood.
- Only makes the correct moral decision if its consequences only affect others' incomes and lives.
- Doesn't read (And boasts about it.).
- Has an attitude.
- Has a temper.
- Has no humility.
- Categorizes people by class, religion, or race.
- Expresses their individualism through consumption.
- Must have the last word in an argument.
- Never says "thank you" or "excuse me."
- Believes the world makes "special exceptions" for everyone but them.
- Speaks without thinking first.
- Acts completely shocked when you point out their selfish or rude behavior. ("I didn't know!")

Congenital traits all Total Losers share (cont.)...

- Never cuts others a break for a mistake, but feels everyone should forgive their goofs.
- Has no respect for other people's privacy.
- Compulsively lies.
- Never returns anything where they found it.
- Never apologizes.

We're told by psychologists that "lack of self esteem" is the cause for a loser's inferiority complex. These learned observers of human nature note the loser hurts innocents because the subject is lashing at qualities that the loser hasn't resolved or dislikes within themselves. Fine. But, what accomplishments has a loser done to be proud of? The reason these griping sacks of turkey shit have an inferiority complex is simple: they are inferior. Why should these insecure flakes have a high opinion of themselves? Plus, have you noticed that anyone with an inferiority complex uses it to suck other people down into the loser's private hell?

Come on, think about it! Even bums who allegedly have "no where to go" fit into this philosophy. These disenfranchised individuals have been on this planet for thirty years or more, and yet they never made one friend or relative who loves or cares about them. But, what Fred finds interesting is most allegedly mentally disturbed losers are balanced enough to know where to apply for government disability benefits, or, if they're not subsidized by an agency, they have a strong tendency to panhandle. Somehow they figured out it was more convenient for them to survive by *taking* from their fellow man instead of giving.*

*****World Of Fred Note:** A bum prides themselves on never holding a job. Yet, they see nothing humiliating in holding out their hand to beg for bucks. They snarl at you for refusing to give them money. Their reasoning: you have more money than you need so you should give it to them. But, even if you give them money, the bum hates you for feeling superior about yourself for helping them. After all, who do you think you are? Then, when the bum gets drunk on your money, what do they proclaim to the indifferent world? They yell, "I don't need anybody!"

Why should we even feel guilty? Losers don't even care about us. Their limited adversarial vision only sees people in relationship to the loser's goals and desires: people are either "for them" or "against them." So, losers are fond of saying things like, "You can say what you want about *(Insert name of a prick.)*, but he's been good to me."

This motivation for self-preservation costs the loser many friendships. But, the loser denies these breakups are their fault. In fact, anytime a loser's inconsiderate behavior destroys a friendship, instead of apologizing and asking forgiveness, the loser gives the ex-friend the silent treatment. After a few weeks go by, the loser claims they're willing to "forgive and forget," adding the ex-friend is wrong for "holding a grudge" against them! If you get involved as an arbitrator and make the mistake of pointing out the failed relationship was the loser's fault, the loser gets angry because you "took the other person's side." Or, acts betrayed and says, "Why are you picking on me? I thought you were my friend!"

Since no one likes losers, these very limited morons surround themselves with self-improvement philosophical sayings for emotional support, such as a coffee cup that says, "World's Greatest Mom," however, the most common one in loserdom is...

> God grant me the serenity
> To accept the things I cannot change
> The courage to change the things I can
> And the wisdom to know the difference*

High-grade and Low-grade Losers

There is a misconception losers are economic failures but that successful and influential people aren't losers. That's not true. In the World of Fred, losers come in two irritating forms...

---

*World Of Fred Note: Of course, this St. Francis of Assisi motto is incorrectly used to help losers justify their selfishness and competitive aggression. Sure I'm flawed, reasons the loser, but at least I'm faithfully trying to be a better person.

High-grade Loser: 1.) An ignorant and selfish person who earns their pride through social respectability, political prestige, and economic credibility. This distinguished loser derives self-esteemed from how others feel about them.

High Graders get offended on a different level than Low Grader. Here's how they do it...

Situation:
High-grade Loser Behavior
(*A **High-grade Loser Judge** gets pulled over for speeding.*)

Cop
You're under arrest.

High-grade Loser Judge
(*Indignant.*)
Do you *know* who I am?

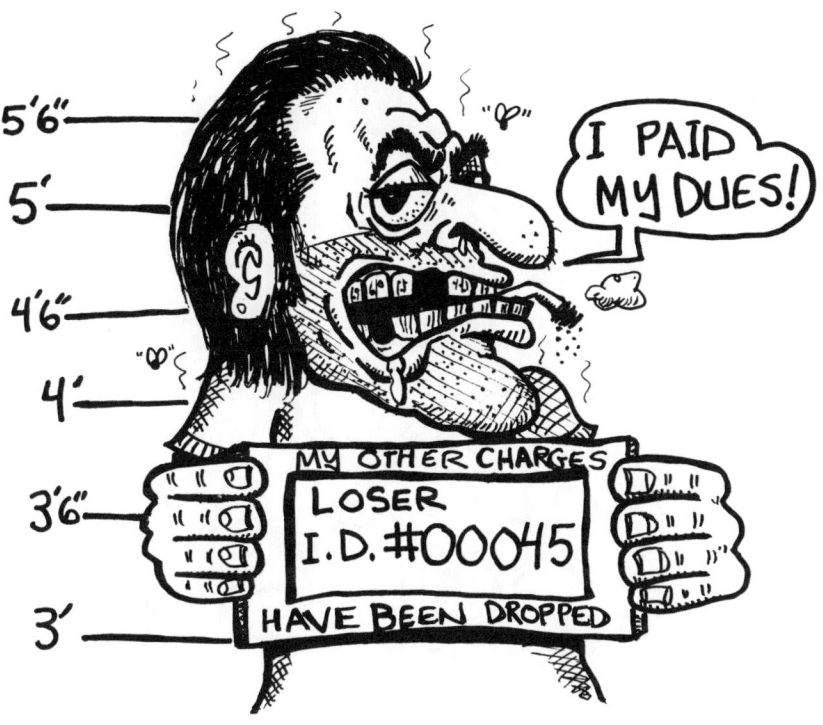

Low-grade Loser: 1.) A person who only has their ignorance to reinforce their pride. This breed doesn't care how people perceive them. This person derives their self-esteem from how they feel about themselves.

Low Graders respond to the problems they bring upon themselves in a different plane than High Graders. Here's how they do it...

Situation:
Low-grade Loser Behavior
(*Typical Low-grade Loser gets pulled over for speeding.*)

Cop
You're under arrest.

Low-grade Loser
(*With self pity.*)
Why are you doing this to me?

The Loser Descrambler

What is said to a Loser isn't what they actually hear
The Loser Descrambler misinterprets reality so the loser can avoid accepting responsibility and blame others.

The most common questions asked about a loser's behavior are...

> **1.)** Why do losers get mad when you tell them the truth about themselves?
> **2.)** How come losers blame everyone except themselves for their problems?

The World of Fred has the answer to these questions. It's all connected to the loser's mental descrambler.

The refined loser descrambler has two denial steps...

1.) Transference of denial: denies responsibility for the loser's actions by blaming other people. This is accomplished by an anger that rails against "injustice."

2.) Denial of guilt through a persecution complex: after shifting blame, the loser sees themselves as an unjustly "persecuted" victim, which enables the loser to justifiably repeat their behavior.

Here's an example of the Low-grade loser descrambler in action...

**Situation:
"Low-grade Loser Biker Meets Cop"**

(Scene: helmetless **Low-grade Loser Biker** straddling his motorcycle. His helmetless two-year old child is perched on the handlebars. They have been pulled over by a **Traffic Cop**.)

Traffic Cop
(Gives ticket.)
You're also responsible for the safety of your child.

Low-grade Loser Biker
(Takes the ticket and yells at the officer.)
The law violates my freedom. I like to feel the wind through my hair. It's the principle of the thing. That's the *real* issue.

Traffic Cop
Having children is a responsibility that limits your freedom. Isn't that a *choice* you already made? Don't you want to be around for them instead of ending up a vegetable?

Low-grade Loser Biker
I hear what you're saying, but you're missing my point. *(Pause.)* I'm bringing up my kid the same way my old man brought up me. *(Yelling at the departing officer.)* Why should I be penalized because assholes don't know how to drive?

Descrambler Result: The loser sees themselves as a misunderstood crusader. Why should he listen? He's a victim of injustice!

When put in their place for a stupid mistake, or caught perpetrating an irresponsible act, the descrambler enables a Low-grade loser to deny blame.

For example...

Low-grade Loser descrambler denial phrases

- "Well, we all make mistakes."
- "I guess we can't all be as perfect as you."
- *(Shrugs and says.)* "So?" or "So what?" or "So sue me."
- "I plead guilty with an explanation."
- "But, *you* told me to do that."
- "How am I suppose to know unless somebody tells me?"
- *(Mumbles.)* "Excuse me for living."
- "It's not like I killed anybody or anything."
- "So I made the wrong decision."
- "I'm only human." or "Hey, I'm no saint."
- "Hey, don't ask me, I only work here."
- *(In an offended tone.)* "Sorry, I didn't realize I needed your permission."
- *(Simply lies.)* "No, I didn't."
- "Prove it."
- "When I want your advice, I'll ask for it."
- *(If asked to pick up a mess they made.)* "I didn't put it there."
- *(When caught eating your food without permission.)* "It's not like you have your name on it."
- "Chalk another one up for experience."
- "What are you going to do, make a Federal case out of it?"
- "It's not like it's the end of the world."
- "You have something *personal* against me."
- "What is this, the third degree?"
- "You got a witness?"
- *(In stunned bewilderment.)* "What did I do?"
- "I'm not here to please *you*."
- "I don't make the rules."

Descrambler lines Low-grade losers say behind the back of people who correctly put them in their place.

It's not enough for the loser to deny their responsibility. They must make others are aware of the injustice the world has perpetrated upon them. After the person who admonished the loser leaves, the Low-grade loser salvages their pride with the following phrases...

- "Where does she get the *right* to talk to me like that?"
- "There is no God."
- "It wasn't what he said it was the *way* he said it."
- "I just didn't like her *tone*."
- "I was just at the wrong place at the wrong time."
- *(Defends selfish behavior by saying.)* "No more Mr. Nice Guy, I'm tired of being taken advantage of."
- "Hey, who are they to judge me?"
- "Everybody breaks the law, the only thing I did wrong was get caught."
- "That guy's gotta real *attitude*. What's his problem? I mean, what an asshole!"
- "I don't need to be lectured to."
- "I'm nobody's doormat."
- "I didn't *deserve* to be treated like that!"
- "See you in court."
- "That guy is way over the line."
- "At least I'm not a quitter!"
- "I don't need this!"
- "Blow me." or "Eat me."
- "Can't beat the system."
- "Zigged when I should have zagged."

How the High-grade Loser's descrambler works better than a Low-grade Loser's descrambler

High-grade losers maintain their inflated sense of self worth with a more sophisticated descrambler system that integrates a social and political network.

Here's how this refined system of cruise-control denial works...

Situation:
High-grade Loser Is Confronted By The Media About An "alleged misuse" Of Public Funds.

*(Scene: **High-grade Loser** is leaving the court house after their arraignment. The press swarms around the alleged felon.)*

News Reporter
(Approaches.)
Has the District Attorney filed charges you misused public funds, received illegal campaign funds, and cheated on your income tax?

High-grade Loser
(Drawls any one of the following "denial" lines.)
- "I won't dignify that comment with a response."
- "Consider the source."
- "I don't want this case tried in the media."
- "My lawyers have advised me to refer all questions to them."
- "The press has blown this whole thing out of proportion."
- "I'm just a fall guy."
- "I was just following orders."
- "I don't want to say anything that would jeopardize the case under investigation."
- "We have filed an appeal."
- "There were no laws broken, we followed all the procedures mandated by the government."
- "Why would I risk my reputation to steal such a small sum?"
(The "small sum" is usually $20,000 or in the low millions.)
- "To the best of my recollection, I don't recall the incident."
- "I resent being treated like a common criminal."
- "It was a screw up by my staff."

High-grade Descrambler Result: When confronted with the "appearance of impropriety," the High-grade loser's sophisticated descrambler system disavows these allegations as "unproven legal charges." This unique mental device not only denies personal responsibility but initiates political and legal processes to avoid public accountability and protects the High-grade loser's "image" from the "determination of criminal wrongdoing" in these ways...

1.) Files a libel suit against a newspaper or TV news show (as if it was the "media" who perpetuated the crime).
2.) Claims "executive privilege" to avoid criminal prosecution.
3.) Has investigatory officials give the High-grader enough legal delays to shred evidence, or falsify documents.
4.) Hires a civil-liberties lawyer to find a legal flaw in the litigation process that violated the High-grade loser's constitutional rights.
5.) In exchange for immunity or a reduced sentence, provides information to arrest others, or does a "sting" operation for the prosecutor's office*.
6.) Classifies and seals incriminating documents from public eyes because of "national security." They also claim the release of the files would "compromise" informants effectiveness or endanger undercover agents lives (translation: gives the crook a way to avoid naming their culprits.)
7.) Uses their financial clout or calls in political markers to have public officials pardon the High-grade Loser in the name of "social stability."**
8.) Divorces, but only provides alimony with the agreement their spouse doesn't speak to the press or write a book about the marriage.
9.) Says they've "found" God and beg forgiveness.

So, the High-grade Loser either beats the rap, pleads nolo contendere, gets pardoned, settles out of court, plea bargains and gets a suspended sentence or serves on a tenth of their prison time in a minimum security prison, pays a fine that's a fraction of what they stole, receives probation or light community service.

---

* **World Of Fred Note:** The sting operation usually reveals the immune loser is the central culprit. So, the sting only snares the loser's gullible underlings. Ironically, the High-grade squealer is praised for their "honesty" in cooperation with law-enforcement officials.

Another World Of Fred Note: These politicos justify their indefensible pardon of an obviously guilty High-grade Loser by saying the following: **1.)** "We have to leave the past behind us and look toward the future." **2.)** "It's time for us to rebuild." **3.)** "It would do more damage to the country than good to prosecute them." **4.)** "This is a time for healing." **5.)** "We can't let one bad apple ruin it for the whole bunch."

But, it doesn't end there! Regardless of the outcome, the High-grade loser holds a press conference to deny their guilt and claim they've been "victimized."

For example...

Situation:
How Guilty High-grade Losers Maintain Their Innocence.
(Scene: Press conference. High-grade Loser, stands by their lawyer behind a podium on a dais in front of reporters.)

Lawyer for High-grade Loser
(Stoutly)
I feel my client suffered enough from their exposure of this incident in the press. They want to get on with their life. Their "reputation" has been tarnished. The guilty verdict doesn't reflect on the integrity of what my client was trying to achieve. This has put a strain on their family. Isn't that punishment enough? What would society gain by putting this upstanding citizen in jail? Let my client address this subject.

Convicted High-grade Loser
The criminal charges made against me were politically motivated. The prosecutor has a personal vendetta against me. They weren't interested in enforcing the law, they were looking for publicity to use this case in a bid to seek higher office for themselves, sell a book, or movie rights.* I did nothing wrong. I was set up. I'm the victim of a witch hunt. I'm was furious at being entrapped and harassed this way, but I feel sorry for the District Attorney, she's the one who should be arrested. This case was a farce. A media circus. My plea isn't an admission of guilt, I'm simply trying to avoid my having my reputation smeared and my family unjustly hurt by innuendoes and rumors. I don't want the people I love to go through that.

---

* **World Of Fred Note:** Through the publicity of the controversy, the High-grade loser profits on the lecture circuit, and sells book and movie rights. But, they aren't exploiting the controversy or profiting from their crime, they're trying to "set the record straight" or to "tell their side of the story" because their alleged crime was "distorted" by the press.

Descrambler Conclusion:
What Low-grade and High-grade losers have in common

Regardless of income or social standing, all losers see themselves as the "persecuted victim" and the other person accusing them of a crime as the guilty offender. The only difference is a High-grade loser has legal and political pull to avoid the punitive consequences of their actions, salvages their "image," and goes off to romp in Europe for the summer. But, the Low-grade loser must "be made an example of," and serves time in jail trying to avoid the lusty probings of a 360-pound cellmate named Cletis.

How Losers Justify Their Ignorance

In their youthful and unformative years, losers reinforce the power of their ignorance force field by absorbing all their parents' flaws; for example, a loser might say, "Why should I graduate from high school? You didn't."* We're basically talking about a student who views art class as a chance to polish their clay-fighting abilities. The only activist stand this teenage loser has is: demanding a student smoking lounge because "the teacher's have one so why can't we?"

Losers defiantly deny the importance of anything they don't know. A loser's first bud break of ignorance emerges in high school English class. Losers hate literature. Fiction is the loser's first introduction to a life-long enemy: abstract thought that isn't related to the gratification of their physical needs or financial gain.

---

*__World Of Fred Note:__ And does the loser parent decide to redeem their past mistakes by insisting their child attend school? Do they decide to be an adult? A true parent? No. They shrug and say, "Well, you got a point there."

For example...

Situation:
"Rebel-without-a-clue Loser Rejects Literature"

*(Scene: A high school English class. The **English Teacher** is discussing the symbolism in Nathaniel Hawthorne's "The Scarlet Letter." **Rebel-without-a-clue Loser** is seated in the far left corner of the room, the back of his chair against the wall. In his notebook, he is drawing a woman's breasts.)*

English Teacher
The "A" Hester must wear stands for adultery. In *The Scarlet Letter*, Hawthorne states—

Rebel-without-a-clue Loser
(Interrupts in a bewildered and irritated voice.)
Don't you think you're reading too much into this? How do you know Hawthorne just didn't write this stuff and it just came out that way? He just picked the letter A! It coulda been any letter. *(Pause.)* Why should I learn this stuff, anyway? I'm not going to be a teacher? After I graduate, I'll be making more than you.*

Result: Most of these blunt-brained losers grow up to become editors or "shock" disc jockey.

Loser defensiveness about their intentional lack of education

Losers are regressive personalities intimidated by any distinctions that show them in a lesser light; therefore, everything around them has to been reduced to their basement level. They arrogantly display this trait with pride throughout adolthood.

*****World Of Fred Note:** Loser children enjoy humiliating the teacher and disrupting their authority, but if the teacher ridicules the student, the pupil complains they're "being singled out." Then, the loser's parents call and blame the teacher for "not being able to reach" their child.

For example...

Situation:
How Losers See Their Ignorance As A Strength

*(Scene. The **Loser** becomes a radio winner. He won a dinner for two at an exclusive four-star restaurant. Of course the **Loser** and his **Loser Date** didn't get dressed up; in fact, he sits down at the table with his cowboy hat still on. He wears a tee shirt with a rock group's name on it, torn bluejeans (which reveal his boxer shorts.), and scuffed snakeskin boots. She is dressed in jeans and a halter top that shows a slight gut as well as the butterfly tattoo above her left breast. They are chewing gum. The **Waiter** shows the couple the menu.)*

Loser
(Scanning the menu.)
Hey, what's this Phil-let Mig-Non?

Waiter
Filet mignon? It's a cut of steak.

Loser
(Contemptuously.)
If it's steak, why do you hide it behind that fancy name?*

Loser's Date
(Jeeringly.)
Yeah.

*****World Of Fred Note:** Interestingly, losers boast about any outstanding ability they possess, but deny that talent to others. For example, a loser dismisses a connoisseur's ability to distinguish various bordeauxs, but in the same expelling breath, the loser brags about their pallet's ability to tell apart different colas.

Various ways Losers strut their ignorance

If you bring up a contemporary figure or a news event, the loser quips, "Big deal, I never heard of him." or "If it's so important, how come I don't know about it?"

Believes "words can never describe an experience."

Ignores the importance of reading by...
- labeling anyone who reads a "bookworm."
- assuming a reader is "doing nothing" or reading because "there is nothing better to do."
- dismissing a bookworm's points by saying, "Well, you read a lot so you'd know that." or "Well, there's book smart and there's people smart."

Maintains color movies are better than black-and-white.

When a traveler talks about the beauty of a foreign land, the defensive loser counters that there is a more beautiful sight in their hometown: "I can show you a sunset from the hills over Lake Topenemus behind the landfill that's better than sight you'll see in Paris."*

If you rent a classic movie from a video store, loser says, "Why did you get that? It's *old*."

Dismisses their ignorance of vocabulary words by airily grunting, "Explain that word to me because my parents couldn't afford to send *me* to college." Or, when asked about the meaning of word, say, "What do I look like? A dictionary?"

If the loser has an addiction to drugs or alcohol it's okay because "everyone has an addiction to something."

---

*__World Of Fred Note:__ The loser feels no need to travel anywhere, because "people just talk about the weather wherever you go." Or says, "There's nothing for me in (*fill in exotic land*), everything I want is right here."

Various ways Losers strut their ignorance (cont.)...

Anytime their favorite radio station plays a song the loser dislikes, they call the disc jockey, shout, "What is this fucking shit?" and hang up.

If you talk about an old popular song or a major historical fact that happened twenty years ago, the loser says, "That was before my time." or "Boy, are you dating yourself!"

Says, "I don't want to sound prejudice but...*(And says something racist.)*; or, if you give a loser an example of racist or sexist behavior, loser says, "But that's *true*."

Ignorant and insensitive sayings Losers use to dismiss a death or tragedy

- "When your number's up, your number's up."
- "It's nature's way of weeding out the species."
- "It's God's will."
- "I guess it was their time to go."
- "Life is for the living."
- "They're better off."
- "Nothing will bring them back."
- "It's a blessing."
- "Nobody lives forever."
- "They're happier now."
- "They must have done something to bring it upon themselves."
- (*When they hear the casualties in a war.*) "More people die on the highways each year."*
- "That's the way they would have wanted to go."
- *(If a combat veteran commits suicide or becomes a drug addict.)* "They were probably that way *before* they went in."

***World of Fred Note:** Of course, the highway death toll would be higher if the drivers are trying to speed through a war zone, or dying from hunger. Or worse, dying from hunger as they drive through a war zone.

Proverbial Loser

Most losers are acutely aware of their social and professional limitations, so they defensively use the same proverbs to justify one or all of the following...

> 1.) their dead-end jobs (as well as career the loser knows other people hold in low esteem, such as insurance, car sales, or being a lawyer.).
> 2.) the futility of any progressive action.
> 3.) ignorance about themselves or others.

The loser effortlessly deflects any criticism, or denies the endless variety and choices life offers, by pulling out any tired saying from the dried-out and fished-out stream of their consciousness.

We have constantly heard these eroded and defective pearls of wisdom, and when they are uttered, the remarks deserve to be slammed with an insult.

Here is a sampling...

Ignorant Loser quotable quotes to justify underachieving or being petty

"You can't be everybody's friend."

(When asked how life is going.) "Same old shit, different day."

"If you can't eat it or screw it, piss on it."

"Out of sight, out of mind."

"Do as I say, don't do as I do."

"There's nothing new under the sun."

"Big deal, in one hundred years who'll know the difference?"

"Don't bullshit a bullshitter."

"I'd complain, but who'd listen?"

"Why aren't words spelled like they sound?"

"It's the squeaky wheel that gets the grease."

"Is the screwing I'm getting worth the screwing I'm getting?"

"You're not really a success until you've been sued."

"Damned if you do, damned if you don't."

"I'm old enough to know better, too young to care."

"Close only counts in horseshoes and hand grenades."

"Hindsight is 20/20."

"Life's a bitch and then you die."

Ignorant Loser quotable quotes to justify underachieving or being petty (cont.)...

(If it's they hear about a rape victim.) "If she was dressed that way, she was probably asking for it."

(Ways they justify their job.) "It pays the rent." or "It's a living."

"What you don't know can't hurt you."

"You "assume"? You know what "assume" is? It makes an 'ass' out of 'u' and 'me'."

"Better to be pissed off than pissed on."

"It would be a dull world if we were all the same."

"Fuck'em if they can't take a joke." (Option: "Joke'em if they can't take a fuck.")

"If I knew then what I know now."

"Anything over a mouthful is wasted."

"My friend, right or wrong."

"I've been accused but never convicted."

"No good deed goes unpunished."

"Opinions are like assholes, everyone has one and most of them are full of shit."

"Don't take a piss, leave one."

"Hey, it's six of one half a dozen of another."

"I know I'm going to heaven because I'm in hell now."

Ignorant Loser quotable quotes to justify underachieving or being petty (cont.)...

(If they hear of a mugging.) "They shouldn't have been in that neighborhood at that hour."

"He has to put his socks on one at time like everyone else."*

*World Of Fred Note: It means nothing to the loser that Einstein put on his socks on one at a time and developed the theory of relativity, while the loser put their socks on one at a time and could only guess two out of nine picks in the football pool at The Gloworm Bar and Grill.

Losers assume ridiculous intellectual arguments to provoke people into conversations.

How to slam an ignorant loser

The overwhelming amount of losers are very sensitive about their lack of education, so, they compensate for their inadequacy by arrogantly taking indefensible positions in a debate with someone who the loser knows is better educated than them. Regardless of how eloquently a person argues their point and backs it up with facts, the ignorant loser stubbornly clings to their outlandish point of view. Why? Because it's the loser's way of contemptuously saying, "If you think you're smart, and I'm so dumb, how come you don't have the intelligence to change my point of view?"

Recommended tactic: Don't try to reason with this shithead. A loser's stupidity is their strength and power. It provokes confrontations that sets them apart from others, which enables the inadequate loser to feel superior. Go to the source! Insult and dismiss the importance of their existence!

For example...

Situation:
Insulting A Loser Who Takes A Ridiculously Inflexible Positions In Alleged Intellectual Argument

Loser
That black guy deserved to be beat up, the cops were doing their job.

You With The Power Of *Insult And Live!*
(Attempting to reason.)
You're saying one guy gets stopped for speeding, has no weapon on him, and someone captures on film over 20 cops standing around, watching other cops knock him to the ground, and then, while the man is down on the ground, use a taser gun on him, which would give a cardiac arrest to a yak, and slam him with nightsticks to beat the crap out—

Loser
You don't know what the cops deal with every day. They know how to make their decisions. Hey, that guy had a criminal record a mile long. And you telling me a guy like that gets it all on film? That was a set up. Where's a black guy like him going to get a video recorder? He's just suing to get money. Besides what if it was a *white* guy and he got beat up in a black neighborhood? Everyone would say he was "looking for trouble."

You With The Power Of *Insult And Live!*
Some people are born again, you're still-born again.

Post-insult Outcome: You won. The loser has taken the pipe! The shrunken cranial couldn't get you to admit defeat or become aggravated.

Losers On Wheels

The car and the open highway give losers an opportunity their personality denies them: a level playing field with everyone else. It's a loser's rare chance to control reality. They have a life and they want to get on with it and you're in their way. They're denial in motion. You see, Losers on Wheels are powered by one solid belief that fuels their questionable motor skills: they are the only ones who know the right way to drive.

Loser on Wheels traits

- Refuses to let you pass them.
- Honks horn longer and more often than they have to.
- Flashes their brights at anyone in their way.
- Plays their car stereo too loud.
- Tailgates or causes gridlock.
- Cuts others off.
- Rubbernecks, but gets mad at others who do it.
- Pulls onto roadways without looking.
- Jumps their turn at a four-way stop intersection.
- Waits until the last possible moment to drive across three freeway lanes to make an exit ramp.
- Parks and boxes you in between another parked car.
- Denies driving mistakes by flipping people off.
- Never properly merges and causes bottlenecks (The worst ones ride on the shoulder to get ahead of the jam.).
- Intolerantly shouts out their window at elderly drivers.
- Takes up two parking spaces, uses your reserved space, or steals a spot you waited for.
- Accelerates so you can't pass them.
- Recklessly speeds through narrow openings in heavy traffic (some do this during hazardous road conditions).
- Doesn't use turn signals or uses them too late.
- When lost, never pulls over to let a motorists pass. Instead they slow down to look at a map; or, block you while they stop and ask directions; or, stop to read each street sign .*
- Instead of having their token or change ready, the loser waits until they stop, and then look for their toll payment.
- Goes too fast in parking lots.
- Tailgates you, then passes you, but once in front of you, drives slow. Yet, when you try to pass, they accelerate.
- Blocks traffic for several minutes to get a parking spot.
- Passes on blind curves.

---

*World Of Fred Note: If tourists, losers drive slowly to see the sight; or stop their car in a on-going traffic lane so they can get out and take a picture of a scenic view (Their favorite place for this move in just after a blind curve.).

Warning: Never insult a Loser On Wheels*

If you yell at a loser or flip them off, they might tailgate you and blind you from behind with their brights. Maybe they'll drive you off the road, shoot you with an unregistered handgun or crossbow (Yes, someone actually did thump an arrow into someone's chest). And, what's even more frustrating, sometimes by getting angry at the Loser On Wheels you stop paying attention to your driving and get into an accident with an innocent person.

So, if you can't insult a Loser on Wheels, how can you hurt them? You don't have to. These losers in transit punish themselves! Because no matter where a loser drives, "some idiot who doesn't know what they're doing" is eternally in their way.

And, console yourself with this World Of Fred Truth...

World of Fred Loser Truism
If you don't confront a loser, they will somehow find and get into an argument with another asshole who is just like them.

By practicing this form of passive resistance, the Loser On Wheels will meet up with another Loser On Wheels. Instead of you getting injured in a wreck, they'll attack each other and weed themselves out. Of course, you can practice this form of passive resistance in any situation. But insulting losers feels so good.

---

*__World Of Fred Note:__ The worst Losers On Wheels drive landscaping trucks, or any dilapidated vehicle with more than three rakes or shovels. These types have no respect for other vehicles. Their favorite move is to cut in front of you on a main road, drive fifty feet, and then turn off the road. They love slowing the world down to their pace.

Loser Humor

Losers constantly inflict their irritating sense of humor upon us. We are persistently badgered by their tired moronic jokes. Nearly every adult outgrows these tortuous jests, i.e., snapping wet towels at people, making cracks about your body odor if you raise your arms, having someone page "Dick Hertz" on a public address system, stepping on the back of your shoe to make it come off your foot, slapping you somewhere on your body and claiming they hit a bug ("Got it!"), or pointing at things that don't exist, and laughing when you turn and see nothing there ("Made you look," they snort. Ho Ho.). If you get angry at the alleged joke, it only increases Captain Obvious' merriment. So, you need a insult to expose these jokers for the humorless morons they really are.

For example...

Situation:
Joking Loser Humiliates You With A Childhood Trick

Joking Loser
(Pointing down at your shirt.)
Hey, you got spaghetti sauce on your shirt.

You With The Power Of *Insult And Live!*
(Looking down.)
Where do I—

Joking Loser
(Running their finger up your shirt and flicking your nose.)
Ha! I can't believe you were so stupid to fall for that!

You With The Power Of *Insult And Live!*
(Angry.)
I wasn't stupid to fall for that old trick, I just couldn't believe an adult was *dumb* enough to do it.

Joking Loser
What's the matter? Don't you have a sense of humor? *(Mocking.)* I didn't know you were so sensitive. I mean it's just a joke.

You With The Power Of *Insult And Live!*
When you were born, I bet the doctor carried you to your mother, shrugged and said, "Shit happens."

Joking Loser
(Offended.)
Fuck you if you can't take a joke.

Post-insult Outcome: You won! Dish-it-out-but-can't-take-it pranksters get really honked out when they are on the receiving end of any joke. They think a sense of humor means laughing at other people. They hate it when other people laugh at them.

Obvious and dumb Loser repartees that demand an insult

Losers go through life with a limited repertoire. Many of us have used these lines, but matured to a point in our lives where we develop our own witticisms. But not the loser, they predictably access the same repartees over and over and over again.

For example...

>**You:** "Excuse me."
>**Loser:** "There's no excuse for you."
>
>**You:** "See you later."
>**Loser:** "Not if I see you first." or "Thanks for the warning."
>
>**You:** "My friends threw me a party last night."
>**Loser:** "What did *he* give you?"
>
>**You:** "What are you up to?"
>**Loser:** *(Says their height.)*
>
>**You:** "What's up?"
>**Loser:** "The sky, the sun, the clouds."
>
>**You:** "What's new?"
>**Loser:** "New Jersey, New York, New Zealand, etc."
>
>**You:** "What do you say we go to (<u>*Insert place*</u>.)?"
>**Loser:** "Let's not and say we did."
>
>**You:** "What are you looking at?"
>**Loser:** *(Staring at you.)* "Not much."
>
>**You:** "Well--"
>**Loser:** "That's deep."

Dumb Loser repartees (cont.)...

You: "Do you have a piece of gum?"
Loser: *(Sticks out their tongue with the chewed up gum still on it.)* "Yeah, this piece."

You: *(On New Year's Eve.)* "See you tomorrow."
Loser: "See you next year."

You: *(See loser heading toward the stairs.)* "Going up?"
Loser: "For what? Up a chicken's ass for an egg sandwich?"

You: "Go to hell."
Loser: "I been there, I don't like your mother's cooking."

You: "What's the show about?"
Loser: "About an hour."

You: "Do you know *(Insert any name or phrase.)*?"
Loser: "No, but if you hum a few bars I can fake it."

You: *(with a clipboard.)* "Can you sign for this?"
Loser *(Says one of the following)*:
- "How much is this going to cost me?"
- *(Pointing at the package)* "As long as it's not ticking." (Get it? It might be a bomb.)
- "I don't give autographs."
- "What's the damage?"
- *(After signing it)* "You ought to keep that paper, that signature is going to worth money some day."
- *(To an approaching mail carrier.)* "Bringing my check?"
- *(Pointing to a long and large package.)* "So is that how you got rid of the body?"
- *(To the person signing for a package.)* "Just write your X."

Dumb Loser repartees (cont.)...

You: "Get a haircut?"
Loser: "No, I got them all cut."

You: "Things aren't going well."
Loser: "Hey, things could be worse."
You: "How?"
Loser: "It coulda happened to me."

You: "Gotta match?"
Loser: "Your ass and my face." or "Your breath and a buffalo fart."

You: "Got any kids?"
Loser: "None that I *know* of."

You: "Well, his car wrecked--"
Loser: "Rectum, damn near *killed* him!"

You: "I feel like a cheeseburger."
Loser: "You don't *look* like a cheeseburger."

You: "What time is it?"
Loser *(says one of the following)*:
- "Same time as yesterday only a day later."
- *(When the sun is out.)* "Day time."
- *(If dark.)* "Night time."
- "What time do you have to leave?"
- "It's time for you to get the hell out of here."
- "Time for you to get a watch."

You: "I was out with my girlfriend last night."
Loser: "What was *his* name?"

You: "Where's the party?"
Loser: "In your mouth, everyone is coming."

Loser verbal humor

When a loser accidentally rhymes two words says, "I'm a poet and I don't know it."

If you're leaving on vacation or exiting with a date to the bedroom, the loser says, "Don't do anything I wouldn't do."

Greets tall people with "How is the weather *up* there?"; or, short people with "How is the weather *down* there?" (Option: if the short person is of the opposite sex, the loser points to their groin and flirts by saying, "While you're down there.")

Anytime a loser sees an expensive car drive by, quips, "I knew I shouldn't have sold that car."

Discusses a date from the previous night and says, "Yeah, we went to a real class place, my treat, you know, something nice *(Names a fast food restaurant.)*."

Asks, "Do you know anything about real estate?" You answer yes or no. Loser points to their crotch and say, "Is this a lot?"

As you bend over, loser looks at your butt and says, "I think I found your best side."

When you are beating them in a game, the right-handed loser says aloud, "I guess I'll switch back to using my *right* hand." (Get it? You were losing to them because they claim they were playing left handed.)

Loser says to a friend whose wife just gave birth: "So how's my child?" or "I notice your kid bears a strong resemblance to the mailman."

If a siren or an alarm goes off nearby, the loser says: "Better start running." or "Break out the strait jacket, they're coming to take you away." or "Guess someone called the cops on you."

Loser verbal humor (cont.)...

Loser has an answering machine with a message that goes: "Hello...Hello...Can you speak louder?" You think you're talking to them and the phone isn't working. You shout. Then, the recorded message says, "Gottcha. I'm not here now, but if you want to leave a message..."

Sizes up your athletic abilities and says, "You throw like a girl." (Loser finds it funnier to say this to a female.)

Anytime a loser leaves, they imitate Arnold in "Terminator" by saying, "I'll be back."

When a loser throws a crumpled piece of paper in a wastebasket, declares, "Not bad for a *white* guy!"

Anytime you say a line with slightly sexual connotations, the loser deftly adds, "That's what *she said.*"

When you're holding an item in your hand, loser says, "Hey, don't point that at me unless you intend to use it."

When you're searching for a nickel or a penny to pay for a purchase, the loser hands you the change and says, "Don't say I never gave you anything." or "Don't spend it all in one place."

Loser goes over to a fashion model standing beside a car at an auto show and asks, "So, do you come with the car too?"

"Got a watch?" loser asks, pointing to their watchless wrist. "Mine's a little off."

If you point out that the loser is hard of hearing, or should get their hearing checked, the loser acts like they can't hear you by saying, "What did you say? What?" (Variation: if you are in a real loud place and shout to the loser that it's hard to hear someone, loser acts like they are saying something to you, but is just moving their mouth without speaking.)

Restaurant jokes Loser yucksters pull

After the waitress presents the bill, the loser hands it to you and says, "Thanks for picking this up."

If there is a "No animals allowed" sign at the entrance door, loser quips, "I guess you'll have to wait outside."

Loosens the top of the salt shaker so it falls off and pours a mound of salt on your food.

Loser says to the waitress...
- "What's safe to eat here?"
- *(If the waitress says, "Would you like the check?")* Loser quips, "No, you can keep it."
- "Are you on the menu?"
- *(When asked for their order.)* "Just pick up what's on the kitchen floor and cook it up."
- *(If there's a screw up.)* "We'll just take it off your tip."

Allegedly funny one liners Losers irritatingly use

"With friends like you, who needs enemas?"

"I never forget a face, but in your case..."

"Nice hat. You get a free bowl of soup with it?"

"Why don't you squeeze that pimple?...The one on your neck."

"I used to have clothes like that, but then I got a *job*."

"Your parents threw you away and kept the afterbirth."

(For a weather announcement.) "Chili today, hot tamale!"

"The great lies are: the check is in the mail, the parts are in the truck, it's only a cold sore, and I won't come in your mouth."

(After they hear a disparaging description of a person.) "Hey, I resemble that remark."

(Say after a good deed.) "That's awful white of you."

"I'd beat your brains out, but someone beat me to it."

"The more hair you lose, the more head you get."

"Did your parents have any children that lived?"

"Stand up and give your mind a rest."

"The best part of you ran down your mother's leg."

(After you borrow something from them.) "I'm not worried about getting it back, I know where you *live*."

"How do you know it tastes like shit? Did you ever eat it?"

Allegedly funny one liners Losers irritatingly use (cont.)...

"You look like a poster child for birth control."

"If you write to me, write slow because I don't read too fast."

"This is an A to B conversation, why don't you C your way out?"

"I woulda been your father but the dog beat me over the fence."

"Let's do the 68, I'll owe you one."

(If loser hear's their name.) "That's my name, don't wear it out."

"It's for me to know and for you to find out."

"You think you're hot shit, but you're warm diarrhea."

"You know what? That's what."

"If you love ice cream so much, why don't you marry it?"

"Hey asshole!...You turned around!"

"Say it, don't spray it."

"I know you are but what am I?"

(If unable to be to think of a comeback.) "I'm rubber and your glue so whatever you say to me bounces off and sticks to you."

"You're so full of shit you're eyes are brown."

"Takes one to know one."

(Pointing to an open fly.) "Did someone die in your family? Then, how come your flag is flying at half mast?"

Loser car pranks

Loser gets into the driver's seat. You stand on the opposite side. Loser doesn't unlock the door. They start the car, wave, and act like they're leaving you.

If you are following them somewhere, instead of driving at a casual pace, the loser goes fast.

Upon opening the car door for you, the loser pulls the car away from the curb. You hurry to jump into the front seat. Loser hits brakes. You bang your head or arm on the dashboard or door.

You're walking along the side of the road. You see the loser driving the opposite way. Suddenly, loser gets a panicky look on their face, as if they have lost control of their car, and veers toward you, then, at the last moment, veers away.

If the loser is your friend and sees your car stopped at traffic light, they slowly drive up and...
- tap your rear bumper.
- jokingly hit their brights.
- when the light turns green, honk their horn as if they're mad, and flip you off.

Loser is driving by a golf course and sees someone trying to line up a putt. Loser furtively stops their car. They wait until the precise moment the golfer is going to strike the ball. Loser hits their car horn, which makes the startled player miss the putt.

If you are sitting in the back seat, the loser cranks up the volume on the radio or tape player and shouts, "Is that too *loud* for you back there?"

Loser hits deep puddles to splash pedestrians.

Loser comic routines meant to irritate or humiliate

Greets you with "How are you doing?" and sticks out a hand. You reach out to shake it. Loser pulls their hand away.

Loser belches, looks at someone else and says, "Excuse you."

Makes obvious jokes or puns about your name.

Shakes your hand and says, "My name is shit, have a handful."

If you make a collect call to the loser and the operator asks if they will accept the charges, loser says, "Who? Never heard of him. *(Pauses.)* Oh wait, I know him. Well, okay, I'll accept it."

Loser routines meant to irritate and humiliate (cont.)...

Loser sees you in a restaurant or bar and snaps, "I guess they let *anyone* in here."

Laughs at anyone's embarrassing hygienic problems, such as the lingering fumes of a fart or bowel movement ("Who died?" etc.); bad breath ("Dragon breath, etc."); bad skin ("Crater face," etc.); or a running nose ("boogers!" etc.)

Loudly points out food on your teeth.

After a loser says, "Knock wood," they rap on your head.

Anytime you tell a story of something wonderful that happened to you, loser adds, "And then you *woke up*."

Loser blows out all candles on their birthday cake and says, "I guess I didn't get my wish, you're still here."

If you're scanning a newspaper, loser incredulously inquires, "Hey, you can read?"

You're with a date. Loser comes over and says...
- "Nice to see you're dating women again."
- "Hope that hepatitis clears up."
- *(To the date)* "Didn't I meet you last week? Oh, that was someone else."
- "I see that sore on your lip is gone."

If you say,"Hey!," loser says,"*Hay* is for horses."

When you're not looking, loser takes your keys or wallet. The loser, gleefully watches you frantically pad your pockets. Loser holds up item and says, "Looking for this?" (Option: When everyone is looking for a lost item, the loser bends over and shouts, "I found it." *(Everyone turns.)* "Just kidding.")

(When loser greets someone.) "What's up Chuck?"

Loser routines meant to irritate or humiliate (cont.)...

After you return from the bathroom the loser says...
- "I bet that's a load off your mind."
- "Everything come out all right?"
- "You took so long, I thought you fell in."
- "What were you doing in there, shaking hands with the unemployed?"
- (*Points to your crotch.*) "Nice stains."

Pats you on the back and says, "You're a nice guy, I don't care what everyone else says about you."

If you ask for a sip of a loser's canned beverage, they say, "You can have the rest." You grab the can: it's empty.

When you're dialing a phone number, loser shouts out several different numbers to get you confused so you forget the number you want to call. (Option: the loser does the same trick when you're trying to open a combination lock; or, if you're counting money, doing an inventory check, or counting spoonfuls of coffee.

As you leave a party the loser loudly says...
- "I thought he'd never leave"
- "Now that they're gone we can have some fun."
- "I guess we can break out the cocaine and dope now!"
- "Don't let the door hit your ass on the way out."

If you are sitting on the toilet and have an embarrassingly difficult and loud bowel movement, loser gives a play-by-play: "Good one!...Nice!...What did you say?"

You tell the loser not to touch an object, loser suspends their hand just above it and says, "I'm not *touching* it."

Loser leaves you in a crowded elevator, just as the door closes they say, "Did you tell your parents you're *gay* yet?"

Loser slapstick and gross-out bits

When someone is discussing a topic, the loser says, "I look at it this way," and tilts their head at a weird angle. (Variation: says, "On the other hand" and sticks out their other hand.)

Enjoys farting and watching people's revulsion; or, tells a person to pull their finger, and then, the loser farts.

Loser shakes up a carbonated canned drink and hands it to you. You open it. Can sprays on you.. Or, Loser shakes can. Points it at you. Opens it. Sprays you.

When the loser goes through a doorway first they...
- try to close the door behind them so you can't get in.
- lock you outside and laugh at your helplessness.
- trap you within a revolving door.
- when you are trying to open a door, the hidden loser holds it from the other side.

If a loser's hands are ice cold, they press them against your warm body.

During a meal, a loser tries to ruin your appetite by...
- opening their mouth to show you the chewed up food on their tongue as they say,."I like seafood: *see* food!"
- popping a retainer or a false tooth out of their mouth.
- talking graphic about bodily functions or disgusting physical sights to make your food less palatable. Such as...
    1.) "This food looks the same way going in as it's going to come out."
    2.) "You know, corn doesn't get digested."
    3.) "Last time I ate that it was coming out of both ends."

Waits until you're drinking, then tries to make you laugh to watch it come out of your nose.*

---

*__World Of Fred Note:__ Fred has a fondness for this one..

Loser slapstick and gross-out bits (cont.)...

Hides in a spot. You enter the area thinking no one is there. Loser jumps out. Makes animal noise. Scares you.

If you're in stretch pants and standing in front of a large group of people, loser sneaks behind, and pulls your pants down.

Stands next to you and says, "I went fishing today, caught one this big!" (Loser rapidly extends their hand to show how big the fish, and thumps the hand against your chest.)

If your feet are elevated, loser unties your shoelace.

Has a wet hand, fakes a sneeze, and flicks the water from their hand onto you.

Loser is behind you, taps your left shoulder. You turn around. The loser holds their hand slightly above your shoulder. Your cheek hits the loser's extended finger.

Loser carries a cup past you and says, "Watch out, it's hot." Then drops the cup in your lap. You jump. It's empty.

When a loser pours you a drink they do the following...
- says, "Say when." But after you say "when," the loser still fills your glass fully to the brim.
- You ask for a full glass. The loser just pours a drop in it. You tell them to fill it. Loser acts like they are going to refill it. And loser just puts in another drop.

Loser hands you an object. But, just as you try to grab it, the loser withdraws it from your reach; or tantalizingly holds it beyond your grasp.

Just before loser leaves an elevator, intentionally drops a smelly fart (Another elevator trick: just before you get out, pushing all the buttons so elevator must stop on every floor.)

Loser slapstick and gross-out bits (cont.)...

You ask the loser to dial a phone number for you. The loser intentionally dials the wrong number and hands you the phone.

Loser walks in front of you, suddenly stops, so you bump into them. (Variation: walk alongside you and surreptitiously try to angle you off the sidewalk into the mud or dirt.).

You have to sit next to a loser. You ask, "Can you move over?" Loser slides the opposite way, giving you even less room to sit.

Losers harass swimmers by...
- shoving dry bathers into cold water.
- if the bather is slowly entering chilly water, loser splashes them.
- when a bather is sleeping or comfortable on an inflatable raft, loser flips it over.
- swims underneath you and pulls you under the water.

If you're wearing a nice felt hat, the loser grabs the brim and pulls it down. Or, takes it off your head and punches out its shape (after ruining your hat, loser says, "I thought it just goes back into shape naturally.").

You ask the loser to carry a large or fragile item. You're walking in front of the loser with your back to them. Loser bangs their leg against an obstruction. You turn, thinking the item has been damaged by hitting something. Loser laughs.

Loser sneaks up behind you, pushes their foot against the joint behind your knee, which causes your leg to buckle.

If you drop the loser off somewhere and start to drive away, loser hits your vehicle with their arm, and jumps up and down to give you the impression you ran over their foot.

Loser slapstick and gross-out bits (cont.)...

You are in a room. Loser knows you are in the room. Loser turns off the light. Then, feigns ignorance by saying, "Oh, I didn't know anyone was in there."

Tries to make you cringed by cracking their knuckles or neck.

If you give them a drink from your glass or bottle, loser makes a big show of wiping it off first.

When you're going to a show or some big event, just as you near the entrance booth, loser gets a panicked look on their face, pads their body, and acts like they don't have the tickets; or, they ask, "I gave the tickets to you, right?" Of course, they have the tickets the whole time.

Asks you, "What's green and goes backwards?" You say you don't know. Loser snorts mucous back into their nasal passages.

If you're sitting at someone else's desk, or standing in someone else's cubicle or office (Let's just say the someone else is named Bob). Loser enters, does a poorly executed double take, and says, "Why, you're not Bob!" (Loser finds it even more hilarious to do this if you are the opposite sex of the person the loser expected to find in the office.)

When you have a picture taken with them, a loser does the following...
- sticks their finger in a V-sign behind your head (to indicate you have horns).
- reaches for your groin.
- *(Says.)* "Better not take that picture unless you want the camera to break." or "Hope that camera is insured."
- sticks thumb out an open fly, as if they had their penis out.
- stands behind someone and grabs their breast.

Insult and Live! by Fred Reiss

A Loser Review

A Loser Review

1.) Why does a loser take a razor and rip someone else's car convertible top?

Answer: Because the loser doesn't have one.

2.) Why does a loser break apart benches in parks, carve initials in trees and fences, or intentionally clog public restroom toilets?

Answer: Because at work, losers feel they have to take everyone else's crap, so now someone has to take theirs.

3.) When you confront a loser for acting like a child, why doesn't the loser respond in an adult way?

Answer: Let Fred give you an example. Say, you take a roommate's unwashed dishes, which have been in the sink for a week, and throw the plates in their bed. Does the loser clean the dishes? No! They take the dishes and throw them in your bed! The loser's rational is simple: "If you're going to treat me like a child, I'll act like a child."

4.) Why do losers complain about being broke but refuse to work overtime or take a second job?

Answer: After losers are done working, the loser sees any moments after that as "my time."

5.) How come losers vandalize works of art?

Answer: Because a loser feels putting graffiti or damaging a work of art makes their vandalism equal to the art form.

6.) Why do losers tell you gossip that will upset you?

Answer: Losers resent anyone who is happy, in love, or has a higher standard of living. Since the loser's life is messed up, they attempt to ruin yours. Once any loser accomplishes this task, it proves to them there's nothing wrong with their own life because everyone is miserable.* Hey, look at it this way, a dump truck is a dump truck, it just dumps on everything but itself.

7.) Why do losers live beyond their means and "max out" their credit card limits?

Answer: Losers believe they deserve to "treat" themselves to a good meal at a restaurant, a weekend getaway, or a first-class vacation.

8.) If people are waiting to use a public pay-phone, why do losers engage in very long personal conversations about nothing?

Answer: Because losers have nothing to talk about but themselves and their relationship to other people. So, they find themselves fascinating, important, and dramatic. They love the sound of their own voice. They assume you will too!

---

*World Of Fred Note: Gossips are heavily into denial. For example, if you accidently catch one in the act of gossiping about you or a friend, the gossiping loser gets mad at you for eavesdropping; or, complains you should have warned them that you were within hearing distance.

9.) Why do Losers On Wheels speed through residential areas?

Answer: Losers are jealous they don't live there. These losers reason that just because you have a house in a nice neighborhood doesn't entitle you to special privileges. You see, somehow, losers have determined your success was derived from making them miserable. Since you allegedly caused the loser's problems, you shouldn't be able to enjoy your life either. They see it as "payback."

10.) Why don't losers have a sense of humor?

Answer: It's simple. If you have a sense of humor, you're able to view yourself in a situation from the outside. Losers are only concerned with their own needs so they can't see beyond themselves. If losers could see beyond themselves, they wouldn't be rude or selfish because they'd be more attuned to the concerns of other people's plights.

That's why, instead of laughing at themselves or their comic situation, losers only see how the world is making them miserable, so, they take every humorous comment literally or personally. They get indignant because they feel you're "rubbing it in" and "mocking" them.

11.) Why do losers go on rampages with an automatic weapon, seize hostages, rant about the world, and then kill themselves?

Answer: When you read in the newspaper about some despondent loser or disgruntled employee who goes on a killing spree, their victims are decent people who did the following "unjust" things...

- Divorced the loser.
- Slapped the loser with a restraining order.
- Fired the loser for incompetency.
- Refused to date the loser.
- Filed criminal charges against the loser.
- Evicted the loser or foreclosed on their mortgage.
- Garnished the loser's wages because the loser didn't pay their bills or child-support.

And what's the common thread that links these victims? Each one forced the loser to acknowledge responsibility. Again, remember the loser descrambler formula: confrontation with reality leads to denial of responsibility, which in turn motivates the misfit to conclude they are the unjustly persecuted victim. The loser becomes a mental case because they *never make an effort* to compromise, understand, or accommodate anyone else.

But, in this extreme state, the rampaging loser takes their persecution complex a step further. They feel "someone must pay" for what the world has done to them. Another variation on this theme is killing what they love because losers can't endure sharing their loved one with anyone else. In both cases, these misunderstood losers seek an apocalyptic salvation through their failures. They see themselves as martyrs and have a mission to kill their oppressors. After the grisly task is completed, these maniacal missionaries leave a note or a recorded message that justifies the loser's crime, their disavowal of guilt, and how in the afterlife a "superior being" (alias God as these losers conceive Him to be.) will understand how the world has made them suffer and forgive the twisted loser. Then, the loser takes their life, and if possible, also kills the person trying to "talk them down."

12.) Why do physically attractive losers passionately pursue lovers who are cruel to them?

Answer: Physically attractive losers have an easy time attracting potential lovers. So, since it's easy, most losers have contempt toward their admirers. But, at the same time, losers enjoy the misery their rejection inflicts upon those admirers. Therefore, when losers aren't pursued by a potential lover, or treated with indifference, these beautiful losers feel a pain, which they see as a sign they are a good person who has the capacity to love. But, what this particular loser really loves is their own misery, a torment they know their beauty causes others.

13.) Why are famous celebrities who have a wholesome and caring public image such scumbags in real life?

Answer: These always-look-for-the-good-inside-people celebs found it was easier to make money by presenting a wholesome image. Everyone has a dark side. No matter how hard a phony tries to suppress it, it'll come out. And the harder a person tries to hide it, the darker and uglier it is. These phonies become successful with a deceiving image of themselves, so they hate their fans. Why? Again, it's denial transference in action. Instead of having contempt for themselves, they are contemptuous toward fans dumb enough to believe in their false image. Every compliment they receive reminds the celebrity they are living a lie. So, they lash out at their fans instead of themselves. This celeb actively seeks out the media to perk up their career during lulls, but when they're hot again, these same celebs rail against the press for not respecting their "privacy." This type also holds vindictive grudges against anyone who criticizes them. Why? They view valid criticism as something that could take away from their income.

14.) Why do you always see a couple comprised of a nice person and a complete loser?

Answer: Loser couples only love what the other person can do for them. They form a "team" against the world. Sometimes a loser joins with another loser to do something they can't do without the help of someone else: satisfying their own needs. That's why you see I-don't-know-what he/she sees in him/her couples. You know, people who seem like they're a mismatch, because one is a arrogant jerk and the other is sackcloth saint. But, if you see them as one individual with two faces, they're easy to figure out.*

A typical you-and-me-against-the-world Loser Couple never lets go of each other's hand, mowing down people in their path.

*****World Of Fred Note:** Opposites detract. Before this type of loser finds their perfect co-dependent, they go through several relationships. The loser complains of their failed relationships, blaming the other person or saying how it reflects the behavior of the opposite sex, but neglects to note the loser only looks at another person for what the loser can get out of them, not for who the person is. Sometimes two manipulating losers have a relationship and embarrass others by fighting, criticizing their partner's flaws, or trying to get a bystander to take their side.

15.) Why is the number of losers growing?

Answer: These unviable tissue masses produce more children than decent people. Think about it. The overwhelming majority of well read and intelligent couples rarely produce more than one or two kids (If any.). But, Fred guarantees, every insufferable loser you know has at least five whiny wet-lipped kids who "take after the old man."

Basic Losers

How a loser wants to be perceived by others, or through the media...

But if shown without their uniform you see what a loser *really* is.

Part Two:
Basic Losers

Purpose of this section: Points out the basic forms losers assume in the World Of Fred, and provides you with insults to slam them.

Losers always see themselves as persecuted saints.

You've learned loser basics, now let's focus on the basic losers who share fundamental characteristics that transcend race, class, or sex. The World of Fred has isolated these qualities in the form of total losers, moochers, loser coworkers, schmoozing sales jerks, loser bosses, and evil old farts.

Typical Total Loser tip offs

During job interviews asks, "When are my days off?"

Has a car in danger of repossession.

Is over thirty, still lives at their parent's home, and is considered the "baby" by an overprotective parent.

When a loser moves, no one helps them move in.

Grumbles about not having any money because the government hit the loser up for back taxes--again.

Lies and misrepresents themselves to get a good deal on a purchase. After the sale, loser brags to others, "Look what I bought!" But, if the loser discovers they made a bad deal, the loser brings the merchandise back to the salesman and says, "Look what *you* sold me."

Doesn't have any friends for longer than two years (If they run into anybody from the past, the person still dislikes them.).

Gets uncomfortable when the conversation's topic shifts away from the loser's personal life.

Blames their parents' flaws for the loser's own limitations and professional shortcomings.

Boasts about all the things they "could of had" but don't have.

Every where the loser goes, the loser manages to get into a fight with "some idiot."

Tries to pay off debts by gambling instead of working them off.

Asks for your advice and then challenges everything you say.

Never sends "thank you" notes from their wedding.

Typical Total Loser tip offs (cont.)...

Anytime the loser screws up, they have an apologist friend who claims the loser "means well."

Says friendly things but never does them.

Always seems to be having "just one of those days."

Their wisdom isn't based on successful experiences, it's based on their mistakes.

Takes out their job frustrations on people.

Makes up stories of their own importance or confrontational triumphs over others.

Has nowhere to go on holidays.

Never celebrates their birthday because the loser knows no one really likes them.

After you treat losers to a meal, they don't offer to buy you a drink or cover the tip.

Throws away reusable possessions instead of giving them to others.

Thrives in groups and becomes dumber and even ruder.*

---

* **World Of Fred Note:** If you take a jerk and it joins forces with another jerk, loser fusion occurs. They grow into a club, neighborhood association, zoning board or mob. Within a group, the loser can briefly dominate the moment. The world becomes their world where the binding loser curve of energy acts out all its fantasies, gratifies whatever hunger it has, and strikes out at any rule. This congealed loser group commits vandalism, beats or bullies people, steals, forms a political party, or dominates a surf spot.

Typical Total Loser tip offs (cont.)...

Has a boring service-oriented job but says their experience with humanity is so vast that "I could write a book" or "I could tell you stories." (But, when pressed, losers can't come up with any interesting tales.)

Blames the school system for flaws in their children.

Talks about their job and exaggerates their importance or position.

Bitches about being broke, but always has money for booze.

Gets consistently fired from jobs for arguing with a boss who the loser claims "doesn't know jackshit."

Always has some upcoming business opportunity that involves making a lot of money, but the deal predictably falls through for mysterious reasons.

Total Loser's annoying habits

Never cleans up their messes.

Writes a lot of bad checks (But, claims it was somebody else's fault the funds didn't clear.).

Asks you a question about a certain topic so the loser can interrupt your answer to tell you how they feel about it.

When sick or injured and brought into the hospital, the loser demands the best medical treatment. Afterwards they bitterly complain about the bill.

Rarely flushes the toilet.

Total Loser's annoying habits (cont.)...

When legally forced to pay a debt or an overdue bill, loser pays the entire sum in pennies.

Believes that loudly talking about a subject makes them seem more intelligent.

Always boasts they know where you can get a better deal on an expensive purchase, medical procedure, or litigation matter, but the loser never tells you where to find it. ("I know a lawyer who'd do it for nothing." or "I have a friend who can get you a real deal on..." or "It's sold out, but...I can get tickets.")

After you tell losers what you sold something for, they say, "At that price, you gave it away. If you told me you were going to sell it that cheap, *I'd* have bought it!" (Yeah, right.)

If asked to do something they don't want to do, the loser deliberately does it badly to insure you will never ask them to do it again.

Never admits they don't know what they're talking about. (Variation: Whatever subject comes up, they always happen to know something about it: "Yeah, that happened to me once, let me tell you...")

Offers their professional help on your project to save you money, then takes forever to do it, which causes you so many delays, you actually lose more money than if you paid someone.

Avoids living up to their potential by seeking out people who are no good for them or treat loser like dirt.

When caught-in-the-act stealing from an employer, the loser rationalizes the crime by saying, "You can afford it;" or, "I help you make a lot of money so I'm *entitled*."

Total Loser's lack of people skills

If you're in a crowd and the loser is the only one who knows where the car is, the jerk wanders off without you.

Never offers their seat to an infirm person.

If they call on the phone, losers...
- ask to talk to the person you live with, but never acknowledge you.
- inquire if a person is there, and if you say no, they immediately hang up.
- refuse to leave their name or a message.

Gets angry or physically attacks the person their lover had sex with, but doesn't do anything to the lover for cheating.

Never gives anything to someone unless they get something of at least equal value in return.

Loves to gossip and dwell on other people's failures.

If the loser can't score with a member of the opposite sex, loser tries to "block" you from scoring.

Interrupts conversations without apologizing.

Bluntly asks what your income is.

Jokingly points guns or pellet weapons at you (Losers defend this by saying, "The safety is on....It's unloaded.").

Instead of giving you a social out by introducing themselves with their name and where you met, a loser makes you feel awkward and simply says, "Remember me?" or "You don't know who I am do you?"

Never wants to hear about your personal suffering.

Total Loser's distortion-of-reality signs

Lives their life without listening to anyone, but never hesitates to tell you how you should run your life. Losers preface their free and unsought advice with...
- "You know what I would do if I were you..."
- "I wouldn't let them do that to me. Why, if they did that to me, I'd..."
- "They can't do that. If you went to court you could..."
- "You know what *your* problem is, you ought to..."

Believes life "owes" them something but losers feel they don't owe anything to anybody else.

If you point out their selfishness, the loser defensively snaps, "Hey, it's my life."

Thinks the number of people they sleep with proves how many people love them.

If losers don't get their way, they mimic what the other person wants to do and make fun of it the whole time. (For example, they'll sarcastically grumble, "Boy, we're having some fun now." or "Oh, this is *great* isn't it?")

Confuses developing a personality with making radical changes in their physical appearance or their way of dress.

If they misplace something, losers blame the object, not themselves. For example: "Where are those *dumb* keys?"

Never gives anyone a sexually transmitted disease. Someone always gave it to the loser.

After a juvenile act, loser grunts, "Yeah, I'm *mature*."

Is well in their thirties and glumly says, "You know it's hard to believe our high school years are gone."

Total Loser's distortion-of-reality signs (cont.)...

Harshly criticizes others, but is extremely thin-skinned if anyone dares to criticizes them. They'll complain they're being "made an example of," "made the scapegoat," or, "shut out because everyone is so cliquey."

Crummy to a person in life, but when the person dies, the guilty loser loudly cries at the funeral, tries to pull the body from the coffin, or jumps into the grave.

If loser has symptoms of any highly contagious terminal disease, says they won't go to the doctor because "I don't want to know what's wrong."

Sues anyone or any organization to avoid accepting responsibility or the financial costs that were the end results of their own stupidity or selfishness.

Total Loser's car passenger manners

Puts their feet on dashboard but doesn't clean their footprints from it.

Without asking, changes the heat, air conditioning, or the stereo's channel and volume.

Leaves their garbage behind.

If someone else on the road isn't driving properly, loser takes it upon themselves to honk your horn at them, or flip strangers off.*

While you're trying to drive, the loser finds it amusing to...
- turn on your wipers.
- hit the windshield washer-fluid button.
- switch on your turn signals.

When you're stopped at a traffic light, the loser waits until you're not looking, and shifts the car out of gear, or puts your emergency brake on.

If you get stopped by a cop, the loser passenger starts an argument with the officer, which leads to an incident that gets you into more trouble than the loser.

---

*World Of Fred Note:** But, if you do honk a loser's horn while they're driving, the jerk gets angry and yells, "What are you *doing?* "

Moochers

The moocher is life's great taker. What's yours is theirs and what's theirs is always theirs. They never repay loans, return your tools, or buy a round of drinks. They consistently bum cigarettes, cold medicines, drinks, rides, stamps, pizza slices, newspapers, or help themselves to your french fries.

Moochers freeload so often they *expect* people to pay the moocher's way. If you reject their loan request moochers get offended, then indignantly say...

- "Hey, I'm always looking out for you."
- "Come on, I don't ask for much."
- "If I had it, I'd give it to you."
- "When's the last time I asked for anything?"
- "I don't want something for nothing."
- "You know I'm *good* for it."
- "If the situation were reversed, I wouldn't be treating you the way you're treating me."
- *(If you turn them down for a ride.)* "You're going that way, anyway." or "It's not that far out of your way."

But the truth is moochers are rarely in the position to give anything to anybody, or co-sign a car loan. And, if they do have money (Usually from a car insurance settlement.), they blow the entire wad on themselves because the deprived moocher has been "doing without" for too long. Yet, moochers assure themselves they're generous people because if they win the lottery or "when their ship comes in," they pledge to "make it up" to everyone.

Ways Moochers sponge at parties

A moocher is a polished sponger. When a moocher brings something to a party it's always the cheapest beer, wine, appetizer, or food item. But moochers never eat or drink what they bring. For example, a moocher brings a two-dollar bottle of wine, but drinks the better one. Or, brings hot dogs to a barbecue but eats someone else's steak. Or, brings cheap, metallic-tasting beer, but quickly slams down any imported brew from the fridge. The other tactic is showing up at a party with only "what I'm going to drink," or, "just enough for what I'm going to have." (Of course, moochers wind up eating and drinking other people's food and booze.)

Moochers consistently shows up empty handed at parties,* tailgate bashes, barbecues, softball beer games and use excuses like...

- "You told me you didn't need anything."
- "I wanted to stop and get something but all the stores were closed."
- *(Show up uninvited with two friends who bought something and says)* "I was just tagging along and these guy asked me to come." Or, lies, "I chipped in for the stuff they bought."
- "I didn't have time to stop at the store because I wanted to get here on time."

---

*World Of Fred Note: When invited to a party, potential moochers give themselves away by asking, "Should I bring anything?" If they weren't moochers, they'd say, "What do you need?" or propose a list of items they would bring to the party.

Moochers reveal themselves at parties with these tactical moves...

1.) Mysteriously disappear when someone is collecting the money for a late-night beer run or pizza.
2.) Follow people around who they think have drugs.
3.) Sees you doing well with a potential sexual partner and tries to snake in on your action.
4.) If there are drugs around...
- Takes more than their share and says, "Oh, I'm sorry, I thought you said do *two* lines." or takes longer hits from the group joint.
- After they've done cocaine with a group, the moocher tries to steal the rolled-up bill used to snort the drug.
- Act like the hash pipe is spent and taps its ashes in a napkin, however, there is still an unburnt chunk within the ashes, which the moocher pockets.

5.) Always nearby when someone else is buying a round of drinks.
6.) If there is a collection for food and drink before the party begins, moocher gives less than others because, "I don't drink or eat as much as everyone else does."
7.) When someone offers to buy a round of drinks or treat to a meal, moocher changes their order and asks for a more expensive drink or dish.

How Moochers deny they're thieves

Most moochers are thieves in a perpetual state of denial. They steal by borrowing items and never returning them. But, they can't admit this to themselves. That's why they get angry when you ask them for your possessions back.

Insult technique: First point out to the moocher you're asking for an item they haven't returned in a long time. Their descrambler will kick in. Again, they can't say hello the themselves, so, they'll just avoid it by saying goodbye to you. This is why these moochers attempt to reverse the situation so you're at fault. When moochers are done wailing their tirade, insult them. But, add an observation that sums up the moocher's twisted logic.

For example...

Situation:
Insulting A Moocher After Asking For An Item They Borrowed But Never Returned.
*(Scene: **You With The Power Of Insult And Live!** approach the Mooching Borrower.)*

You With The Power Of *Insult And Live!*
Say, you remember that hedge trimmer I lent you six months ago, I need it back.

Mooching Borrower
(Indignant.)
I was going to bring it back, I just forgot. What are you trying to say? That I wasn't going to return it? That I was going to steal it! Take it if you need it so badly. All you had to do was *ask* in the first place. Instead of going off on me like that. *(Storms away.)*

You With The Power Of *Insult And Live!*
I'm certain Jesus loves you, but I bet in your case, He's probably seeing other people. *(Pause.)* Does that mean I can't lend you anything for six months and ask for it back again?

Post-insult Outcome: You win! Instead of being intimidated by the moocher's behavior, you slammed them and summed up their crime. The moocher's defensive response is their confession. Yes, they did intend to keep the item and never return it.

Ways Moochers use other people

Moocher says, "I'll fly if you buy."

In a move to soak relatives for gifts or money, moochers send their children's wedding invitations to relations who live so far away they can't possibly attend the event.

Invites themselves up every weekend to your beach house, or to use your pool in the summer.

Is never around when you need their help to move; however, if a post-move beer/pizza party is involved, the moocher strategically avoids heavy lifting, or shows up late.

During the holiday season or when someone's birthday comes up, moochers are "too broke" to buy anyone gifts. (This doesn't stop moochers from accepting gifts; which they feel entitled to because they are so broke.) Sometimes they give you a present they used, or was given to them, but didn't like.

Tries to get something for free by complaining.

Makes toll calls from your house.

Never gets off their behind to get anything but says to someone, "While you're up can you get me a (*Fill in blank*)?"

Gives you a present that's some type of food or candy, then after you open it, they eat all of it.

Treats themselves well, but is a cheapskate to others.

If you catch them wearing your clothing, the moocher says, "You never wear this anyway."

Gives or shares anything that's not theirs, such as exorbitantly tipping with your change from a meal you bought for them.

Moocher ruses to duck out of paying their way*

Has a tendency to accidentally leave their wallet at home.

Consistently brings less money than they need to go out (this ensures others will cover for them).

If they take an item from a business without paying for it, moocher justifies the theft by saying, "They'll never miss it." or "I spend a lot of money there anyway."

Refuses to pay phone companies for expensive sex-calls numbers on their bill with the excuse that "I didn't make those calls, someone must have broken into my house and made them."

Borrows your car and returns it with a nearly empty gas tank, or gets a parking ticket and doesn't tell you about it.

Says they'll chip in for somebody's present; then, after they share credit for buying the gift, never pay you back.

Pays most of their loan to you, but never repay the rest.

Keeps change from a purchase the moocher made for you with your money.

Cause a scene to get a discount.

---

*World Of Fred Note: Interestingly, if you owe a moocher they either relentlessly harass you for payment, immediately demand the return of a favor or the item you borrowed ("Hey, you get this meal, I gave you $1.42 for a hamburger three weeks ago."). But, if you hit on a moocher for the money they owe you, the moocher feels you embarrassed them, which entitles them to delay paying you even longer. What's even more irritating is that moochers are usually cheapskates with huge savings accounts, a trust fund, or concealed real estate holdings. These moochers complain they're broke, then suddenly show up with a new car or purchase an incredibly expensive luxury item.

Moocher ruses to duck out of paying their way (cont.)...

Denies paying their costs of utility or phone bills by saying "according to their records" they owe you far less. (If you insist on payment, the moocher gets offended because "you're yelling at me." The moocher sneaks out because they "feel threatened" by your aggressive behavior, which further justifies why they should stiff you.)

Arrives with no money because the moocher expected "an ATM to be nearby." (Variation: after you pick a moocher up to go out, moocher says, "I have to stop at an ATM to get some cash." (Knowing you won't stop and will front the money, which moocher will never pay back.)

If you ask a moocher to repay you for concert tickets, the moocher says they gave the money to someone else who is suppose to pay you.

When a moocher returns a borrowed item in broken condition, the moocher...
- doesn't reimburse you for it because it "would have broken anyway." or "I was just the straw that broke the camel's back."
- claims it "was that way when I borrowed it."
- replaces the broken item with something of lesser quality.

Reneges on lost bets by saying, "I didn't think you were serious." or "We didn't shake on it."

Ducks out of giving you money for gas by innocently asking, "So how much do you need for gas?" They know most people feel uncomfortable asking for cash, and let the gas money slide.

Calls radio station listener lines, hoping there's a contest, and just says, "Did I win anything?"

Carries large bills they "don't want to break" so they ask you to pay or cover the tip with your smaller bills.

Moocher ruses to duck out of paying their way (cont.)...

When asked to repay money, the moocher laughs and says...
- "I got you back for that a week ago."
- "You said you were treating."
- "Come on, you weren't going to use that (*Fill in the amount.*)."
- "I didn't bring my checkbook."
- "I'll have to get you next time, this has been a rough week."
- "I thought you were coming tomorrow for the money."
- (*If caught sneaking out before the check arrives, says*) "I wasn't leaving, I was just going out to my car and coming back in."
- "I can't pay you, I need the money to go out this weekend."

Ways Moochers sponge meals in restaurants

You're in a restaurant with a party. The moocher in the group orders numerous drinks and eats several appetizers. When the bill comes, the moocher says, "All I had was a *cheeseburger.*"

Moocher calls you up and says, "Let's meet for lunch." Then after the meal is done, tells you they "don't have any money."

Party-of-twelve moochers promise the waiter a "big tip." But, the moochers spend all their money on liquor, and stiff the waiter. They rationalize their selfishness away by saying, "The food was overpriced, and it wasn't that good, so the hell with them. They made a profit." They leave a huge mess.

Lets everyone else buy rounds of drinks, but leaves before it's their turn to buy.

Agrees to split on a dish, but tries to eat more food than you.

Treats you to a breakfast (if the bill is cheap), but the next time, when the breakfast bill is expensive they ask you to pick up the check because the moocher "got the last meal."

Encourages others on expense accounts to treat the moocher.

Losers at work

One thing a loser definitely hates more than their own life: their job. These losers are "nice" until it comes to "work." Their whole purpose is to make everyone else's job even more difficult. They always know more than the boss and make their own decisions without clearing them with anyone, which screws up other people's departments. These miserable perfunctories are spiteful, highly inept, malicious, and turn every task into drudgery. Their motto: if you're not making progress, slow down (A credo practiced by union and government employees.) Oddly, the simpler the position, the more important the loser feels about it, and the more job pressure the low-leveler feels at work. *

*****World Of Fred Note:** Most miserable losers have been employed by one company their entire life. They've never been out of work, so, they take their job for granted, and turn every dispute into a personal confrontation. Most of the time these miserable losers don't get fired because no one else wants their dead-end position, and management feels the next person they hire for the post will be the same or worse.

Insult technique: Give the loser every possible chance to be optimistic or productive. Then acknowledge their negative mood, but attach an insult to it.

For example...

Situation:
Insulting Losers At Work

*(Scene: It's Monday morning in the break room by the coffee machine. The hungover **Loser At Work** is drinking coffee and glumly staring at the rain through the window. Enter **You With The Power Of Insult and Live!**, the ambitious and professional employee.)*

You With The Power Of *Insult and Live!*
(Approaching loser at the coffee machine.)
How are you doing today?

Loser At Work
(Sullenly grunts.)
I'm here. *(Pause.)* If you really want to know how I am, ask me at five o' clock. *(Sips coffee.)* Well, it's Monday. Four more days to go. *(Looks outside.)* It's raining.

You With The Power Of *Insult and Live!*
Yeah, but it's going to clear up in a few hours.

Loser At Work
Great and we're stuck in here all day.

You With The Power Of *Insult and Live!*
Look on the bright side, you could be back at your old job shoveling dead animals off the highway.

Post-insult Outcome: You won! You acknowledged the loser's attitude problem without really confronting it. Sure, they're still miserable and depressed, and possibly offended by the remark, but it doesn't matter. They're losers. They won't do anything to make your job easier anyway. You can't trust them. So enjoy!

Loser workplace habits

Arrives late to work and is the first one to leave.

Expends more effort to avoid work than the time it actually takes to do a particular task.

Chews gum and talks with their mouth open.

Quick to give a reason why any proposed task can't be done.

Intentionally misfiles information so they can eventually blames the system for being inefficient.

Never does anything until someone asks them to do it.

Complains about their job so often they don't pay attention and make mistakes. When the loser's errors return to them, they blame it on the office's disorganized system, which of course would run better if they "were in charge." (This is usually said by low-rung employees, i.e., mail-room staff.)

Loudly does their tasks or thinks aloud as they do them.

Processes paperwork and loudly groans, "This shit belongs in someone else's department."

Never does more than the job requires because their boss don't pay them enough.*

When you explain a job procedure, loser interrupts you, claims they "know how to do it." (Later you find the loser does it wrong because they didn't know how to do it.)

---

*__World Of Fred Note:__ But, the loser never admits their counter-productiveness is why they never advance. Instead, these losers complain people get unfairly promoted over them because of "seniority," "office politics," "brown nosing," or a "quota system."

Loser workplace habits (cont.)...

Makes personal phone calls during business hours, takes long lunches, as well as frequent smoking or coffee breaks "because I need to get away from my desk to think."

Always has to be told what to do. (When they do the task incorrectly, the loser claims they were incorrectly told how to do a project.)

If their boss lets the loser do a job without interference, the loser says there's "no leadership." But, when a loser has a demanding boss, the loser grumbles they can't properly do the job "with someone always looking over my shoulder."

Sends out mass-mailed letters without proofreading them.

When they leave the job, steal a lamp, calculator, etc.

Loser At Work break-room behavior

Takes the last cup of coffee, but never refills the coffee maker.

Steals someone's milk from the refrigerator for their coffee.

Complains about their work load by saying, "I'm not used to working like this."

Returns depressed from vacation and grunts, "Boy, I need a *vacation* to get over my vacation." (They also say this about their weekend or say, "The weekend wasn't long enough.")

Proclaims, "Boy, if I ever win the lottery, I'm gonna put a couple people in their place before I go."

Mentions people by name and loudly accuses them of screw-ups or criticizes their professional limitations so other coworkers in the room can hear them.

Rude ways Loser workers treat fellow employees

Takes their personal knowledge of a coworker and uses it against them. For example, "You know why they left early? They're going to a ball game."*

Never chips in for someone's birthday or going-away present, but is around for a free piece of cake.

When a loser feels they are doing more work than someone else, they quickly point it out to the boss.

Never covers for a coworker's mistakes.

On pay day, goes through wastebaskets to find out if an employee makes more than them.

If a coworker is looking for information in the wrong location, loser doesn't tell them.

Anytime the loser screws up, they attempt to divert attention from it by unjustly accusing someone of a larger goof.

Meddles in other people's work but doesn't spend any time on their own job; then complains they can't "get anything done because nobody knows what they're doing around here."

Without telling you, goes over your head.**

***World of Fred Note:** Office losers never learn from their mistakes. For example: A loser maliciously gossips about a coworker. The unjustly maligned employee finds out, and reports the loser to management. A supervisor yells at the loser. But does the loser learn gossiping serves no productive purpose in the work place? No way! Instead, the loser tries to discover which coworker confidant "betrayed" them.

**Another World Of Fred Note: Some losers because of their personal wealth don't need their job, so, they don't have to play office politics. They're contemptuous. They jeopardize other people's livelihoods by bluntly exposing coworkers flaws and screw ups.

Rude ways Loser workers treat fellow employees (cont.)...

Develops a snarly disposition so coworkers are afraid to ask the loser to do anything.

If sick, leaves their used tissues all over desks.

Walks into work and never says "good morning" to anyone.

When they can't find something, the loser accuses you of removing it. (The missing item is often found on the loser's desk because they never really looked for it.) Sometimes the loser finds the item, and tries to escape blame by sneaking into your office, and leaving it.

Dumps the particular responsibilities that they hate in their job onto a new employee.

When it's their break or lunch time, they immediately leave the office (even if you're swamped with a customer rush or need someone to cover the phones.).

Accuses anyone who is courteous and professional as being a "phony" or an "ass kisser." (Option: loudly makes ass-kissing sounds behind the person's back.)

Loser At Work phone skills

If a client asks to be transferred to another department, loser says, "I'll transfer you right now," and hangs up.

Anytime someone is away from their desk, loser never answers the coworker's phone.

Answers the phone but never identifies themselves or the work place, instead, the loser indifferently grunts, "Hello" or "Yeah."

Schmoozing Sales Losers

Sales jerks believe they can sell you anything. They won't take no for an answer. Instead, it's a challenge to hit the right pitch to hook you into their "doable" deal. These slick sharpies are always trying to sell you on something. They don't even have to believe in it! The important thing is convincing you to believe in it! Really, it can be anything: an idea, an incorrect fact, getting you to change your opinion, or even seducing someone. The sales schmoozer wants to prove to themselves they can do it. In fact, these client-cultivating hustlers who always know the latest joke, are so busy sucking up for a sell, they never develop an identity. That's why, when the schmoozer gets drunk, they turn into a crude beast.

If you're a polite person, the schmoozer cheats you on a sale by promising more than they deliver, passes off damaged merchandise as new, charges you more than they should, or sells you a defective product or of lesser quality. They figure if you're so naive to trust them, you deserve to be taken.

Insult technique: These intimidating salesmen collar you into listening to their spiel by making you feel like a bad person if you say no to them. It doesn't matter if you insult them. They don't even take it personally--it's a game to them. These schmoozers don't even think it's their insincere personality that turns people off, they think they just used the wrong sales approach.

Situation:
Using Insults To Get Rid Of A Schmoozing Sales Jerk

Schmoozing Sales Jerk
Hey buddy, I have this once-in-a-lifetime deal. You gotta act fast. Just between you and me, you oughta take a look, it'll make you a lot of money. *(Senses they're losing you so they ask a question you'd be embarrassed to say "no" to.)* I'm not boring you? We're still friends?

You With The Power To *Insult And Live!*
Well, let me put it to you this way, you're what happens when a dialysis machine backs up.

Schmoozing Sales Jerk
(Slapping you on the back.)
Funny! Look, I can see you're busy right now. We'll talk later, buddy. Over lunch. My treat.

Post-insult Outcome: You win! These glad-handing schmoozers can't reveal their smarmy act. You've thwarted their attempts to exploit your decency.

Loser Bosses

Loser Bosses often confuse leadership with bullying their staff. They never give compliments because "you're doing what I paid you to do." These hard-balling bosses conceal their incompetence by flying into rages and bellowing phrases like...

- "I'll get to the bottom of this, heads are going to roll."
- "I'm not running a country club here."
- "I'm going to rip someone a new asshole."
- "I'm not out to win any popularity contests."
- "It's time to kick ass and take names."
- "Let's throw it against the wall and see what sticks."
- "It's time to shit or get off the pot."
- "When I ask you to jump, you say, 'How high?"

*World Of Fred Note: The lowest form of Loser Bosses are sleazy nightclub owners who underpay their staff, abuse them, shabbily treat customers, never pay their bills on time, and cheat performers on pay.

How Loser Bosses make their employees miserable

After someone leaves, instead of filling the position, the Loser Boss dumps the work onto other people.

The without-a-life Loser Boss is a workaholic who doesn't "demand anything from their employees that I wouldn't demand from myself." (Which somehow entitles the boss to overwork their staff to "get the best" from them.)

Hires an incompetent friend from the "outside" to a supervisory position that should deservedly go to an employee who has been with the company for twenty-five years; then, squeezes the loyal employee out because they won't go along with their new supervisor's dumb ideas.

Takes your commission from a deal.

Replaces your Christmas bonus with a gift certificate for a turkey or company merchandise.

Downgrades their staff to make them feel they're not entitled to a raise and "lucky" to even have a job.

Pays you late to collect extra interest in their account.

Turns down your requests for personal days or vacation time.

Removes you from any job you're comfortable, productive, and efficient at.

When times are allegedly tough, the Loser Boss denies you a raise because "I'm not making any money."(But when times were good they never shared it.)*

---

*World Of Fred Note: Yet, they drive an expensive luxury car, live in an elegant house located in an exclusive neighborhood, or go on exotic and exorbitant vacation.

Loser Bosses are tyrants to helpless underlings, but are notorious butt-kissers to those above them.

Loser Boss job performance review

Takes an efficient department and runs it into the ground because they want to "make their mark on it."

Only likes doing something different if it's *their* idea.

Never gives you enough information to complete a task, this way they're still the boss because you can't finish the job without consulting them.

Nice to you as long as you're not a threat.

***World Of Fred Note:** Worst butt-kissers are aides who pucker for generals (It's known as the Lieutenant-colonel factor).

Loser Boss job performance review (cont.)..

Stays late after work so they can be one step ahead of everyone else in their office the next day.*

Never delegates (This protects their job.).

Drives women to tears during a project, but after the work is completed gives them a gift to show the employee their boss "is a nice person who means well."

Complains about you arriving late or leaving early but never notices you worked without a break or lunch.

If the Loser Boss is going to be away all day, they never tell their staff, because they want their employees to "be on their toes."

Goes through your files and takes something, never returns it or misfiles it, and blames you for not instantly producing it; or, request old files and figures they don't need.

Doesn't know how to talk to people--they *tell* things to them.

Gets furious if they're not consulted in advance about anything.

Believes "no one would know what to do" without them.

Doubts everyone else's ability but their own.

Establishes a dress code that doesn't apply to them.

Takes long lunches.

---

*__World Of Fred Note:__ Most employees who never take a day off, or come into work when nobody else does, are thieves. They fear their absence will enable another employee to catch on to what they're doing. Tip off: when someone unexpectedly enters their office, the loser flips over their papers so no one sees what they're working on.

Loser Boss job performance review (cont.)...

Speaks too quickly for you to understand their policy, orders or directions; then, gets mad at you for asking them to repeat it because what they told you is allegedly "self explanatory."*

Promotes you to a managment position so they can overwork you and not pay you overtime.

Devises a system where the loser boss can takes credit for your work or blame you for their mistakes.

How to downgrade a Loser Boss with insults

Insulting your own boss is a very delicate matter. You could get fired, written up for a bad attitude, accused of being unprofessional, or risk a good job reference. But, you're perfectly safe to insult a loser boss if...

1.) you belong to a strong union.
2.) you're leaving your job and going into a different field.
3.) the boss you're insulting is the head of another department or company and is belittling your department or company (in this case abuse is seen as a plus because you're standing up for the people you work with.).
4.) you're an office temp; or, nearing the end of your summer job.
5.) you're denied a bonus or partnership (meaning: there's no future for you at the firm.).
6.) you don't even work for the boss, but see the boss abusing a friend of yours, or some hapless employee.
7.) your job is protected by a contract.
8.) you have a protector in a position above the Loser Boss.
9.) you run into a former boss at a social occasion or public event.

---

*__World Of Fred Note:__ Actually, Loser Bosses talk rapidly because they *don't know* what they're talking about, this way they can blame you for any screw up by saying, "That's not what I told you!"

Insult technique: The only difficult part about insulting a Loser Boss is deciding to insult them. A good touch is to follow up the insult with one of the Loser Boss' pet tyrannical phrases.

For example...

Situation:
Laying Out A Loser Boss

*(Scene: **Loser Boss** blusters into your office without knocking. You're a **Union Employee With The Power Of Insult And Live!** You are at your desk. The boss is waving about a report.)*

Loser Boss
(Barking.)
I'm not asking for your opinion, I'm telling you what I think.

Union Employee With The Power To *Insult And Live!*
You know boss, until now, I never knew a prostate gland could speak. *(Pause.)* And if you don't like it there's the door. Believe me, there are plenty of incompetents out there who would kill for your job.

Post-insult Outcome: You won! By insulting them, you've proven the Loser Boss has no power over you and must treat you with respect. Most will grudgingly admire you for standing up to them.

Selfish young people become selfish old people.

Evil Old Farts

Losers age like a cheap jug wine. Evil Old Farts never develop depth and dimension. Old age has made these unesteemed seniors even more demanding. They act like spoiled little children. If Evil Old Farts are widowed, they expect everyone to dote and pamper them the same way their spouse once did.

In an Old Fart's youth, they were disrespectful to elders who " had their time." But, when the loser is old, these self-involved geezers become even more inconsiderate because they "don't have much time left."

They've always been selfish. When these Old Farts were in their income-earning prime years, they did nothing for their offspring.* Instead of saving money to give their children a benefit the loser never had, they made them work to buy whatever they needed, including an education. This doesn't stop Evil Old Farts from refusing to live in a retirement community and impose themselves upon their offspring, who are now adults with their own lives, raising their own children, or trying to enjoy their own retirement.

These Old Farts live with their children's family and become too much of an emotional burden. Sadly, the spoiler is reluctantly placed in a home. Then, as it must come to all lesser people, they pass away. In child-like spite, the spoiler bequeaths their life savings to the "nice girl" who cut their toenails every Thursday.

Evil Old Fart traits

Discusses their regular bowel movements.

Is indifferent to the person who pampers them, and praises another relation (who never visits or does anything for them.).

Repeats the same story over and over again.

Never prepared for their retirement, but complains their pension or social security doesn't provide them enough money.

Urges you to undertake a career they hated.

---

*World Of Fred Note: If the Evil Old Fart's children returns the favor by neglecting to come to their parents aid, the old timer complains their "ungrateful" family has abandoned them.

Evil Old Fart traits (cont.)...

Is overly possessive of pigeons they feed in the park.

Gets overly concerned about cars that are parked for more than two days straight on the old fart's block.

Has bad eyesight but continues to drive their car until they kill themselves or someone else.

Has a camera that doesn't work or is equipped with a flash that never goes off.

Says they're lonely but refuses to visit the Senior Center because they don't "want to be around all those *old* people."

Believes everyone loves them.

Creates a highly inaccurate portrayal of how wonderful their deceased spouse was.

Talks to pictures in the hallways.

Annoying Evil Old Fart eccentric behavior

Is more patient and understanding with their grandchildren or pets than they were with their offspring.

Insists they're not too old to shovel snow.

Smokes too much in doughnut shops or diners.

Interferes with people's personal affairs but sees themselves as a perfect person who is "only trying to help."

Calls apartment-complex security and complains you're too loud in the evening, but think it's okay to allow their running and squealing grandchildren to wake you up at 7 a.m.

Annoying Evil Old Fart eccentric behavior (cont.)...

If you have a burden-free life in your thirties, the Evil Fart snarls, "When are you going to grow up?"

Observes how old you are getting, but vainly note about themselves, "I'm in great shape for my age."

Brings up a screw-up or embarrassing moment from your past. (This is done in front of people you want to impress.)

Recites a litany of various friend's deaths, such as "Bea died from a clot in the head three years ago."

Insists you remember obscure relatives in the past that you never met or were way too young to notice.

Takes up all the seats on the casino bus tours.

Tries to get you to be their personal servant (bathing, shaving, wiping them, clipping their nails, etc.).

Criticizes you by saying, "I hope when you live as long as I have so you'll know how hard it is."

Suddenly discovers religion, lectures you about it, and then adds, "I'll pray for you."

Establish retirement communities in towns and then control the political spending.*

Constantly recalls how they discovered their dead spouse.

---

*World Of Fred Note: This group of elderly people forms a substantial voting block in local elections and budget hearings. These grouchy and selfish Evil Old Farts vote down any school or recreational improvements (It doesn't matter they received their free education and used parks in their youth.).

Tedious Evil Old Fart attention-getting moves

Pouts like a child if they're not included in everything.

Never mingles at social gatherings; instead, sits in a corner and glumly complains "no one comes over" to them.

Makes you wait longer in line while they have prolonged conversations with the clerk over routine purchases; or, get on a bus, talk to the driver, and fumble around for change.

Calls emergency numbers for minor illnesses or injuries.

Is melodramatically grief-stricken at funerals.

When anyone has a physical ailment, they have to top it.

Has nice clothes, but dresses like they're poor.

Tedious Evil Old Fart attention-getting moves (cont.)...

Frequently lapses into self-pity for attention by saying, "I'm just in the way...Things would be better if I weren't here...I've lived too long...I hope I go in my sleep...when I'm gone..."

Prides themselves on saying what's on their mind, regardless of how they hurt another person's feelings.

When you leave them or say good night, the Evil Old Fart implies this might be the last time by saying, "I hope I'm around to see you." or "Maybe I'll see you tomorrow."

If you don't call for awhile, Old Fart says, "Hello, stranger."

When you ask them if they need help, the evil old codger grumbles, "I'm not helpless." But, if you don't ask them, they get angry you didn't offer because "I shouldn't have to ask, you should have noticed I needed help."

Complains "no one listens" to them.

If they live alone, the evil elder expects their children to do things around their house for them—even if their "kids" are in their sixties.

Selectively afflicted with various physical ailments.

Wishes they had more children (But if they do have several children, Evil Old Farts emotionally play them off each other.).

Keeps going to different doctors until one of them agrees the Old Fart's imaginary ailment is a medical problem.

After the Old Fart finishes speaking, they continue to stand and aimlessly stare at you for several seconds.

Intentionally wets their beds in nursing homes because the nurse isn't paying attention to their needs.

How to insult an Evil Old Fart

An Evil Old Fart's demanding disposition drains us, raises our blood pressure, causes friction within the family, gives us headaches, adds stress to our lives, and reduces our life expectancy. You need to insult them once in awhile to establish that your life isn't their life.

For example...

Situation
Deflating An Evil Old Fart

You With The Power Of Insult And Live!
I want to introduce you to my date.

Evil Old Fart
(Looks at your date and then says to you.)
I remember you when you had a load in your pants.

You With The Power Of *Insult And Live!*
Where's an aneurysm when you really need one?

Post-insult Outcome: You won! But, you might ask, "How can I really win? After all, these elderly losers are too old to change their ways. So, what is accomplished by slamming them in their sunset years?" Insulting these Old Farts gives you an emotional outlet! Endangering their social security relieves *your* blood pressure. It lengthens your life so you'll outlive them.

Insults for any situation with a Loser

I'm certain Jesus loves you, but in your case He's probably seeing other people.

When a woodchuck has a wet dream, you're what it probably experiences.

Were you born under the sign of Zodiac Killer?

Why do I have the feeling a UFO crashed near here, and they're looking for the one loser who flew coach?

Are you a side effect looking for a disease?

Before I met you, I didn't know erosion could walk.

So, what's it like to be limited?

What brought you in here?...
- Chum?
- Live bait?
- Are they cleaning your tank out?
- Flushed out your place with a gopher bomb?
- Frat drop from a slow learner's class?
- Gas leak at the trailer park?
- They close the bus terminal lobby?
- Celebrating first place in the carp-spearing contest?
- Are they raffling off a chainsaw?

I never knew pus could assume human form.

Until now, I didn't realize a prostate gland could speak.

For you, cosmetic surgery is getting silicon frontal-lobe implants.

Insults for any situation with a Loser (cont.)...

You're a person of great convictions: manslaughter and fraud.

This scene going on between us should be in your book: "Motocross, when the cheering stopped."

A terrorist wouldn't use you as a human shield.

Are you cranky because no one changed your litter box?

What's it like being a gland without a purpose?

Are you irritated because your mother never removed the thermometer out of your butt?

I don't know your background, but I bet you can recommend a good bail bondsman.

You're a good argument for denying rights to the common man.

Don't worry, I'm certain some day they'll find an antidote for your personality.

Incredible, your tumor is benign but I see that your personality is malignant.

Wow, I've never met a stool sample with motor functions!

You know, if you applied yourself, you could be an under-arm deodorant.

Usually I don't meet a person like you until I press the "trouble" button in the bowling alley.

Insults for any situation with a Loser. (cont.)...

You're real impressive. Let me guess what you do for a living. Do you...

- Adjust fan belts?
- Fold laundry?
- Scrub burn victims?
- Cut live bait?
- Sell fill?
- Rearrange sprinklers on the fairways?
- Remove the lint filters from dryers in the laundromat?
- Clear shopping carts from the parking lot?
- Install gutters?
- Unplug catch basins?
- Hand out prize tickets to high scorers in skee ball?
- Illegally dump hospital waste?
- Disinfect rented bowling shoes?
- Clean out gym lockers?
- Rake up golf balls with the driving range truck?
- Draw blood?
- Screen top soil?
- Filter sludge?
- Run a forklift?
- Vacuum out rental cars?
- Match dental charts to airplane-crash victims?
- Repair public-housing stairwells?
- Process wastewater?
- Salt roads to melt ice?
- Label and weigh fish packets?
- Slice deli meat?
- Chalk tires for the Parking Authority?
- Work at a rendering plant?
- Run a homeless shelter?
- Bath the elderly?
- Martinize suits?
- Run a linen service?

Insults for any situation with a Loser (cont.)...

You're real impressive. Let me guess what you do for a living. Do you...

- Reload vending machines?
- Open up a nightcrawler shack?
- Work the self-service pumps?
- Shovel dead animals off the highway?
- Steam clean exit ramp signs?
- Siphon out septic tanks?
- Replace dispenser cups in water coolers?
- Spray down lettuce in the vegetable section?
- Take inventory at the auto parts store?
- Refill the protective toilet seat wrapper containers in the bathrooms?
- Shampoo poodles?
- Shake out public pool hair traps?
- Collect tolls?
- Clean out the bull's eye target in the urinals?
- Lay chalk base lines on the ball field?
- Perjure yourself on the witness stand?
- Make correct change at the video arcade?
- Announce sales over the mall's public-address system?
- Wipe sweat off the exercise-machine cushions at the spa?
- Lay fresh newspaper for the pet store's puppy display?
- Hold someone's crotch to get their inseam?
- Hit the "hot wax" button in the car wash?
- Press someone's toe and tell them if the boot fits?
- Wipe off the sneeze guard above the salad bar?
- Provoke guard dogs?
- Monitor sewage outflows?
- Put the tarp down over the tomatoes in the truck?
- Carry shrubs to cars?
- Stock salmon?
- Seal driveways?
- Trim grass around tombstones in the cemetery?

Insults for any situation with a Loser (cont.)...

You're real impressive. Let me guess what you do for a living. Do you...

- Tune-up dirt bikes?
- Remove the gum left in water fountains?
- Bleach needles for the poor?
- Hire strike breakers?
- Assess video-cassette rental fines?
- Supervise migrant workers?
- Run a storage locker center?
- Put plastic tips on the ends of shoelaces?
- Turn back odometers on used cars?
- Go through suit pockets in the dry cleaners?
- Blend the *Big Mac* special sauce?
- Shake out the powder on the vomit to clean it off the floor easier?
- Knock cows on their heads with a hammer in the slaughter house?
- Put people on hold at the rape crisis center?
- Bag potting soil?
- Attach motel shower curtains?
- Sponge out soap racks in the YMCA bathrooms?
- Chlorinate pools?
- Clean air conditioner ducts?
- Construct warehouse pallets?
- Clean dried gum from under tables?
- Seal boxes in shrink wrap?
- Empty out wastebaskets?
- Assemble gas grills?
- Refill propane tanks?
- Separate plastic containers from aluminum cans?
- Glue velcro strips onto running shoes.
- Put in utility posts?
- Sign off pig's feet deliveries at the warehouse?
- Suck the sperm out of dental dams?

Insults for any situation with a Loser (cont.)...

How's your correspondence course in escalator maintenance going?

What's your job perk? Getting to keep an extra sand eel?

Why do I feel you went to vocational school to learn to say, "Unleaded on pump two."

I know you have to get back to your job: drinking beers in front of the television and testing adult diapers.

After you polish a pair of shoes, do you leave them in front of a golfer's locker?

Do you get job stress from working the fryer without the timer?

You seem like a real comer, I bet there's a future for you in...
- custodial management.
- telemarketing.
- security guard work.
- scientology.
- highway construction.
- the school crossing guard squad.
- the auto parts business.
- mini-bike rentals.
- the hall monitor field.
- night manager at a Catfish Farm.
- pizza delivery.

Did you get a promotion because you can say "You want fries with that?" in two foreign languages?

When you hear voices do they say "For here? or "To go?"

Insults for any situation with a Loser (cont.)...

Why are you speaking that way, have you been inhaling too much lime when you clean the stables?

You know, being qualified in computer management doesn't mean being able to give out correct change in a video arcade.

Are you the one who has the "I'd rather be welding" bumper sticker on your car?

Don't be so negative, I think you can eventually develop the technical skills to cut chicken fryer parts.

You seem nervous, does a feeling of insecurity overwhelm you when there's no grill to clean?

One thing that's wonderful about being a *(Insert loser's real job occupation here.)* is your children will never be overshadowed by your accomplishments.

What was the hardest part of your last job application? The true or false section? Or the coloring?

If you're here, I bet somewhere there's an empty chair at the recycling center.

What's skilled labor for you? Asking people if they want paper or plastic?

In high school, were you voted most likely to drive a waste-management truck?

You can't hear me? Probably because you don't wear protective ear muffs when you run the leaf blower.

Insults designed to attack a Loser's ignorance

Did you think *Boyz In The Hood* was a movie about the klan?

I think we've determined that your brain cells have a shelf life.

I've never met a pre-school drop out.

There's a future for you in the energy field, as a fossil fuel.

You're a frozen embryo whose brain hasn't thawed yet.

On the scale of one to ten, I know you could count up to five.

Does your brain suffer from vapor lock?

So, I see a mucous membrane can lip sync.

I bet, on a land-use map, your brain would be undeveloped space.

Do you need "Cliff Notes" to read *Hagar*?

So, I see disposable waste does have the power to think.

When you graduated from high school, did your cap have tassels or fuzzy dice?

You have no self doubt, that's the great thing about being brain dead.

Is there a sign in front of your home that says, "Slow Adult"?

Insults designed to attack a Loser's ignorance (cont.)...

If a cannibal ate your brain, he'd be vegetarian.

Why don't you go home and bore yourself?

Do you rent out your skull as a sensory deprivation tank?

If your mind was...
- a.) written in Braille it would read, "See Dick run."
- b.) a song, it would be a Neil Diamond record.

It must be tough when your skull is gutted by a fire.

You're what happens to slow learners when they grow up.

If I had a depth gauge, you couldn't give me a reading.

I'd like to insult your intelligence, but I'm afraid I'll have to go after something else.

You're making me suspect that *McDonald's* does practice selective breeding on humans.

Why do I feel like I'm talking to a person whose brain is still in the fetal position?

You could have your brain classified as a blunt object.

Yeah, you're streetwise, *Sesame Street*-wise.

You're from the old school: illiteracy.

For you, food for thought is a *Mounds* bar.

You're an argument against white supremacy.

Insults designed to attack a Loser's ignorance (cont.)...

I feel like I'm talking to Lenny in *Of Mice And Men*.

I see you've taken autism to the third power.

Here are lines to use when a loser flips you off...
  a.) I'd give you one, but you'd want to sit on it.
  b.) I'm sorry but you'll have to rotate on that yourself.
  c.) Look at that, a fart that can pull its own finger.
  d.) Are you trying to show me you wiped yourself?
  e.) So, is your prostate a quart low?
  f.) Lose the other fingers in the band saw?
  g.) Are you trying to look like a gay rotisserie?
  h.) Who removed the altar boy?
  i.) Hoping a scoutmaster will come by to sniff it?

When you die, they'll break your skull open and only find pennies.

I bet you thought urinalysis was a taste test.

Origin-of-birth insults to reveal a Loser as a dumb and emotionally defective human

When you were born...
  • I bet you left a dirt ring.
  • was your mother hitting the reset button?
  • your parents had to file an environmental impact statement.
  • the doctor didn't say "Push," he said, "Pull pull."
  • they didn't check the invoice for an IQ.
  • your mother got fined for littering.
  • it was an easy delivery because your mother ate a lot of bran.
  • were they filming *Damien*?

Origin-of-birth insults to reveal a Loser as a dumb and emotionally defective human (cont.)...

In your case, fetal development cut a few corners.

When your mother was pregnant, did she take up kickboxing?

In high school, when the debating team discussed pro choice, did they all point at you?

Were you born through the Hemlich maneuver?

You're the result of *Unplanned* Parenthood.

Your parents don't have a birth certificate for you, they have a breeder's permit.

You're the reason anesthesiologists now have such high malpractice insurance.

Did you have a teething ring with lead paint?

You're here, so I guess condoms can't stop a toxic waste discharge.

When you were just a three-month fetus how did you manage to unscrew the jar and survive?

After being with you, I know there's a thin line between birth control and pest control.

Were you a failure in the placenta-recycling experiment?

I didn't know they made DNA without chromosomes.

If you were born a twin, was it crowded in the pod?

Origin-of-birth insults to reveal a Loser as a dumb and emotionally defective human (cont.)...

I bet your mother still suffers from post-natal depression.

As a child were you attacked by a spray and neuter crew?

How did you crawl from the dumpster to the orphanage?

You wouldn't be here if a wombat womb had a recall.

After talking to you, I understand why some people are against abortion and *for* capital punishment.

I guess ultrasound didn't tell your parents everything they wanted to know about you.

I don't believe in the after life, but since meeting you, I now believe in after birth.

Some people are born-again, you're still-born again.

Is your umbilical cord still attached to a woodchuck?

Now I know why doctors no longer use forceps to deliver babies.

I bet the best thing about your mother's umbilical cord was that it doubles as your leash.

When you were born, did the doctor spank you, or grab you by the ankles and bang your head against the wall?

Does your creator know you're out of the lab?

Insults for Loser couples

You've been married that long? Wow, so you've learned to compromise. He has his limitation and you have no standards.

I guess they really do get better looking at closing time.

Did one of you forget to wear an "I'm with Stupid Shirt."

How did you two meet?...
- Poaching?
- Reptile touch tank?
- He liked the way you rubbed him in the petting zoo?
- Did you pull a thorn out of his paw?
- Bumped heads when you licked the salt block in the woods?
- Slid into each other on the slow learner's curve.
- Freed each other from the No-Pest strip?
- Fighting over the possum on the highway?
- Is there a crack dealer catch and release program?
- You don't have to tell me, I don't want to violate the confidentiality of psychologist-patient relationship.
- Did you raid her village?
- Did her Dad trade her for a new tractor?

Is this how *Walmart* and *Mary Kay* people cross-pollinate?

Obviously, I guess it's this place's "bring-in-a-slow-learner-get-in-free night."

Why do you call this person your x? Are they like an algebra problem you never got over?

Who introduced you guys? Pimp placement service?

Insults for Loser couples (cont.)...

It's reassuring to see that after years of not speaking to each other, "null" and "void" are back together.

If I was your date, and driving you home, I'd wonder what type of damage a freeway abutment would do to the passenger side.

You look like the first couple that gets killed in a slasher movie.

Why are you dating her/him?...
• Just trying to turn your crotch in a handicapped parking space?
• Is this your way of sheltering stray animals?
• Trying to get accreditation for a course on disproving Darwin's theory?
• Did Mother Teresa give him to you as a penance?
• Did you get nailed for drunk driving and they're part of your community service?

Is the dating service just giving out loaners?

You look like an Amish couple waiting to raise a house.

It's a good thing people don't pick up their trash on the beach, otherwise you wouldn't meet anyone to go out with.

I see you two have learned how to make do with less.

Just going out with her long enough until you get a good video?

You probably schedule your vacations around ball games and she schedules hers around fleet week.

Pile Driving Stud Muffins and Macho Nerds

Typical Macho Loser:
Coaches who believe sports builds character but will deviously undertake any unethical tactic to win.

Macho-flexing loser list

Car mechanics who use technical knowledge to overcharge their customers.

Tyrannical chefs who maintain there is "only one way" to cook.

Company officers who married into the family business and want to prove they're no longer in their father-in-law's shadow.

Theatrical military officials who make a spectacle of their arrival.

Bullies who know just enough martial arts to beat you in a fight.

Vain and egotistical lead singers whose "untapped talent" breaks up every band.

Arrogant airline pilots who view everyone on the flight crew as a lesser, and go out of the way to treat them as imbeciles.

Exercise instructors who injure clients with gruelling work outs.

Bulked-out Beefcakes who try to compensate for inarticulateness by over-developing their body to intimidate people.

Ferry-service sailors in resort areas who parade their nautical abilities over landlubbers.

Hawkish muscular draft-age cowards who never enlist, but prove their manhood by beating up anti-war demonstrators.

Frustrated dads who try to overcome their shortcomings by living through their sons.

Gloating tow-truck drivers who enjoy your helplessness and take you to corrupt repair shops (which give the trucker a kickback.).

Weekend warriors who try to relieve their tensions by ruining everyone else's fun.

Purpose of this section: You'll learn machismo isn't restricted to bulked-out hulks, rowdy male bonders, and chauvinists. This virile strain of testosterone poisoning also inflicts itself upon us in the forms of professional nerds, frustrated jocks, emotional retarded experts, and CEO egos.

Tough Macho tip offs

Most Tough Macho Losers gravitate to manly jobs involving landscaping, plumbing, law enforcement, warehouse employment, firemen, construction, pumping gas, assembly-line work, pool cleaning, wrecking and towing, public works, refrigerator or air conditioner maintenance, as well as car, kitchen appliance or television repair, utilities tasks, and delivery truck driving.

His job involves the use of the following...
- Hot-tar mop
- Riot gear
- Tool belt
- Compressor
- Gun
- Union card
- Jumpsuit
- Hairnet
- Name tag
- Hardhat
- Goggles
- Radar gun
- Drop light
- Protective clothing
- Helmet
- Waders
- Snowplow or backhoe
- Steel-toe boots
- Rangers hat
- A curved tile knife
- Key ring with way too many keys
- Wallet with a chain running through it
- Dropcloth

Tough Macho Losers walk naked around in the men's room way too long, and talk to you with your face at their crotch level.

Tough Macho Loser vanity signs

If a girl is approaching, or if someone is taking a picture, Mr. Macho sucks in his gut.

Surrounds his workplace or home with pictures of himself:
- beside celebrities or professional athletes.
- doing something rugged.
- holding an animal he killed.

Displays trophies, plaques, and awards.

Only plays games he's good or can win at.

Tough Macho Loser vanity signs (cont.)...

In gyms, asks attractive women to "spot me" while he tries to bench press poundage to heavy for him.

Atop his desk has models of equipment he's ridden, designed, or has repaired, such as airplanes, cars, ships, and tanks; or has his get-tough philosophy displayed on a motto or desk plate.

Wears pants too low, because he refuses to admit he can't fit in the same jeans he wore in high school.

If he's married and at a bar with single men...
- points out the available women in the joint and says, "I can't believe you single guys aren't hitting on the talent in here, when I was single..."
- shows his wedding ring to the guy and says, "When women see this it's like a magnet."

Believes he can do the same activities a younger man can, but he doesn't have the "time to stay in shape."

Walks around the supermarket without his shirt.

Believes he's an invincible ironman.*

If Macho Loser's girlfriend says a movie star is attractive, he declares the actor is a fag.

When sick, becomes a whining little baby.

Never stops at gas stations to ask directions.

Thinks pain is good for the body.

---

*World of Fred Note: For example, why should he go to a doctor when the loser can run ten miles? He can drink a case of beer every night, do drugs. After all, he's obviously in great shape: he can still run *ten miles*.

Tough Macho Loser vanity signs (cont.)...

Jokingly says he won't do certain sports or activities because they're not "manly" enough.

Brags about his sexual conquests, adding, "Once a woman gets it from me, she always wants it."*

Tries to point out he's an expert and you're a layman by using highly detailed and tediously long descriptions on how to do home repairs and auto maintenance.

Must be referred to by his professional or academic title.

Tough Macho Losers are vain about their trucks. This amphibian-like vehicles specifically designed for off-road terrain. Yet, the macho guy never takes his "baby" off a paved road, keeps it spotlessly clean, and goes ballistic if a shopping cart nicks the finish in a parking lot.

*****World Of Fred Note:** Usually said by dateless and divorced men.

Tough Macho Loser vanity signs (cont.)...

Wears too much cologne when he plays sports.

Is very big on monogram ties and initialed jewelry (He always has a vanity license plate with his initials followed by a number for each vehicle he owns, such as JR-1, JR-2.).

Dismisses professional compliments by smugly saying, "Just doing my job."

Lack of depth readings on a Tough Macho Loser

Maintains a firm handshake means something.

Says how an adrenaline rush helps keep him "focused."

Hunts animals he knows can't hurt him; however, if he does hunt dangerous animals, he shoots them from a safe distance.

Says, "I'm a nice guy, but don't get me angry."

Adamantly likes one type of music, anything else "sucks."

Quotes his high school coach to justify cutthroat behavior in the market place or in amateur sports.

Brags he can fix any appliance or vehicle; then, he takes it apart, and never puts it back together (Usually it's someone else's appliance or vehicle.).

Authoritatively addresses people by gruffly barking their last name.

When he does any job for someone else it's always second rate.

Before he sharply criticizes a buddy, he prefaces it with "Don't get me wrong, I love the guy like a brother, but..."

Lack of depth readings on a Tough Macho Loser (cont.)...

Only likes movies that have a car chase, violence, a high body count, sex, or a monster in them.

If you tell an interesting story, talk about a beautiful place, say a joke, or make an insight, macho guy won't end the conversation until he can "top" you with a more interesting story, funnier joke, keener insight, a more beautiful place, or bring up a subject you don't know anything about.

When participating in any outdoorsmen activity, believes he's "challenging nature."

Takes any drug as long as he can still have an erection.

Lack of depth readings on a Tough Macho Loser (cont.)...

Thinks the best period in life was when he was really close and dependent upon a group of men.

Concludes his views on a subject with definitive phrases like "case closed...end of story...need I say more?"

Turns every professional task or athletic situation into a personal challenge or a competitive situation.

Instead of developing a personality, defines himself through uniforms, heroes, literary quotes, and myths.

Disparagingly labels any man who refuses to fight as a "pretty boy."

Vulgar Tough Macho Loser moves

When you say a remark he doesn't have an answer for, he mockingly grabs his crotch and repeats the subject. For example, "Algebra? *(Grabs crotch.)* I got your algebra right here."

Chews tobacco and squirts it in a cup while they are speaking to you.

Belches words.

Loudly announces his toilet functions, such as "I have to have to take a dump...pinch a loaf...time for me to drain the dragon...guess it's time to water the plants...roll a log."

Has a nickname for his weenie.

Makes fart sounds with his armpits.

Vulgar Tough Macho Loser moves (cont.)...

Blows his nose without using a handkerchief (sometimes he uses his shirt.); or, refers to his nose as a "snot locker."

When macho loser heads toward a bathroom says, "I have to urinate standing up because the doctor told me not to lift heavy objects." (Variation: in crowded men's rooms says, "More than two shakes is masturbation." or "I hate this place, all the dicks hang out here."

Hawks mucous loudly and spits.

Describes the futility of any difficult task by using a gross anal image, such as "It's like shoving spaghetti up a rat's ass."

If asked a question, he substitutes a "yes" answer with these phrases...
- "Is a frog's ass water tight?"
- "Is the Pope Catholic?"
- "Does a bear shit in the woods?"

Incredibly inconsiderate Tough Macho Loser conduct toward women

Are live-in boyfriends or husbands who...
    a.) leave discarded clothes or underwear on the floor where they took them off.
    b.) doesn't put the toilet seat back down.
    c.) never shares the housework.
    d.) refuses to relinquish the TV remote control so he can channel surf.
    e.) never cooks.

Farts in bed, pulls the covers over the woman's head, and yells, "Dutch oven!"

Sees sex as something he "got away" with.

Incredibly inconsiderate Tough Macho Loser conduct toward women (cont.)...

Associates being "romantic" as a sign of weakness.

Refers to his mate in public as the "old ball and chain" or someone who has them "by the short hairs."

Insists all dinner reservations be made in his name not the woman he's dating.

Describes their mustache as a "flavor saver."

If a woman kids him, he calls her a "bitch" because she's not in awe of him.

If he gets divorced from his wife, he tries to set fire to the house.*

After having sex never calls women back.

Loudly makes these comments about a woman's big breasts...
- "You'll never drown."
- "I bet she can't see her shoes."
- "Better hope you never get a chest cold."
- "Here comes Hooterville."
- "She could feed a whole country."
- "Mama!"
- "Hey look, the Grand Titons."
- *(Stares deeply.)* "Looking is free."

***World Of Fred Note:** Most men set fire to the structure of the house, while women prefer to throw the man's clothes on the bed and set fire to their "home."

Tough Macho Loser Phrases

- "What's it to you?"
- "You got a *problem* with that?"
- "Ask me if I care?"
- "What are you looking at?"
- "You want to *do* something about it?"
- "You talking to me?"
- "Who died and left you boss?"
- "You wanna *make* something out of it?"
- "Why don't you stick it where the sun don't shine?"
- "You think your shit don't stink?"
- "You trying to be a wise guy?"
- "What do you think I am, *stupid?*"
- "You want to *tell* me something I don't know?"
- "You telling me?"
- "Why don't you eat shit and die?"
- "You and what army?"
- "Wanna knuckle sandwich?"
- "You want some of this?"
- "What's it to you?"
- "Wanna mouth full of teeth?"
- "Is *this* what you want?"

Tough Macho Loser phrases (cont.)...

- "You kiss your mother with that mouth?"
- "How's it hanging?"
- "Why don't you take a picture, it lasts longer?"

Obviously, these are men in need of answers.

Most cruising-for-a-bruising macho men are cowardly bullies who sometimes meet a real tough guy...

The pummeled Macho Jerk tries to save face by allowing his friends to break up the fight. As his buddies pull him away, he struggles to give the impression this unwelcomed intervention is the *only* reason the fight ended. Or, Macho Loser backs down from a fight by saying, "I'm a lover not a fighter." Another technique: Macho guy motions with his fists and says, "Come on!" but takes one step backward for each forward step of his opponent.

Dumb Cop Macho
Worst type of tough guy machismo

This badged breed allegedly "puts their lives on the line every day." So, these bullet-for-brainers see themselves as the "thin blue line" that protects citizens from the "criminal element." This loyal brotherhood is dutifully tolerant of their own tribe's drunkenness, criminality, overtime abuse, or brutish behavior, but is completely intolerant of any "civilian" who displays the same duplicitous behavior towards the law.

Dumb Cop Macho assume three official forms...

1.) Rookie cop without a mature tolerance or compassion for the people he serves.

2.) Small-town cop in a low-crime area who are insecure because he never fights "real criminals" so he compensates for this deficiency by strictly enforcing drunk-driving laws and cracking down too hard on rebellious kids (Oddly, these little boy blues seem to forget they were the rowdiest dirtballs in high school.).

3.) Security guard are want-to-be a cops who take their job too seriously.*

Irritating Tough Cop Traits

Pulls your vehicle over and tauntingly asks: "Do you *know* why I stopped you?" or "Do you know how *fast* you were going?"

Expects to drink, eat for free, or receive huge discounts from merchants because he "provides a service" for the community.

Never bust drug dealers but fines teenagers for skateboarding.

Drinks and drives off-duty but harshly busts others for it too.

Tickets your car for parking too far away from the curb in the middle of nowhere, or after midnight.

Enjoys flicking his patrol car's brights at couples who are humping in parked cars; or interrupting thrusting lovers to tell them the park is closed.

Overreacts when you challenge his authority (which usually involves claiming your constitutional rights).

Drives his patrol car recklessly. (Such as peeling out as he leaves the station or driving too fast on a rough road.)

Uses black humor within the earshot of a victim.

***World Of Fred Note**: Wannabe cops sport ridiculously large badges, wear broad leather straps, tote a huge scuffed-up club, and are equipped with mace, lots of bullets, and an enormous gun. (All this law-enforcement equipment comes in handy when the empowered centurion has to tell someone to move their car from the "company" lot to the visitors parking garage.) The worst variation of this breed: airport parking authority types and hotel security; or, guards at pro baseball games who prevent children from getting foul balls that drop on the playing area near the stands.

Irritating Tough Cop traits (cont.)...

Stops your car because a tail light is out, but is really hoping to nail you for a drunk driving charge.

Unjustly shoves or verbally abuses you, and covers for his mistake by threatening to charge you for some other offense, or for "interfering with the duties of an officer."

Sets up speed traps at the bottom of hills and tickets you for going forty in a twenty-five mile an hour zone.

Is cynical and suspicious of anyone who isn't a cop.*

If you criticize their bungling of a criminal case or riot control, he accuses you of "second guessing" because you weren't there.

Pulls a woman over for an alleged traffic violation, but really wants to ask her out.

Gives parking tickets to parents who briefly use a no-parking zone in front of a school to run inside to pick up their kids.

If their union contract isn't promptly settled, they endanger the public by having all union members call in sick (known as the "blue flu"); or, they complain "morale is low."

*****World Of Fred Note:** After all, cops are entitled to be judgemental. Many only hang out with other blue knights in sleazy bars, are overweight, cheat on their wives, smoke too much, drink to excess, as well as moonlight a second job. Then, when they get a heart attack or injure themselves at another job, they make a cheesy claim it was a "job-related" to obtain medical disability benefits, which gives them more free time to work on their boat. Or, they get an early retirement, which of course, includes a pension at full-salary because their union lets the amount of overtime in their last year of service count toward their total salary from which the pension's percentage is derived. (For example, normal income: $40,000; with overtime $80,000; pension formula of half their salary is isn't $20,000--it's based on their last year: $40,000).

How to insult a Tough Macho Guy

The Tough Macho Loser is physically intimidating to hide his self doubts about his own virility. He uses bullying and overly demonstrative toughness to conceal the following insecurities he has about himself...

- Inability to measure up to his own masculine standard.
- Latent homosexual desires.
- Impotence/or other sexual inadequacies.
- Self-conscious about his lack of mental agility.

When you insult a tough guy, it's important to hit one of those insecurities to expose his weakness.* In the following scene, we'll take an approach that ridicules the macho guy for being a primitive mental slug.

For example...

Situation:
Spiking A Tough Macho Loser Bouncer/Doorman

(Scene: **Tough Macho Loser Bouncer / Doorman** is at the door of a club. He is humongus, but mostly fat, and has a confrontational nature because he can deny access to people who want to have fun. He is sitting on a bar stool near a lecture that has a guest list of people for the sold-out show. **You With The Power Of Insult And Live!** attempt to enter the club with your date.)

You With The Power To *Insult And Live!*
Yes, I'm on the guest list for tonight. Bill Robinson plus one.

Tough Macho Loser Bouncer/Doorman
I don't see your name here. *(Enjoying your discomfort.)* Oh, yeah, you can go in.

*****World Of Fred Note:** This is why the insults that follow this section attack either a macho guy's sexual performance, accuse him of latent homosexual desires, or ridicule his alleged toughness.

You With The Power To Insult And Live!
(After getting your ticket and entering.)
Are you cranky because someone stole your chewbone?

Post-insult Tough-Macho Outcome: You won! How? Well, you didn't respect the bouncer's bullying quality.* You aced the toughie by stripping his prestige. But, remember, don't insult these guys until you've gained access to the club.

---

*World Of Fred Note: Another type of obnoxious steroid sentinel is the no-neck doorman who works at the hottest nightspots and keeps you waiting outside the club while they allow *hipper* people in.

Insult and Live! by Fred Reiss

Nerd Macho

When nerdo commutes to work he's quickly sipping coffee, scanning readouts, frantically hitting keys on his calculator or computer lap-top. He acts like tension and job pressure are weights he lifts above his head. You see, he is working while others aren't because his job is so much more important and demanding than yours.

Full-On Nerd Macho

A Macho Nerd has a below-average physique. He is frustrated, balding, and short; or skinny, gawky, and has an unruly mass of hair (Untrimmed beard optional.). In childhood, the Nerd was picked on by a bully, or roughed up for his lunch money. He never got over it. Instead of acquiring wisdom from the cruelty he experienced, the Nerd becomes a born-again bully in adulthood; it's his chance to avenge childhood slights.

Since the inadequate Nerd can't pride himself on his physical strength, he shows off his cerebral abilities by becoming an arrogant experts in these jobs and fields...

- accountants, investment bankers, stockbrokers, etc.
- coroners
- nearly everyone in the medical or science field
- circulation managers
- roadies for bands
- militant environmental activists
- school administrators
- head librarians
- lawyers
- historical society archivists
- 96 percent of symphony musicians
- computer programmers, electronic technicians, etc.
- graphic artists, special effects movie designers, etc.
- photographers
- comic book store owners
- science fiction novelists
- 97.9 percent of people who wear lab coats
- engineers/inventors/architects
- winemakers
- nutritionists, herbalists, etc.
- traffic reporters/traffic-flow experts
- consumer-affair experts
- ballistics
- news reporters and 93. 6 percent of sports announcers/writers (the attitudunal gleepy ones)

(Nerd fields cont.)...
- volunteer fire department*
- radio call-in talk show hosts (especially public-affairs shows on Sunday mornings.)
- survivalists

N erds want to be like tough guys, but they can't, so, nerds create "alternative realities" where they can be bullying tyrants.

---

*World Of Fred Note: This Macho Nerd has a fog-light bedizened truck with a CB-scanner and portable flashing light. He is basically a glorified rubbernecker who goes to accidents or fires, gets in the way of officials, and enjoys preventing other people from seeing the scene.

Macho Nerd tip offs

Macho Nerd flexes his machismo through these activities...

- Chess, pinball, or complex video game moves
- Stamps and coins
- Nature: bird or whale watching, spelunking, butterfly collecting (Better known as the "Nabokov syndrome".), etc.
- Baseball card values, or comic book artists
- Star Trek or any type of fiction with "alternative realities."
- Yoga and muscle stretching
- Music, movie or television trivia
- Financial investments.
- Wine tasting
- Computer systems*
- Ham radio
- Tag sale bargains/antique knowledge
- Gardening
- Kennedy assassination theories
- Taxidermy
- Model rockets, trains, airplanes, and boats
- Restoring and collecting antique cars
- Fighting famous battles which he reenacts on game boards with perfectly scaled paper-mâchè terrain and the use of meticulously painted soldiers, divisions, and equipment
- Any activity that involves a lectern, lecture notes, and a slide projector
- Extensive knowledge of symphony or opera movements, classical composers, sculptors or painters
- Improper language use
- Citing religious scripture
- Ancient history
- Environmental terrorism
- Tax laws
- Gun collecting/or, knowledge of explosives

---

*World of Fred note: Perennially compares the strengths and weaknesses of various computer systems. (A Nerd always possesses an expensive computer or stereo system he is always upgrading.)

The Empty Suit:
Company bureaucrats design a system where everyone but them is responsible for mistakes.

Macho Nerds most common way to flex their muscle: Becoming an Empty Suit CEO Ego.

A Macho Nerd becomes a man of business. This CEO Ego sees himself as a "green lighter" or "stand-up guy" or a "take charge" executive. He's really a pass-the-buck bureaucrat, a perk-addicted-team-playing corporate executive, a paper-trail making administrator, or a short-term visioned vice-president who fears the stockholders and the Board Of Directors. This Empty Suit loves employee handbooks, bar graphs, marketability surveys, slide-show presentations, spreadsheets, memos, demographics, feasibility studies, one-to-one customer focus groups, management-training seminars, prospectuses, annual reports, and forming task forces or fact-finding committees. He intentionally causes confusion by incorrect management decisions that justify his existence. The CEO Ego claims the confusion caused by his policy change is proof of "miscommunication" between departments and "demonstrates the need for his leadership" to create a more efficient organization. Before this unworkable system can be set in motion, the Empty Suitor is promoted, and yet another Empty Suit takes his place and the whole process starts again.

Like a true Nerd, the Empty Suit can't dominate a situation unless he can create his own alternative reality. Since this hard-lining exec knows every employee loses their citizenship as soon as they park in the company lot, the power-ravenous Nerd sees this as his chance to be a totalitarian who rules a private corporate world.

Nerdy Empty Suit CEO Ego business traits

Every stellar success they have made is cancelled out by a failure of equal magnitude.*

Only makes his "strong" opinion known after everyone else has stated their views. (This way he's not risking anything.)

Surrounds himself with financial people who endorse short-term profits and don't understand long-term investments, capital expenditures, marketing or product development.

When the CEO gets a chance to make any decision that's strictly within their department and won't get to their supervisor, the Ego has to make that ruling.

If the company is doing well the CEO Ego solely attributes it to his department; but, when the company is doing badly he blames every other department except his.

Never came up from the factory so he has contempt for plant operators and the sales force.

---

*__World Of Fred Note:__ This is Fred's I-must-see-the-monster-at-full-strength theory. Let His Fredness explain, Dr. Frankenstein reanimates a dead body into a living man. But, the creator isn't satisfied. He says, "I must see the monster at full strength!" So, he gives his creature more power than it needs and creates an unmanageable monster who kills its creator, destroys the laboratory, kidnaps a woman, and carries her into a swamp because the monster can't cope with rejection.

Nerdy Empty Suit CEO Ego business traits (cont.)...

Blindly adheres to the company line with rulings that make his employees' lives difficult, but justifies it by saying, "This isn't *me* doing this, it's just company policy." *

Asks for "feedback" at meetings, but if anyone criticizes the Nerd's policy, they're fired for not being "team players."

Has his secretary call to invite you to a party, or to ask you for a personal favor.

Acts tough but never fires an employee to their face; he has a subordinate do it.

Believes in a mandatory retirement age but not for him.

Views a sense of humor as a sign of weakness.

Only reads trade publications.

Raves about the company, but is the first one to leave his job or sell it out.

Acts unaware his second-in-command is making your life miserable. (See Loser Boss section.)

Stands by his bad decisions by saying, "I can take the heat, that's what I get paid for."

Uses company funds to decorate his office with expensive furniture and art work, then, when he leaves or retires, takes these goods with him.

*****World Of Fred Note:** Of course, the CEO made the policy, such as hiring you through a temp agency to work full-time and deny you benefits; or, making budgets cuts which laid you off, but also created expensive golden parachutes to management to ensure a big buck exit for all the incompetent CEOs (his power-structure buddies).

Nerdy Empty Suit CEO Ego business traits (cont.)...

When the CEO Ego gives you a job review, he...
- doesn't offer you a raise because the purpose of the session is to "benefit the employee with input on how management views their performance."
- denies you a raise or a promotion but presents you with a "lateral" move that will "reward you with fresh challenges."
- gives you a promotion but no raise.
- awards you a raise lower than the cost-of-living increase.*

Is always on the phone (He has no life so he creates friendships through business contacts with other no-life CEO nerds.).

Has a predictable fondness for these phrases...
- "Let's ramp up."
- "Let me bounce this off you."
- "Run it up the flagpole and see if anyone salutes it."
- "Let's run a sanity check."
- "Let's make sure we're on the same page."
- "We need a paradigm shift."
- "I can't fit that in, my plate is full."
- "Are we on the same bandwidth?"
- "This is an action item."
- "Let's take this off line."
- "He doesn't bring much to the table."

Ensures your hard work doesn't produce any recognition or sense of accomplishment.

Transfers the frequent-flyer mileage from employee business trips to his personal account not the company's.

---

*__World Of Fred Note:__ Your raise was computed by a consulting firm the CEO ego hired to evaluate and adjust salaries in comparison to other companies. Oddly, the same study indicated the CEO was grossly underpaid. (Of course, the fact that the CEO gives the consultant further job references as well as other research projects, has allegedly has no influence upon his particular salary-hike statistic.)

Emotionally-Retarded-But-Professional Male Nerd profile: spent his twenties studying for a degree, such as medicine, architecture, engineering, and law, etc. He inaccurately and impertinently interprets life through the same methodology he uses in his profession. His mental faculties are fully developed, but emotionally he's a repressed teenager. When this retardo gets out of debt and becomes a success, he spends the rest of his life trying to playing catch-up on all the experiences the Nerd believes he missed during his youth. He gets a "really fast car," drops the woman who helped him through hard times, and frolics amok in a field of high-breasted bimbos.

The worst Male Nerd:
The Emotionally-Retarded-but Successful Professional Doctor)*

These warped medicine men are the lowest of the low because their self-involved callousness is inflicted upon patients who are undergoing true emotional and physical suffering, which magnifies

---

*World Of Fred Note: Lawyers are the lowest over-billing immoral scuzzballs on the planet. But, everyone expects a lawyer to be that way! The key difference is a lawyer makes their living keeping a wound open and a doctor is supposed to be a kind healer.

the probing Nerd's cruelty. These degree-holding males see themselves as God-like with a power of life over death, so why should they care about your petty pains? The more important the organ he specializes in, the more arrogant the doc. They justify their callousness as their only way to "survive" and function in a profession filled with so much tragedy and personal horror.*

Nerd medicine man's insensitivity to patients

Instead of looking and talking to you, the intentionally overscheduled doc checks his beeper and records his diagnosis into a cassette recorder.

Treats you as a disease not as a suffering human.

When you call him to find out a result, the call isn't returned for hours (When you get a return call, it's from his secretary.).

Tells you a procedure won't hurt and it does, or says he'll stop if it hurts you and doesn't because he's "almost there."

Isn't available on Wednesday or weekends (Why? he's golfing and asking club members stock market questions.).

Duplicates painful tests to prevent malpractice suits.

Respects his medical and science peers but is contemptuously dismissive of other professions (Why? Because those "other" professions serve him.).

Tries to do more than their specialized field to prove they can do anything, such as a heart expert who boasts that he still delivers babies.

Lets you sit forever in waiting rooms.

*****World Of Fred Note:** Notice how another person's tragedy only gives the pill-rolling MD a self-centered reason to develop indifference to patients, instead of compassion *toward* a suffering human.

Nerd medicine man's insensitivity to patients (cont.)...

Pops in for a six-minute visit in your hospital room, asks how you're doing, and bills you $75.

Insists you repeatedly fill out the same form over again.

Screws up filing your medical-insurance claim and sics a collection agency on you.

When you're in a vulnerable position during treatment or an exam, the emotionally retarded doc drills you on a payment schedule.

Where Tough and Nerd machismo meet:
Frustrated Jocks (the Unnaturals) and Wannabe Athletes

The Frustrated Jock is in all amateur adult athletic activities. This marginal-growth male takes competing so seriously he can't draw pleasure from any sport. He just loves winning, because winning isn't everything, it's the only thing.

The more frustrated Unnatural sees sports as the last place in life where he can cheat, lie to himself by doctoring his performance statistics, and still come out ahead by winning or beating someone on a point. That's why, when his view of himself doesn't match up to his athletic performance, he really goes off!*

Nobody even likes the Frustrated Jock—even his own team mates root against him. In fact, no one plays with this active jerk, they

---

*__World Of Fred Note:__ These guys usually have a beat-up car with a dog in it, and bitch about their two ex-wives.

play *against* him. If this jocular-strapped jerk is so despicable, why does anyone even play with him? Because we want to enjoy beating the guy! We know he hates to lose!

Frustrated Jock tip offs

Loudly espouses his theories on how a sport should be played, or criticizes a coach's strategies or a team's trade.

When he plays a sport, adopts a particular professional athlete's personal ticks, philosophy, and imitates his hero's style of play (he even wears his hero's number or uniform).

Yells at a coach for not putting the Frustrated Jock's child in the starting line-up.

Explains his business decisions through sports analogies, such as showing his "game plan" to "touch base" with other "team players" in the organization who "go to bat for us." (This gives the Jock the impression he's a financial athlete. Of course, he looks down at any coworker who "drops the ball.")

If he's benched, gripes about it during the game and loudly finds faults in the person playing in the Frustrated Jock's place.

Is in his thirties and still says, "You know, I'm playing better ball now than when I was in high school." (Variation: laments his coach didn't play him enough in his senior year.)

Erroneously believes he could have been a professional athlete, but didn't succeed because the Frustrated Jock...
- had his growth spurt too late.
- was unjustly cut by the coach from the team.
- experienced an injury early in his playing career.

Does a play with more muscle than grace.

Is a notorious ball hog.

Frustrated Jock tip offs (cont.)...

Compensates for his athletic shortcomings by becoming a rabid sports fan.

Yells at himself for making mistakes. (Usually it's "Damn it, why don't you give them the game?" or reenacts the correct move and beseechingly to cries out, "What are you doing?")

Becomes his team's manager so he can get more playing time.

Makes an easy play look difficult.

Enrolls adult fantasy camps where he competes against faded pro athletes (reinforcing his belief he could have been a one).

Throws a ball too hard to you at close range.

Has his name boldly emblazoned on his sports equipment.

Admires athletes who "play hurt"; or are "money players" (meaning they perform when there's a lot of money at stake), but yet he complains pro athletes are paid too much.

Cites sports statistics like they're original thoughts.

Frustrated Jocks sportsmanship traits

Dismisses cheating charges by saying "you're just a sore loser."

Enjoys rubbing his victory into a defeated opponent by...
- mocking his opponent when they score against them.
- hot dogging plays to show he doesn't have to try to beat you.
- laughs at his opponent's errors.
- after winning, insists on shaking your hand and says, "Hey, it's just a game. It docsn't mean anything." or "Better luck next time."

Frustrated Jock sportsmanship traits (cont.)...

If he's winning, the Frustrated Jock never disputes an official's call; in fact, he compliments the official to upset an opponent. But, if the Jock begins losing, he starts complaining.

If losing, he tries to mentally throw his opponent's timing off by changing the game's pace (stalling, arguing, etc.).

After he loses, quickly leaves to avoid shaking your hand.

Intentionally hurts opponents during the game by claiming he was "only going for the ball" or "trying to make the play."*

Has a quick temper and heaves sport equipment around, or gets thrown out of games for yelling at officials.

Ways Frustrated Jocks deny defeat

Says you cheated.

If you make an excellent play, he grunts, "Luck." or "Pulled that one out of your ass."

Complains officials made bad calls or were on the "home team's" side (known as a "home job"); or, believes the victor had an unfair or home-field advantage.

Blames the playing surface or the weather for his errors.

Says he lost because you were "due to win sooner or later" or won because of the "law of averages."

If losing, he has sudden injury and can't finish the game.

---

*__World Of Fred Note:__ He offers to help the injured player or asks, "Are you okay?" so everyone will think he's a "good sport."

Most Macho Nerds take up solitary non-contact sports.

Frustrated Jock Mutation:
Second-time-around Wannabes

The Macho Nerd is a frustrated athlete who was never good at sports in his youth,* but as an adult, he takes up one particular athletic activity with a vengeance.

With the exceptions of slow-pitch softball and bowling, Nerds take up non-contact/teamless activities, such as jogging, rock climbing, backpacking, white-water rafting, hackysack, teatherball, sail/rollerblading, cross-country skiing, bicycling, golf, paintball,

---

*****World Of Fred Note:** In childhood, the Nerd never made the team. So, he carried the first-aid box, was sports equipment manager, or became the official team score keeper. His athletic highlight was leading the varsity team in calisthenics.

martial arts, kayaking, hiking, camping, fencing, tennis, games involving Frisbee-throwing, surfing longboards on two-foot waves, or flying gliders, hang gliders and private planes.

Instead of practicing and honing a sport's fundamentals to play the activity better, the Frustrated Jock's attempts to take a shortcut around the fundamental skills: he thinks using the finest equipment will improve his performance. That's why...

- in golf, buys the best drivers with the newest alloy or the latest putter design.
- in tennis, has three racquet models used by the most recent victor at Wimbleton (also, uses special stick'em grip).
- in bowling, has metal wrist clamps to throw a better hook.
- in jogging, has the most expensive sneakers.
- in softball, uses $150 bats.
- in fishing, has the latest casting reel, most expensive graphite rod, fish radar, or a highly-equipped bass boat.
- in surfing, has webbed gloves for better paddling and a specially shaped board with latest performance designs.

And what's the end result of all the equipment? He still stinks!

In an effort to at least have some dominance in a sport, a nerdy wannabe joins a club. Since he lacks physical talent, he does what comes naturally to life's benchwarmers: political and bureaucratic maneuvering.* He becomes the organization's president. Why? So he can stage rigged tournaments where the Wannabe Nerd designs the entry rules and sets up contest heats to prevent the better participants from winning. And who emerges with a trophy? The triumphant and psychologically redeemed Wannabe.

---

*World Of Fred Note: If a Nerd can't get known for his ability in a sport, he assuages his ego in these two ways: 1.) Organizing various local events so he can be known for his "contribution to the game." 2.) Because he can't gain recognition for his skill in a sport, he wants to be know for his collection of rare memorabilia connected to it.

How to insult a Macho Nerd

Nerds are very similar to a Tough Macho loser, because they both have an insecure hold on their masculinity. But, the main difference is a tough guy is trying to conceal his mental and emotional inability to be a total man from others, while the Nerd is angry he can't physically look like a tough guy *to* others.

Nerds have these weak spots...

- Angry he's not a physically strong hulk.
- Denies he's a Nerd by acting professionally tough.
- Bitterness about his nerdy adolescence.
- Embarrassed he's *still* physically uncoordinated.

When you insult a Nerd, bring up the simple fact that no matter how arrogant he is about his professional abilities or philosophy of life, you are still superior to him because he's a Nerd.

For example...

Situation:
Demoting A Loud CEO Ego Macho Nerd
(You With The Power Of Insult And Live! are in town for a business conference, lounging in a hot tub at a plush hotel, but you have to listen to a bellowing CEO Ego Macho Nerd trying to impress a client.)

CEO Ego Macho Nerd
(Almost shouting his opinion in the hotel hot tub.)
You have to know how to motivate people. Let me bounce this off you, when I undertake a game plan the only players I'm interested in are the ones who carry the ball and run with it.

You With The Power Of *Insult And Live!*
(Exasperated and leaving the hot tub to come back later.)
Wow! You're a tough guy. I bet phlegm hawks you up. *(Always add under your breath.)* Nerd.

Post-insult Nerd-Macho Outcome: You won! You feigned awe at the nerd's hall-monitor trumpery, slammed him with an insult related to the image he portrayed of himself, and then called him a Nerd. This last touch is important because the Macho Nerd is spiraled back to his adolescent memories. The twerp is furious he can't hide his nerd stigmata. Plus, the unmasked Nerd is even more enraged because he's not physically strong enough to defend his views.*

Male Bonders

Most Macho Losers thrive in a herd to form a buffer zone against reality. Their egos annex. They pick on loners. Aside from professional types who form committees, this primitive breed believes their physical abilities and strength gives them the right to disgrace lesser specimens.

World Of Fred Note: A Macho Nerd is all mouth, but when forced to physically back up his threats, he says, "Touch me and I'll charge you with assault."

Typical Male Bonder:
Frat Guy (age range 17 to 28.)
For seven years at college, Frat Guy parties with his bros.

Insult technique for Male Bonders: Go for the leader of the macho herd. He's easy to find. He's the loudest. Take him out and you win over the group.

For example...

Innocent Male Meets Boomer And His One Brain-Celled Gang In The Mens Locker Room

*(Scene: The locker room. **Boomer** and the guys are standing around their lockers, wearing towels around their hips, powdering up their bodies, blow drying their hair, and admiring themselves in the mirrors. **You With The Power Of Insult And Live!** enter the locker room, your physique and athletic abilities don't measure up to theirs.)*

Boomer
Hey, do you know what a guy with a big dick has for breakfast?

You With The Power Of *Insult And Live!*
(Feeling awkward and out of place.)
No.

Boomer
(Squeezes your thinner arms and says.)
I figured *you* wouldn't know. *(The gang laughs.)* Come on, I'm just busting stones. You get those marks on your face from getting poked with ten foot poles? *(Group laughs.)* If we didn't like you we wouldn't be giving you a hard time. Hey does you face hurt? It's killing me! *(Group laughs.)* Just trying to keep you humble.* I wouldn't want to bend over and pick up the soap in the shower with this guy around. Did you have to wear a pork chop around your neck so the dog would play with you? *(High fives his buddies.)* We're not laughing with you, we're laughing *at* you!

*****World Of Fred Note:** Ironically, a guy who forms male bonds by "busting stones" is intimidated by a woman who busts his stones. If a woman verbally burns him, the Macho Loser gets defensive and complains she's "bitching" or not being "supportive" of him.

You With The Power Of *Insult And Live!*
(Shifting into a machine gun delivery.)
Oh yeah, like you're a real stud, when a woman looks at you and says, "Go for it!" she throws a Frisbee. *(Group laughs at Boomer.)* What's your nickname? "Bubba's bitch?" *(With a mocking edge.)* Hey, I'm just busting stones! Just trying to keep you humble! Say, I'm not holding you up. Shouldn't you be heading out to your Impotence Anonymous meeting?

Post-insult Outcome: You won! You vanquished the herd's ruler. And since the group secretly hopes their gangleader's next victim will either punch his lights out or verbally humiliate him, the pack will jeer their deposed king and slap your butt into their testosteronic fold. Plus, Boomer will never bother you again. Why? Because bullies only get in fights they can win.

The next de-evolutionary step of male bonding: callously humiliating women.

Male bonders are easy to spot at hotel lobbies, athletic events, parties or bars. They are on a sports team, belong to the same club, work for the same company, or are childhood pals. They refer to empty beer bottles as "soldiers." They howl after doing shooters. High five for no apparent reason. They belch. These melding males are aggressively rude to women through chauvinistic baiting, crude jokes, or animalistic acts, which they erroneously think gives them an independent and macho appeal. The essential rule to their crude behavior is: their buddies have to see them do it.

For example...

Situation:
Male Bonder Hitting On A Babe

(Scene: A bar in the evening. It's late. Eight guys in softball uniforms are drinking pitchers of beer and eating pizza. One teammate approaches an attractive and professional-looking woman. **The Male Bonder** *is overweight, there is pizza sauce on his shirt, and his baseball hat is turned around.)*

Male Bonder
(Carrying a half-filled beer pitcher.)
Hey, you wanna fuck?

Woman
(Justifiably offended.)
Get lost!

Male Bonder
So I guess a blowjob is out of the question.*
(He goes back to his laughing teammates. The group hoots and high-fives the Male Bonder.)

Of course, when separated from the herd, the male bonder apologizes to the woman, and instead of being boorish, becomes a little boy whose friends allegedly put him up to the task.

*****World Of Fred Note:** Male bonding helps a typical Macho Loser overcome his shyness with women by being rude to them first.

How Male Bonders try to provoke women

Makes sucking or kissing sounds with their lips at a passing woman.

Sees a woman breast-feeding a child and says, "When you're done with him, how about me?"

Loudly uses the "C" word (such as "missed it by a c--- hair.").

In a car, drives past a woman bicycling and smacks her butt.

Waits until a woman passes by and is almost out of ear shot, but says under their breath to the male group...

- "Younger girls are tighter than older ones."
- "I'd fuck her...again."
- "I wouldn't fuck her with your dick!"
- "Do you have fries to go with that shake?"
- "I'll have some of that."
- "The angle of the dangle equals the heat of the meat."
- *(About large woman.)* "Roll her around in dough and try to find the wet spot."
- "Old enough to bleed old enough to be butchered."
- "Tookie." or "Cootchie"
- "Women, can't live with'em can't shoot'em."
- "I think I'm in love."
- "Life's a bitch and then you marry one."
- "I'd make a woman out of her."
- *(If the woman is on a bike.)* "I'd like to be that seat."
- "Must be on the rag."
- "Tuna."
- *(If she received a promotion or has a better job than the male.)* "Who'd she blow to get that?"
- "Wanna mustache ride?'
- "Sit on my face."
- "Hot lunch."
- "More bounce to the ounce."

How male bonders try to provoke women (cont.)...

Tells these anti-female jokes in front of women...

- How do you know when a woman has an orgasm? Who cares?
- Why are there so many battered women? Because they just *won't listen!*
- Why does a doctor smack a baby? To knock the dicks off the dumb ones.
- Why did cavemen drag women by their hair? If you drag them by their legs they fill up with dirt.
- What's the ideal woman? Someone who is knee high with rubber teeth and has a flat head to rest your beer on.
- Why does a divorce cost so much? Because it's *worth* it!
- How many male chauvinists does it take to screw in a light bulb? None. Let the bitch cook in the dark.
- How is a woman different than dog shit? The older she gets the easier she is to pick up.
- Why shouldn't you trust women? Don't trust anything that bleeds for a week and doesn't die.
- What's the difference between women and dogs? A dog can bury a bone without getting its nose dirty.
- What's a sanitary napkin and a woman have in common? They're both stuck up bitches.
- Why is a woman's crotch so hairy? So you won't see the hooks.
- What's a man's navel for? So a woman has a place to put her gum on the way down.
- Why do women rub their eyes in the morning? Because they don't have balls.
- Why do women close their eyes making love? They hate to see a man have a good time.
- How do you make a woman scream after having sex? Wipe your dick on the drapes.
- You know, the term for manslaughter is seven years. If I'd have killed my wife when I first thought about it, I'd be out by now.
- What does a man like in a woman? His dick.

What makes a He-Man Woman Hater?

He-Man Women Haters have it in for women. These are men who equate equality with the execution of grueling physical tasks. They see it as a point of honor not to hold a door for a woman or to offer their seat to her. These threatened males bemoan quotas for women in the work place. Instead of blaming their own personal flaws for failures in female relationships, the He-Man blames women for his shortcomings. After all, a He-Man might say, "I know everything about women, I've been divorced three times."

A He-Man doesn't see women as individuals who can strengthen and contribute to his existence; instead, he either distrustfully views women as a breed intent upon ruining a man's life by limiting his freedom, or as a multi-holed being solely designed for his sexual pleasure. But, when it comes to evaluating a woman's aesthetics, the He-Man's brain is in his crotch. He declares the best way to keep a woman is to "treat her like shit." He loudly boasts to other men about his sexual conquests (he'll even show you pictures of the women.). These He-Man Woman Haters score with a lot of women, but it's always the same type of woman, usually a Bimbo.* In fact, the He-Man never dates or socializes with women who don't reinforce his narrow view of females as a burdensome species.

---

*World Of Fred Note: Ironically, when a woman uses and treats a He-Man the same indifferent way he treats women, the He-Man swain gets furious and never forgives her for it. He uses this offense to justify his hostile view of women. Again, it's the denial transference principle in action. Instead of realizing he's guilty of the same behavior to the opposite sex, he defends his callous behavior based on the way his first love dumped him. He's going to get even.

He-Man Woman Haters Roster
(Alias brain-in-the-crotch males who are all elevation with no sense of direction.)

Chauvinistic coworkers who...
- pulls a woman's bra strap at meetings.
- expects a woman to get him coffee.
- makes a woman's professional life miserable because she won't date them.
- assumes she's incompetent.
- dismisses a woman's valid criticism by saying, "It must be that *time* of the month."
- asks her to get the change out of his pocket.

Insensitive male gynecologists who use cold instruments; or, when a woman's in the stirrups, leaves the examining door open.

He-Man Woman Haters Roster (cont.)..

Muscular hunks in health spas who insists on showing females how to work out on the machine, and leers at her as she pumps the weights.

Alleged randy studs who call a woman a "ballbuster" if she doesn't sleep with them, and a "slut" if she does.

Customers or restaurant owners who pat waitresses' butts.

Unsupportive guys threatened by his wife's talents, education, and higher income who...
- ridicules her job, and belittles her coworkers.
- indulges in childish or rude behavior to make her submissive to his needs. (Such as, getting ridiculously drunk so she has to drive him home.)
- intentionally shows up poorly dressed at his wife's social function or company party and grunts, "What's the matter, you ashamed of me?"
- expects her to attend his team games, but refuses to go to her social functions because he "hates being around those people."

An intriguing and romantic foreigner who never tells the woman he's dating about his fiancé in another country.

Spermatozoa Heads who think when a woman says "no" she means "yes."

Drunks who try to cop a feel from a woman.

Guys who bump and grind too much during a slow dance.

Emotionally defective men who misinterpret overtures of female friendship and accuse her of sexually leading them on.

Unbalanced males who bluntly eyeball a woman's breasts when she's talking to them.

He-Man Woman Haters Roster (cont.)..

Cheating boyfriends who defend their behavior by saying, "Hey, it's not like we're *married.*"

Sir Wandering Eyes who is with his girlfriend or wife and bluntly checks out other women.

He-Man Woman Haters reveals his true attitude towards women in sports. He's an over aggressive and intractable man who...

- never allows a woman to make a play in a game because he "wants the team to win."
- gets angry if a woman doesn't do exactly what he tells her.
- lacks the skill to beat a woman in a co-ed game so he uses his brute strength to win; for example: sliding spikes high into a female catcher at a company softball game; or, (Above.) viciously spiking a ball into a woman's face during a friendly volleyball game.

He-Man Woman Haters Roster (cont.)...

Make-out artists who counter any female resistance to his advances by asking, "What are you? A lesbian?"

Deadbeat ex-husbands who don't send child support to his former wife because...
- "The kid isn't mine."
- "Why doesn't she have the boyfriend who she's living with pay for it?"
- "She won't let me see the kid."
- "She married a guy who makes more than me, what do they need my money for?"

Insincere dates who say, "I had a wonderful time. I'll call you." But, the woman suspects he's never going see or call her again.

Sleazy males in crowds who sticks out his elbow to feel a woman's breasts.

Cheating studs who defends his infidelities by saying, "Hey, don't get me wrong I love my wife...but this woman I met..."

Cruising guys who find out a woman is married and tells her he doesn't want to waste time talking to her because she's "out of circulation."

Married lechers who hit on woman at parties and say, "It doesn't have to mean anything."

Slimy sales guy who makes a move on a "hot nugget" by insisting he's met the woman before; or starts a conversation by greeting her with a different name or insists she is someone else.

Persistent hands-on maulers who spends a lot of money on a date and expects the woman to give him "something" in return.

Some men think it's funny to make extremely crude and obvious innuendoes out of a woman's name.

Why women need to learn the art of insulting macho losers

Most women confuse an insult with sexual rejection. But come on, ladies! Emasculating a man by saying you won't sleep with him isn't an insult. All you did was reject his advances! When you did this, you demeaned yourself by assuming the sexual object role the male sleaze imposed upon you.

Here's a typical example...

Situation:
Woman Getting Hit On By A Male Sleaze
*(Setting: Single's bar/meat rack. The **Male Sleaze** approaches a **Woman Without Insult And Live!** is at the bar. He hits on her.)*

Male Sleaze
How about getting a bottle of what you're drinking and going back to my place? *(Pause.)* You know you want it.

Woman Without *Insult and Live!* **Power**
In your dreams.

Male Sleaze
(Walks away.)
What a bitch!

Post-insult Outcome: You lost, babe. Why settle for a simple rejection by saying the same lines like, "In your dreams." or "You wish."? Instead of turning down a male sleaze, you can use insults to turn upon him. He can't dismiss you with the "bitch" ruling.

Let's replay the scene...

Take Two:
Return Of The Woman Getting Hit On By A Male Sleaze

Male Sleaze
How about getting a bottle of what you're drinking and going back to my place? *(Pause.)* You know you want it.

Women with the power to *Insult And Live!*
From you, be serious. When you want to find a girl's G-spot you have to lift up her tail.

Post-insult Outcome: You won! Your insult rejected the annoying male as a person. You didn't settle for equality. You dominated the male with an in-the-face disgrace! Now, that's equal opportunity!

Insult and Live! by Fred Reiss

Basic machismo-deflating insults

You're not macho, you're testosterone *Lite*.

You're a real macho guy. Yeah, I bet you don't even use toilet paper, you just sit on the rug and pull yourself across the floor.

Was that you speaking? Or is your groin teething?

Big guy, what do you eat for breakfast? Foster children?

Does it strain your back to walk upright?

When the doctor grabs your crotch for a hernia check, do you cough or do you say, "Yo!"?

When it's that time of month for your sweetheart, do you change your Camero's oil?

When I stare at you I feel natural selection missed one.

What's an authority figure to you? A zoo keeper?

You are a man of letters: J-e-r-k.

I bet, you think recycling energy is lighting farts.

You're one ounce of testosterone short of being a man.

The only thing you can whip out and use is a wet towel.

Are you cranky because you lost your chewbone?

Why do I feel like I'm talking to a man who still has his original sperm tail?

Basic machismo-deflating insults (cont.)...

Say is this the longest you've ever spoken without belching your words?

I'd like to make you feel comfortable but I don't have...
- any traffic signs for you to shoot at.
- a small animal for you to hunt.
- any ants for you to burn.
- a chain saw for you to make a tree sculpture.
- a seal to club.
- tires to rotate.
- a highway crew to direct traffic around you.
- a keg of beer for you to tap.
- bottle caps for you to flip.
- a transmission to drop.
- a can for you to spit tobacco juice in.
- cinder blocks to put underneath your car.

Are you edgy because there are no tools in this room?

Why don't you find a welder and spawn?

How do you survive without a root system?

How come you're talking to me?
- No animals to trap?
- No mailboxes to smash?
- No lawns to do car doughnuts on?
- No brush fires to set tonight?

Why don't you go play stoop ball with your testicles?

I guess *Wrestlemania* does have a larval stage.

Where are you going? Migrating to a truck stop?

Basic machismo-deflating insults (cont.)...

A consciousness raising class for you is gym.

One day there will be a way to recycle you into a man.

I bet a doctor conducts your hernia check with tweezers.

You're what happens when the testicles descend without the man.

What are you doing here? Don't you have to bury a Teamster?

Uncomfortable in a room that doesn't have a work bench and a sawhorse?

While you're here, is your VCR taping the televised skeet shooting contest?

For you, road kill is a pizza topping.

Why do I have the feeling you don't understand any sport unless it involves bait?

You thinking "voguing" is mooning.

If they put your original sperm and egg into a super collider, it would come out as a *Budweiser* can.

For you, a wake-up call would be the Bronze Age.

I bet phlegm hawks you up.

Mr. Stud monster. How can you stand the thought that somewhere there's a mirror without your reflection in it?

Basic machismo deflating insults (cont.)...

You're happy because *Hee Haw* isn't pay-per view.

When you go to the zoo, do gorillas try to high five you?

You're wonderful, I never met a Cyborg.

For you, a social climber is a four-wheel vehicle.

Do you work on the assembly line or were you *made* on the assembly line?

Are you the holograph for the *Chainsaw City* credit card?

You look bitter because you don't belong to a union.

For you, raising your standard of living means getting a trailer hitch for your truck.

(If a man starts barking or growling say...)
- Why are you excited? Is there livestock nearby?
- Did you think I was your trainer?
- Oh, for a second I was hoping someone was clubbing you for your pelt.
- Did you just do a trick and you want some fish?

Relax, drag your knuckles on the carpet.

You're the type of guy who can't keep his balance unless you're holding a beer.

For you a wake-up call is the Cro-Magnon period.

I hear you made the Kennel Club's active stud book.

Do you consider bowling a mating dance?

Basic machismo-deflating insults (cont.)...

Look, why are you bugging me?...
- I don't have any *Liv-A-Snaps* left.
- I've run out of food pellets.
- Lose your chewbone?

Celebrating tonight because the nine-year old couldn't identify you in the police line-up?

Yeah, if you're God's gift to women, it's only because when they see you they say, "Jesus Christ."

I have the feeling a fast food snack for you is auto parts.

Insults to ridicule a man's sexual appeal or performance

In a brothel, I bet you use the self-service pump.

The only way you could be in the mile-high club is by flying solo.

You're such a wimp, you're the only man I know who has a yeast infection.

When a woman looks at you and says, "Go for it!," she throws a Frisbee.

I bet you've never spoken to a woman without sticking a twenty dollar bill in your mouth.

Your last date wasn't bulimic, eating and looking at you just simply made her sick.

A hooker would say to you, "I just want to be good friends."

Insults to ridicule a man's sexual appeal or performance (cont.)...

Are you upset because you came home early and caught your inflatable doll in bed with someone else?

If they did a porno picture of your sexual performance, it would be a still life.

When a woman plays hard to get with you, she gets a restraining order.

You're the reason lesbians don't have a sense of humor.

Why are you attracted to me? Do I look like an all-terrain vehicle?

You're not being celibate if people don't want to go to bed with you.

If women didn't lack self-esteem you'd never date.

Hey, buying American doesn't mean cutting down on Oriental prostitutes.

Doing it all night doesn't mean watching the *Sports Channel* till dawn.

When you go to the bathroom, do you get confused over which one is your weenie or your outie belly button?

The only time you could experience sex and bondage is getting a hostage.

In your case size doesn't matter, if you're dating a flea.

You have a way with women: celibacy.

Insults to ridicule a man's sexual appeal or performance (cont.)...

After you complete an act of sex, do you look in the mirror and say, "Was it good for you?"

You have to take sod-laying night class because dirt is the only thing you can score with.

You look a guy who's into power tools: vibrators.

You're so horny you'd get...
- sexually aroused listening to a square dance instructor.
- into a car accident so you could hump the air bag.
- arrested for gridlock at a gang bang.
- excited seeing overturned tractor-trailers on the highway.
- watching the *Discovery* channel?

Didn't I see you on America's *Least* Wanted?

I saw you at the nude beach. You were the guy with the binoculars.

For show and tell in sex education class, you demonstrated limpness.

What stimulates you, seeing a picture of a cupped hand?

Look at you, hormones without a sex life.

By the way, did you know over aggressiveness is one of the first symptoms of impotence?

Say, didn't your last girlfriend have a tattoo that said, "Inflate to 36 pounds?"

Insults to ridicule a man's sexual appeal or performance (cont.)...

When it's a hot day, and you feel like a cold one, do you go down to the morgue?

You probably had your pit bull neutered so he'd lick *your* crotch.

What's a self-improvement book to you: "Fifteen erotic ways to make a pig squeal"?

Do you get excited by the centerfold in *Field and Stream*?

You probably lost your virginity at nineteen, eleven if you count livestock.

When you want to find your girlfriend's g-spot you have to lift up her tail first.

What's a porno number for you? 976-MOO?

When you went to the Mustang Ranch, were you disappointed there weren't any horses there?

Depressed because they're aren't conjugal visits at the petting zoo?

When you're doing it with your right hand, do you imagine you're milking a cow.

For you, putting on sheepskin condom is a sexual experience.

You couldn't score at the Kennedy compound.

Are you angry because you popped your inflated sheep?

Insulting a macho' man's homophobic behavior by inferring their fear is suppressed homosexual lust

Are you disappointed because sperm banks don't have tasting bars?

Do you think a party ball is a guy named Bill?

Do you tip your proctologist extra to exam you with a gerbil hand puppet?

I'm not saying you're not a hetero, but I bet your favorite movie is "Altar Boy's Revenge."

In the Boy Scouts, did you get a merit badge for sodomy?

When you're in a circle jerk, I bet you're the one who wants to sit in the middle.

Why do I have the feeling you know *Preparation H* is tasteless?

Do you think anal retentive is being able to hold in more than   three gerbils?

The only thing that would improve your love life is prison.

Do you tip your dentist extra to find rectal cavities?

Yeah, you're into crack—butt crack.

Did you lay a fake molar under your pillow to try to score with the tooth fairy?

What's your favorite Steinbeck novel, "Of Mice *In* Men?"

Insults for small herds of Male Bonders

If you guys sit there long enough, a gym class will form around you.

Sitting here until your coach shows up?

In this modernized world it's so surprising to discover an untouched primitive society.

You look like a starter set for a slow class.

Feel like I'm staring at a Klingon single's group.

Bummed out because you couldn't attend the Aryan Woodstock?

It's nice when Outreach programs have field trips.

Is this a cast party for *Gorillas In The Mist?*

What is this, a Shop Class Reunion?

Look at this line-up, the Mount Rushmore of alcoholism.

If Darwin were here, he'd feel that he lead an empty life.

Here they are: the *Skoal* poster children.

Don't you have to get back to the rest of your drinking buddies at the tidal pool?

You realize if everyone in this room was one body, you'd be its pap smear?

Were you guys freshly picked by migrant farm workers?

Insults for small herds of Male Bonders (cont.)...

This is probably the closest you boys have sat together without a bait bucket between you.

If you guys just had a duck blind around you, you'd all feel more relaxed.

Why did you guys come here?...
- No tractor pull tonight?
- No televised fishing on TV?
- Slurpee machine break down?
- The softball umpire clinic was canceled?
- The motor pool was closed?
- Is there going to be female mud wrestling here?
- No junked cars to strip?
- Did the Neanderthal theme park lay off a few cavemen?
- Special Olympics conga line outrun you?
- No rats to shoot in the dump?
- Do they have a slow learning class in the Texas glide?
- They fumigate the reptile touch tank?

Say is this the opening scene for the horror movie: "Men Without Dates"?

Is this a van-art think tank?

Say, what are you celebrating? Do special education classes have Spring break?

If I put onions and peppers in between you guys I could make a low-income kabob.

I can only hope you guys are planning a cluster suicide pact.

Insults for small herds of Male Bonders (cont.)...

Look at this, for the first time together, the five warning signs of cancer.

Has someone successfully cloned motocross fans?

(To two guys.) It's nice to meet the poster children for shipping and receiving.

You guys waiting to throw rocks at a Woolly Mammoth?

You guys have come a long way from playing those banjoes in *Deliverance.*

Insult and Live! by Fred Reiss

Giving it Hard to Hostile Femmos

The Femacho

The grim-eyed Ms. Executive Action determinedly strides in her sneakers on her commuter trail to work (Her business shoes are in the bottom drawer of her desk behind her mineral water bottle.). A Femacho's authority actionwear is comprised of a billowy skirt covered halfway by a large blazer designed to conceal her bison-like behind. If she gets married, she immediately cuts her hair to a practical and unappealing length.

Purpose of this section: To teach you how to identify and insult hostile women, such as Femachos, Bitches On Wheels, Bimbos, Vaginal-Centric Penophobes.

Femacho: 1.) A career-driven woman who is independent, goal oriented, and bitter. 2.) A hostile woman who stereotypes male behavior. 3.) A woman who blames sexism for her problems instead of her deficient personality. 4.) A woman who feels men can't understand women, but feels women can completely understand men, who are simple, and usually evil 5.) A woman who is so accustom to her husband or boyfriend obeying her, she can't handle any other man not listening to her, or one who justifiably calls her a pushy moron.

Ms. Femacho

Ms. Femacho is a spike-heeled killer. This diva-like dominatrix is her own person. She has a way with people—her way. In fact, she firmly maintains anyone who doesn't like her is "threatened" by her superior talents. But, like all losers she sees herself as a nice soul who is misunderstood and unappreciated by those around her. When she's accused of being a dominating woman, Ms. Femacho denies it. She firmly maintains "I don't have problems with people, they have a problems with me."

Her social life completely revolves around her job. She sees the people who work with her as "family." She has power lunches and goes on business trips. She has one-night stands. And, when this full-on flaming Dragon Lady has the option to wield power over someone to serve her in any way, she seizes it. Oddly, the hard-charging Femacho sees herself as someone who is challenging a male-dominated field by being a "woman of the nineties," which somehow makes her a unique individual. However, when you examine this woman of the nineties, she seems to resemble a man from the forties.

Femacho traits

Says her hard character protects her "vulnerable" qualities but notes, "I can be a *real* bitch when I want to."

A displaced maternal instinct makes her a fond of a particular creature. Her home abounds with a variety of objects in the shape of this creature, usually it's a flamingo.

Periodically alienates relatives or friends.

Has an unresolved father complex (He was distant.).

Owns two cats that represent her split personality: one that's friendly; the other is nasty and scratches.*

Intimidates others by strutting with a monstrous dog, which is vicious and overprotective. (The beasts helps her "feel safe.")

Her closest male friend is a homosexual.

Maintains she isn't moody—it's job stress.

Throws theme parties or theme-designed evenings that require how everyone must dress or act.

Over uses the phrase "woman friend."

Bullies other motorists by driving a huge vehicle. (She needs the vehicle to "feel protected.")

Although she is in the prime of life, after she buys groceries, she insists a clerk carry her purchases to the car (Especially, if the clerk is a woman her age, or older.).

When men dance with her, she has a tendency to lead.

***World Of Fred Note:** She likes her pets because they are "always glad to see her" and "don't demand anything" from her.

Insult and Live! by Fred Reiss

Ms. Femacho ridicules action-movies as "stupid," but enjoys taking her dates to male-bashing films with implausible plots. (For further comments on male-bashing, see Vaginal Centric Penophobes.)

Ms. Femacho and the opposite sex

Is only interested in men indifferent to her charms, but, once he falls in love with her, she dumps him.

Thinks a geeky or fat man is "lucky to even have a woman," but that men are cruel for not being attracted to a geeky and fat woman because "she can't help who she is."

When men break up with her, Femacho says, "It's his loss, he doesn't know how good he had it with me."

Dismisses any aggressive quality in a male as an example of his sexual shortcomings, or as a juvenile need to prove his virility.

Ms. Femacho and the opposite sex (cont.)...

Sees sex as a submissive or done in "exchange" for something.

Cites "sexist" references made by males, but sees nothing wrong with commenting on a guy's "nice butt."

Believes it's important to keep former lovers as "friends."*

At work, claims she has to be "twice as tough as a man to be taken seriously."

Thinks men are always trying to "prove something."

Justifies unethical business behavior or discrimination against males by saying, "Men have done it to women for years."

Anytime men find an aggressive flaw in her character she labels them a "sexist."

Interrupts a man's conversation by finishing his sentences and thoughts, or retells his story.

Controls her relationships by only dating men who are either: **1.)** dumb. **2.)** emotionally weaker than her. **3.)** total losers. **4.)** married (usually it's her boss).

Without asking, during sex, she rolls the man over and squats on top (Variation: gives foreplay commands.).

Gets angry at men for treating her like a "dumb woman," but she feels free to assume a condescending maternal tone and talks down to men in the same way she'd speak to a child.

***World Of Fred Note:** Of course, none of her former lovers feel the same way.)

Male-to-female topics Femachos forcibly interject in conversations

• Why can't men stay at home and do housework?
• If there was a birth control pill for men, shouldn't they take it?
• Why can't men have the children?
• Why don't men give up their surname after marriage?
• Why is a woman a slut if she sleeps around, but if a guy does it, he's a stud?
• How come an aggressive man is seen as someone who can take charge, but if a woman displays the same behavior, she's called a "bitch"?*
• Don't you think the world be better if it was run by women?
• Why shouldn't prostitution be legalized; after all, isn't a man who doesn't believe in his nine-to-five job the same as a prostitute?
• Who has the right to determine what's "masculine" and what's "feminine"? (Mostly said by unattractive women.)
• Why does sex have to even enter a relationship between a man and a woman?**

These aren't debatable questions to the Femacho, they are decrees that demand men make a concession in the conversation.***

---

*World Of Fred Note: Actually, when a man is over aggressive, he's called an "asshole."

**Another World Of Fred Note: This spin on the "just friends" theory, which is a fraud. Proof: if a guy said to his lover," Honey, I'm going camping this weekend with my friend Monica." Do you think she'd let him go unescorted with that "friend"?

***Yet Another World Of Fred Note: Femachos militantly believe in gender-cleansing every conversation. If a man mentions terms like "Town Fathers," or "firemen," the Femacho snaps, "Excuse me? They're fire*persons* and Town *Persons*." Best way to handle this one, simply say: "You must be divorced." or "I guess I should read more *her*story."

How to insult a hostile Femacho

A hostile Femacho is obsessed with being acknowledged as an individual. The best approach: treat her as frigid. The Femacho gets mad because you're not treating her as a person by attributing her defiant individualism with her lack of sexuality.

For example...

Situation:
Giving It Hard To A Femacho
*(Scene: a sports bar. **Softball Player** in his thirties is dressed in his dirty uniform. He passes a **Femacho**.)*

Femacho
(Caustically.)
Still playing baseball at your age? I thought you'd given it up by now? I guess men don't grow up, they just grow *older*.

Male Softball Player
I bet, if I slept with you, I'd have to wear a condom so I wouldn't get freezer burn.

Post-insult Outcome: You won! Femachos see men as an option they can dismiss, or chose to accept in their life. An insult gives you the initiative to reject the Femacho before she can reject you. But the driving reason an insult defeats the Femacho is this: you're not rejecting the Femacho on physical appeal, you're rejecting the one quality she believes is irresistible to men--her personality.

Typical hostile woman video-tape library:
Hostile women favor male-bashing films. These plot-less movies deal with how a woman's individuality is suppressed by men who only see women as a sex object. Yet, in these hostile-femmo movies, the female protagonist discovers herself when she experiences her first "real" orgasm. If her cathartic orgasm is achieved by a lesbian affair, bondage, or oral sex with a paraplegic, it's an "art" film.

The Bitch On Wheels.

Get you motor running! The Bitch On Wheels mows over anything in her way. She's reckless. A notorious hit-and-runner. The Bitch On Wheels is not insured, leaves the scene of every accident she causes, and is determined to live in the "now." (Mainly because her past is a disaster she can't acknowledge; in fact, like all losers, she gets furious when she's forced to confront it.)

The Bitch On Wheels

The Bitch On Wheels always has half a mad on. Usually, she is a spurned first wife in the mid-thirties and above range. Her hair is short, just like her temper. She gets loud when she drinks. She is assertive, defiant, and overdemanding. And, in most cases, she's divorced or separated. Why? Because the husband left her to marry a younger, more emotionally supportive, and *quieter* woman (who the Bitch On Wheels dismisses as a "trophy wife.").

But, the free-born Bitch On Wheels neglects to note her man left because she...
- let herself go.
- didn't give her husband emotional support which drove him to a woman who believed in him.
- during the marriage made all the decisions regarding the raising of *her* children without consulting the husband. (So, after the kids graduated from high school, he bolted.)
- insisted on living and working near her mother and father, in spite of the fact her husband's family is nowhere near hers and that his career advancement is limited by the move.
- wouldn't let her retired husband sell their house because she insisted on being "near the children." *
- turned the couple's house into "her home" where everyone has to follow *her* rules (Her only concession: giving the man free reign over the garage, a wall, or a basement corner.).
- constantly kept saying she gave up her career for the children or him.
- shares a joint bank account with her husband, but without consulting her equal partner, spends money on anything she desires, such as unnecessary lengthy long-distant calls to her mother, because "I worked and it's my money and I can spend it anyway I chose." (If the husband protests this indulgence, she says he is "inconsiderate.")
- reneges on her pre-marital promise to either have children, or not have children.

---

* **World Of Fred Note:** It doesn't mean anything to the Bitch On Wheels that her mate wants to relieve himself of a financial burden and enjoy his retirement. She defends her action by saying the husband wants it too ("You wouldn't be happy away from the children, I *know*.").

Once divorced,* the souped-up Bitch On Wheels, powered by either her pedal-to-the-medal estrogen, or skidding on post-menopausal testosterone rushes, is primed to achieve a satisfying career and a self-rewarding personal life.

This customized Bitch On Wheels won't let any man determine her future. But, she'll accept what she views as "rightfully" hers from men, such as her ex-husband's property, alimony money, or financial backing from her new boyfriend to start up her own business. But when she talks to anyone about her financial status, she acts like she was completely responsible for her own success.

Some Bitches On Wheels become aggressive medical receptionists. Typical tactic: After a patient sees the doctor, the pateint stops at the receptionist's desk to make another appointment. Then, she bluntly and brutally shakes down the patient for cash. After the doctor's bill has been settled, the dreadnought attempts to conceal her extortion-like behavior by shifting into a false maternal concern for the patient's health by asking "When will we see you again?"

*World Of Fred Note: If The New Bitch On Wheels is still married, her husband cheats, completely ignores her, or is an alcoholic wimp.

Bitches on Wheels business activities and career moves

- Organizing weddings
- Catering companies
- Employment services
- Public relations or advertising agencies (Largely formed by half of her ex-husband's clients.)
- Divorce lawyer
- Real Estate agent*
- Entertainment booker
- Overprotective executive secretaries**
- Health-care or makeup product sales managers
- Bed-and-breakfast or hotel owners
- Part-time journalist at her hometown weekly newspaper
- Managerial number-crunchers in small businesses
- School bus driver (the fat ones.)
- Runs and owns a small "playhouse (this is a middle-aged woman who gave up acting in her youth to marry money.)
- Head nurse (who enjoys limiting visitors to terminally ill patients who want visitors.)

Romantic novelist (Most pose on their book's jacket photo holding their dog.)

---

*__World Of Fred Note:__ This is the top professional choice for Bitches On Wheels.

**__Another World Of Fred Note:__ A Bitch On Wheels who becomes an executive secretary assumes the power of her boss. She does this by deciding who gets access to him. For example, when she answers the phone, she doesn't say, "I'll give him the message," she says, "*I'll* have him call you." Sometimes she will even ask, "What is this in reference to?" Also, when she relays a message from the boss to the employees, she regurgitates it back with a rude edge, as if she's issuing the directive. She feels no need to explain anything she does to anyone because she says, "I report only to Mr. (Blank.)" When no one can hear or see, she ruthlessly pecks on the receptionists beneath her. This secretary considers herself above answering phones or taking messages for anyone but her boss. If her boss is married, she is overly protective and in love with him as well as jealous of his wife who she belittles by saying "She's fat...She's ugly...She doesn't realize all the things *he* does for her."

Bitch On Wheels motor functions

Says "honey," "dear," "darling," and "be a love," to people she doesn't know.

Uses way too much makeup and perfume.

Sheathes herself in jewelry (As if it were armor.).

Collects antiques, or has a diverse collection of artifacts from her travels to foreign countries. (Her house seems more like a museum than a home.)

Has a poodle or chihuahua with a French name.

Anytime she sees a man reclining in a comfortable position, the Bitch On Wheels thinks he's "doing nothing" and should be given something to do.

Carries more luggage than she needs on trips.

Wears furs.

If she has a male child it's an overweight, passive wimp; if it's a girl, she's a spoiled and rude brat.

Is over protective about a room or expensive furnishings (big on slipcovers, never using the "good" silverware, etc.).

Bitch On Wheels interpersonal relationship views

Declares the most important personal quality is "self confidence." (Regardless of being right or wrong.)

Smears children's faces with lipstick from sloppy kisses.

Says she doesn't like a particular political candidate because he reminds her of an ex-husband.

Bitch On Wheels interpersonal relationship views (cont.)...

Never gives you what you want, she gives what *she feels* you need. (She is a notorious underwear-giver to kids.)

Asks you to help her move heavy objects, but never lifts a finger to help. She'll point and say, "I want it there. "

Can't tell the difference between when a man is telling her what to do or simply telling her *how* to do it. (Example: If a male tells her how to get to a destination, she says, "I don't take directions from *men*.")

Bitch On Wheels performance toward her own sex

Believes young women are "stupid" to have children.

Doesn't even like other women, especially if they're younger and slimmer women who men admire.

Asks an overweight woman if she is pregnant. Or says, "You know, you'd be very attractive if you lost weight."

Says to a single gal, "Well, dear, you're not getting any *younger*."

Tells her own daughter that giving birth ruined her mother's figure forever.

Says to a wife she's jealous of, "You don't deserve such a nice husband." or "You're not a good wife."

Overdresses in a loud or revealing outfit at weddings (her purpose to steal attention from the bride.).

If a woman has long hair, she tugs it to see if it's real.

How women can insult Bitches On Wheels

When women insult each other they risk being felinously charged with cattiness or banshee-caterwauling bitchiness. A woman can escape this dilemma is simple: never attack first. This way your self-defense insult can't be interpreted as a jealousy or a competitive remark directed against an ego-guzzling Bitch On Wheels.

For example...

Situation:
How Women Can Cut Off A Bitch On Wheels

*(Scene: wedding. The **Bride With The Power To Insult and Live!** is walking among the guests. The **Bitch On Wheels**, an alleged friend of the bride. The **Bitch On Wheels** has been divorced once, and is clearly jealous of the bride.)*

Bitch On Wheels
(To a guest.)
The marriage won't last a year. I give it six months tops!

Bride With The Power Of *Insult And Live!*
(Overhears conversation and says to the woman.)
You're attacking my husband? He would have married you, but he told me the hardest part of having sex with you was waiting in line so long.

Post-insult Outcome: You won! Not only did you emerge as classier lady, you drove the Bitch On Wheels off the highway of your life. Have a pleasant drive.

The Bimbo

The Bimbo giggles and flirts. But when this coquettish little kitten doesn't get her way, she has a full-on hissy fit. You see, throughout her entire life Daddy has always taken care of her. He has purchased everything for his "little girl" who's use to getting her way. The Bimbo isn't just looking for any man. She's hunting for a man to replace her father. And if her husband doesn't shelter, protect, pamper and cater to her whims like Daddy, she'll make the man's life miserable forever. She doesn't age well--and she's *very* aware of it.

Jobs Bimbos take to meet a future husband

- dental hygienists
- cosmetic clerks
- waitresses*
- radiology technicians
- practicing nurses
- secretaries
- hairdressers
- stewardesses
- receptionists at automotive-service departments
- accountants in their Dad's business.
- dispatchers for police, fire, ambulance, or a cab company
- tambourine player in her lover's band

Bimbo tip offs

She has lots of stuffed animals on her bed. (Sometimes they have names and she talks to them.)

Wears a crucifix in her cleavage (Virgin Mary/Whore look.).

Signs her name with hearts, or dots her i's with them.

Drives a white sports car with a personalize license plate like "4-Babs" or "Thx-Dad."

Is overly melodramatic during every stage of her pregnancy.

Gets drunk and does high school cheers.

Wears makeup and jewelry when she exercises near men.

---

*World Of Fred Note: The biggest female loser is a cocktail waitress in the twenties to mid-thirties range. She is the most emotionally unstable, compulsive, and obsessive human being on this planet. This Bimbo's life is a constant emotional drama. She's usually divorced more than twice, has a bratty kid. If single, the Bimbo has a major drug or alcohol problem, and whines about the guy they are dating (who is in a band).

Bimbos favor reading thick romance novels about young, naive, but promiscuous women who are "looking for love," travelling around the world, and earning a lot of money working with powerful men.

Bimbo tip offs (cont.)...

She lives in a condo her parents allegedly bought for their retirement, but purchased to get the Bimbo out of the house.

Can't cook.

Makes a cartoonish squeaky sound when she sneezes.

She's a slob (It's common to see discarded but unwrapped sanitary napkins in the wastebasket.).

For Halloween, she dresses in a tight body suit as a kitten, devil with a blue dress, or an angel.

Bimbo tip offs (cont.)...

Wears revealing negligees to make up for her deficient sexual talents.

Loves showing off a ludicrously expensive engagement ring.

During the work day, she does her nails at the desk.

Several former roommates don't speak to her because she stole their jewelry.

Her voice increases three octaves when she says hello to one of her girlfriends.

If she's uncomfortable in a social situation, instead of talking to people, she isolates herself from them until everyone leaves.

In women's rooms, she puts on her makeup but doesn't give any other females room to wash hands or use the mirror.

When she asks you if she's overweight, and you say yes, then she gets mad at you.

Bimbo character traits

Gets angry if you don't notice her new outfit.

Doesn't compromise. She only has tantrums.

Only thinks about shopping, partying, and eating.

Chews gum and sips blush wine at the same time. (She chews gum to keep her breath fresh; and hates dry wine because it's "not sweet enough.")

Consistently late and unreliable.

Has a huge poofy hairstyle.

Bimbo character traits (cont.)...

Orders strawberry daiquiris or difficult-to-make-crushed ice drinks from the bar.

Infatuated with attractive male recording artists who sings about never being able to find woman to love him.

Angry if a woman is more attractive or interesting than her.

Uses heavily exaggerated limp-wristed gestures.

Bimbos draw attraction to her average body by revealing cleavage and flaunting her flanks. She gets angry when men gawk. (If she's dating or married, she claims it's how her lover wants her to dress.)

Bimbo's relationships with opposite sex

Believes every man physically desires her.

After making love, she intentionally leaves a personal possession to have a reason to return.

Bimbo's relationships with opposite sex (cont.)...

Never trusts her boyfriend and is always checking up on him or accusing him of infidelity.

Thinks a man's looks are more important than his personality.

If she even suspects a guy of looking at another woman, she points and snarls, "Is that the *type* of woman you like?"

Recklessly drives her boyfriend's sports car or truck.

Dates tough guy macho types and complains about them to other guys she wants to meet.

Gets mad at her mate for the way he treated her in a dream.

Says he would do things for her "if you really loved me."

When travelling, clings or sleeps against a guy so he can't do anything else.

Flirts to make her boyfriend or husband jealous.

When she is pregnant she expects the husband to remain home with her and not to drink.

Anything that gives her lover pleasure apart from her must be stopped, because she feels it shows he doesn't love her enough.

If a guy calls her up on Monday for a weekend date, she says, "call me Thursday." (Translation: she'll date you if no one else asks her out for the weekend.)

Sleeps with men to use their drugs, but defends this practice by saying, "We just partied."

Instead of developing her own independent qualities, she blames men for her limitations.

Bimbo bonding:
The Beauty, Cutie, and The Beast grouping*

Bimbos On The Prowl.
Most Bimbos travel in threes. There is the beautiful one with a bitchy personality who lives to reject men (This type likes to wear white cowboy boots). The cute one with a pleasant personality. And, the fat one who drove; or is unfairly used by the other two to get out of awkward situations with men (They point to The Beast and say, "I'd like to stay, but she has to get up early.")

*****World Of Fred Note:** The accuracy of this group is as valid and as entering a strip-joint or massage parlor and being certain to find a woman named Amber, Brandy, Crystal, Deidre, Candy, Dawn, or Bambi. (A possible exception: any name that ends in "y" is changed to "i"; for example: Candy is spelled as Candi.)

Here's the official World Of Fred breakdown of the bimbette trio...

The Beauty

She is the most attractive and sexiest of the group. But, she's the deadliest. She has a jealous boyfriend who shows up at unexpected moments. Of course, having a boyfriend doesn't stop the Beauty from flirting, dancing, or accepting free drinks from other men (Sometimes she cruelly gives out a made-up home phone number.). After all, she's entitled: "no one owns her." By closing time, the Beauty gets drunk, throws up, schizes out, leaves with a cocaine dealer, or runs into her angry boyfriend. Usually it's all five. Sometimes, she even tries to get her enraged and jealous lover to beat up the unsuspecting guy with whom she has been, flirting, drinking and dancing with all night. Also, the Beauty doesn't hesitate to steal the attention any male makes towards The Cutie.

The Cutie

This female is less sexually flashy than the Beauty. She dresses modestly, uses less makeup, and has a much more attractive personality. The Cutie is a loyal friend who apologizes for the Beauty's behavior by saying, "She's not like this all the time." The Cutie dances together with the Beast.

The Beast

The unattractive one who drives The Beauty and the Cutie to bars. Usually, just when the party gets going, the disgruntled dumpy duenna wants to leave. The blowsy Beast's sole function is to sit around bored while the other women dance or talk to guys. No male hits on The Beast until last call; a hard and brutal truth in her life she has come to expect and heavily resent.

Why Bimbos are the simplest females to insult

All insults work on a Bimbo--even if she doesn't understand them. Why? Because Bimbos firmly follow these tenets...

    1.) All men want to make love to the her.
    2.) Every woman is jealous of her ability to attract men.

Since a Bimbo's entire basis for interpreting life is based on the belief of her flesh-monkey irresistibility, she gets angry at any line that doesn't imply worship, desire, or envy...

**Situation:
Chapping The Bimbo**
(Scene: nightclub. **Guy With The Power Of Insult And Live!** approaches a **Sorority Girl Bimbo** who is standing on the dance floor's edge and provocatively shaking her hips to the music. She is in a tight dress, has poofy hair, and wears spiked red high heels.)

Guy With The Power Of *Insult And Live!*
Would you like to dance?

Sorority Bimbo
(Sipping her daiquiri through a straw.)
With you?

Guy With The Power Of *Insult And Live!*
Now I know Ted Bundy had a legitimate motive.

Sorority Girl Bimbo
(Shrilly.)
Fuck off!

Post-insult Outcome: You win! An insult means she can't control you to get what she wants. So, she behaves like a irreconcilable child by storming away, snarling, or glaring at you. Warning: Bimbos are quick to throw drinks, scratch, pull hair, or slap. They don't want to develop a mature point of view. Why? Because they've always gotten what they wanted by being childish.

The most hostile of all hostile women:
Male-bashing Vaginal-Centric Penophobe

Penophobic "womyn" ape all the worst characteristics of what they conceive as "typical" male behavior. These prehistoric Gynosaures dress in sleeveless shirts, leather outfits, bluejeans, workboots, and janitorially sport a belt ring with numerous keys. They take tough guy jobs. They bully males (some will go to the extreme of throwing shoulders at passing men). They bark commands at their lovers. Their whole purpose: provoke the worst behavior from men, which, when it happens, reinforces her perceptions that men are inherently evil, destructive, erection-driven-rapist brutes.

Male Bashers
(Alias Vaginal-Centric Penophobes)

The Femacho and Bitch on Wheels believes all her problems are caused by men. The Bimbo? Well, she thinks all her problems can be solved by men. The hostile male-hating Vaginal-Centric Penophobe aggressively maintains her emotional difficulties as well as all the world's troubles would be solved if men didn't exist!

These intense Penophobettes obsess out on "having control" of every situation. They view heterosexual sex as one partner being the aggressor (guess who?) and the other one: the victim (who is female). The exception: the female isn't considered a victim if their female partner performs the sexual act with a piece of durable plastic, a cucumber, or inseminates her with a turkey baster.

In The World Of Fred, the Vaginalette's most positive contribution to society is removing folksinging from mainstream culture.

Vaginal Centrists live in university or resort towns and gravitate to these professions...

- mass transit workers
- strippers/painted women
- 92 percent of stand-up comediennes
- government case workers
- physical therapists
- rape crisis or batter "women-center" counselors
- gym teachers or athletic coaches
- 99.7 percent of professional golfers/tennis players as well as 99.9 percent of volleyball/softball pros.*
- sociology college professors or teachers who specialize in courses that begin with "Women's role in..."
- canine control
- fashion modeling (beautiful women need beautiful women.)

---

*__World Of Fred Note:__ Some say the percentage of Penophobes in a sport is the same percentage in general population (Yeah, right.).

Vaginal-Centric Penophobic traits

Penophobes protest beauty contests because the event reduces women to sexual objects for men...

But, it's okay for Vaginal Centrics to attend female muscle-building contests that reduce women to sexual objects for other women.

Vaginal Centric Penophobic traits (cont.)...

Sees herself as an "oppressed" minority group.*

---

*World Of Fred Note: The confrontational Penophobe hasn't accepted her sexual preference. Instead of facing it, she wants society to accept her sexual choice, so, she's exhibitionistic to provoke people.

Vaginal Centric Penophobic traits (cont.)

Everything she's against has some variation of the word "male" or "men" in it.

Can't talk about men without using words "fascist" or "Nazi."

Declares her sexuality defines her as a person, but gets infuriated when viewed as a sexual object.

Has permed road-killesque haircuts; in fact, she usually has more hair on her armpits and legs than on her head.

Denies her militant personality is the sole reason why people dislike her.

Thinks female bonding is male bashing.

Calls inanimate objects by their equivalent female name; for example, a microphone ("mike") is described as a "Michelle."

Intimidates people by walking around with vicious attack dogs that blindly obey their commands (The dog is male, restrained by a painful collar, and is always neutered.).

Wears way too many rings in her ears.

Incorrectly interprets history to have a heritage (this enables her to reinvent herself without developing a personality.).

The best way to slam a male-bashing Vaginal Centrics

A Vaginal Centric conceals her bulging and throbbing hatred of males beneath a feminist's baggy clothing. The best way to slam this separatist rager is an insult that defines her as someone who despises men, which undermines her intellectual integrity and self-esteem.

For example...

Situation:
Exposing A Male-hating Vaginal Centrist

*(Scene: college campus auditorium. The **Male-bashing Female Author** addresses the group. She has written numerous feminist fictional works and ovular sociology studies. She has discussed how men are responsible for all the evils in the world. She allows the audience to ask her questions. A **Bashed Male With The Power Of Insult And Live!** is in the crowd.)*

Male-hating Female Author
(Answering a question.)
I don't see any hope for women to achieve their freedom under the slavery of a male-dominated society. *(Pause.)* Sir, do you have a question?

Bashed Male With The Power Of *Insult And Live!*
Okay, so if men are evil, how can the women who gave birth and raised these men be good? The equation doesn't balance out, after all, if you blame the product, don't you have to blame the manufacturer too?

Male-hating Female Author
(Without hesitation.)
Ovular mergers must have female children because as I see it male violence is institutionalized in society and causes men to become rapists, women batterers, and baby killers.

Bashed Male With The Power Of *Insult and Live!*
What did you do before you became a writer? Work on a Ken doll assembly line and snap off the genitals?

Male-hating Author
That's the kind of response I'd expect from a *man!*

Post-insult Outcome: You won! Verbal slam, bam, thank you madam. When you expose her hostility as the motivational force for her views, she locks into denial and assaults you as anti-female and gets even angrier at you! That's funny.

Insult and Live! by Fred Reiss

Slut insults for hostile women

Didn't I see you at the supermarket? You were trying to suck the cream out of the cupcakes.

I didn't want to say anything to you because you seem like such a sophisticated woman. I mean you look like a woman who has everything: syphilis, clap, gonorrhea.

What do you do for a living? Let me guess: automatic teller at a sperm bank?

Great, the girl with the glow-in-the-dark diaphragm is bothering me.

I hear you're up for the lead in the Greek play *Chlamydia*.

This is probably the longest you've ever talked to a man without sticking money in my crotch.

I know how a guy flirts with you *(act out the counting of money)* ten, twenty, thirty.

What's a one-liner to you Miss? "How much?"

You're so quiet, so demure, but you don't fool me, I bet back home you have a vibrator with cruise control.

Above your bed, do you have a sign that says, "How am I driving?"

You feel tense here, I'll make you feel more comfortable, I'll have the men form a line in front of you.

Does your IUD have a vanity plate?

You're hot, for you a condom is a doggie bag.

Slut insults for hostile women (cont.)...

Don't act so shy. You're sexually experienced. You probably have a diaphragm with an odometer on it.

You look pretty wild. What does a man need to go to bed with you? An insurance waiver?

I bet you've slept with so many men you have warning from the surgeon general on your hips.

What's a mid-term exam for you in college? Positive or negative?

You were probably a real tomboy as a girl, then you were Joe's boy, Bill's boy.

You'd look a lot more familiar if you put a black strip across your eyes and posed nude.

For you, breaking water is wetting the bed.

When you take off your shirt, is the tan line on your chest in the shape of a guy's hands?

I bet your computer dating service matched you up with the Green Bay Packers front line.

What's oral sex for you? Roughage?

Are you yawning or is that an offer?

Didn't I see you on a wanted poster at the VD clinic?

Say, what's a new sexual position for you? Getting the men to form two lines?

Slut insults for hostile women (cont.)...

You don't have an IUD, you have an IOU.

What's safe sex to you? A sponge headboard?

You're a real defensive woman. Does that mean you like tackles, guards, and linemen?

You didn't fail sex education class, I bet you got a D and C.

It's good they have day care for career women, otherwise you wouldn't be able to work the streets.

No doubt about it, if you were an engineering major in college, you pulled trains all the time.

Hey, did *Penthouse* nominate you as carrier of the month?

If you posed nude, you'd be a scratch-and-*itch* centerfold.

For you, pro-choice is deciding which professional athlete you want to sleep with.

Why are you leaving? Did the USS Missouri just pull in?

Do you get an employee discount at the Mustang Ranch?

With all these military bases closing, you must be losing a lot of business.

Do you have a scratching post in the shape of a man's back?

When you decide to see someone else, you go from a cordless to a strap-on.

Didn't you volunteer to be a stunt double in *The Accused?*

Slut insults for hostile women (cont.)...

Did you think a rape whistle came with a safety?

Say, what's the most beautiful hotel ceiling you've ever seen?

What's a long-lasting relationship for you, rechargeable batteries?

For you, being a traditional woman means not taking a personal check.

In high school, were you voted most likely to be impregnated by a gang member?

You got arrested for breaking into a circumcision shop and try to steal the tip jar.

Insult lines to accuse hostile women of frigidity, male-bashing bitterness, or biological moodiness.

For you, sucking the blood out of a man is a sexual position.

A lot of men would die to sleep with you, a lot of men have died because they slept with you.

Is it tough pursuing a family and raising a career?

Why should I blame you for your personality? Life is a bitch and you're just tying to validated it.

You look like *Miss Manners* with cramps.

I'll call you, if I need a thermos.

> **Insult lines to accuse hostile women of frigidity, male-bashing bitterness, or biological moodiness. (cont.)...**

What school did you attend? Was it 'Our Lady of the Iron Hymen'?

Do you often confuse assertiveness with castration?

Bitter because you lost the bathing suit competition in the Miss Unwed Mother Contest?

You have such a wonderful feeling about men, it's nice to meet Miss Penis Envy of 1993.

You remind me of a girl who loved me for my mind. I know she did. It was the only organ she liked to fuck.

Nice attitude, when you buy panty shields do you get a sword too?

What warmth you have, you must be *Chevrolet's* prototype for the new bitch on wheels.

I bet, even a gynecologist couldn't make you say "aaaaaah."

Let's face it, when it comes to sex, the only thing you ever blow is a fuse.

I'm not saying you're a tease, but judging from your charm, around the holiday season, do you just decorate your Christmas tree with only *blue* balls?

Come on, if I slept with you, I'd get hypothermia — and I'm not saying where.

Oh, I offended you. Well, pardon me, Madam Maxi pads.

Insult lines to accuse hostile women of frigidity, male-bashing bitterness, or biological moodiness (cont.)...

Are you cruising for men? I'm not asking for myself, I'm just trying to save the guys in the joint beer money.

There's definitely one thing a man won't experience with you: motion sickness.

Sometimes I think toxic shock was developed to weed out women like you.

Some women belong to NOW, you belong to Not Now.

I bet the first words your baby said were, "Not tonight, I have a headache."

It's chilly in here, did you uncross your legs?

I wouldn't want to have oral sex with you, I'm not into frozen dinners.

I'm not saying you're moody, you're just the first woman I met who has AM and PMS.

You know, Miss, I'm not saying you're a bimbo, but somewhere, out there — there's a butterfly with a tattoo of a you on its butt.

What charm you exude. You know, you're the reason some men's testicles don't descend.

What's do you do for fun? Sing with the other sirens and try to get ships to wreck on the rocks?

Let's make believe you and I are in bed, you lay beside me, and I'll try to chew my arm off from under the pillow.

Insult lines to accuse hostile women of frigidity, male-bashing bitterness, or biological moodiness (cont.)...

What's does your ID bracelet say? PMS?

It's nice to meet the winner of the Betty Crocker testicle bake-off.

You ought to write a cookbook to tell women the correct amount of salt to put in a wound.

Insult lines for a hostile woman's personality defects

I'm not saying you're an airhead, but I bet if you chew gum and try to blow a bubble, the gum just sits there and the back of your skull expands.

Why do I wish your nipples were volume nobs?

Before I met you, I never met a woman with a credibility gap between her legs.

I guess the silicon from your implants has gone to your brain.

You give me an idea what Jackie Kennedy would have been like if she took a bullet in Dallas.

The only way you'd get on your knees for a man is if he was going to say, "Ladies, let's mud wrestle."

Don't worry about the afterlife, I'm certain your soul will go to cat heaven.

Some guys carry a torch for you. I'd carry a flame thrower.

Insult lines for a hostile woman's personality defects (cont.)...

Something is going through your head now: air.

If Hitler ever comes back into power can I use you as a job reference?

You're the reason married men in their forties have a mid-wife crisis.

You know why they're called "trophy wives"? Because most men feel that after being married to a woman like you, they deserve an award.

You're not a Ms. You're a Ms—stake.

What does your gynecologist examine you for? Wind chill factor?

Jodi Foster would shoot you to impress Hinckley.

Insult and Live! by Fred Reiss

Blowing Out Superior Snotheads

Like all losers, Brainiacs love to loudly voice their opinions.

Purpose of this section: Shows you how to identify and verbally snub the snobs who in the form of pseudo-intellectual Brainiacs, pretentious Hip Brainiacs, Right-To-Your Lifers, Upper Crustie Wannabees, Powers That Be-Idiots, and Big Money Dwidheads.

The snobs who assume they are intellectually and culturally superior to you: Brainiacs and Hip Brainiacs.

Brainiac: 1.) A smug person who gives the annoying impression they are more intelligent than you. 2.) A dumb person who hides behind intellectual phrases and politically correct views to conceal their stupidity. 3.) Emotional cripples who are incredibly articulate about their psychological limitations but never have a lame excuse to break their behavior pattern. For example, people who never get over their "first love." (Oddly, they see this limitation as a unique quality.) 4.) Anyone who criticizes or derides art or any issue, but never creates anything better or has a political solution. 5.) A failed artist who becomes a critic, booking agent, recording artist promoter, or clubowner. 6.) Elitists who categorize others but deny they themselves can be categorized as Brainiacs.

The Brainiac profile

Brainiacs fear any similar traits they might share with someone else lessens their uniqueness, so, to maintain a superior view of their existence, these thwarted aristocrats intellectually segregate themselves from their natural desires or the moral consequences of their own actions. But the simple truth is pseudo-intellectual Brainiacs are self-conscious jerks who see themselves on a higher level than the "masses." If these Brainiacs are caught in any act that resembles the behavior of common-denominator drones, these sophisticates concoct a rationalization to snobbishly show they're different than the general populace. *

What follows is a listing of several categories to help you spot Brainiacs and their annoying allegedly cerebral qualities...

*****World Of Fred Note:** Typical example: A stockbroker whiz who thinks he's different because he refuses to wear a tie, and dresses in jeans.

Brainiac tip offs

Constantly refers to themselves in third person.

Isn't a fan of any sports team; in fact, Brainiacs allegedly don't care who wins or loses, they just "enjoy the game itself."

Is in their forties, and still quotes observations made by their college professor.

Glib but never funny.

Describes themselves as a "purist."

Says they are against everything but never commit to one particular passion or principle, they defend this moral limitation by declaring their purpose is to "raise questions."

Boasts about their anagram abilities.

Likes the idea of doing things but never acts on it. (For example, "The *idea* of surfing intrigues me...")

Claims they're not a "joiner."

Is known for their wit but not their humor.*

Speaks one dead language well.

Picks an obscure field and allegedly learns everything about it so they can hold forth on the topic without the fear of anyone correcting an inaccuracy.

Is only interested in global or national politics, but is ignorant of local issues that directly affect their lives.

---

*World Of Fred Note: Wit only proves you can take the dullest knife and sharpen it. But humor shows compassion and true-life experience.

Brainiac Tip offs (cont.)...

Feels guilty for being detached from their emotions so they either date flakes or hang out with ungrateful people.

If you refute a Brainiac's argument with a valid point based on experience, they dismiss it by asking, "What's your source?"

Marries someone they think is dumber than them.

Is unwilling to make the material sacrifices to develop artistic talents. Their hobby is what they really wanted to do with their life. They assume these forms...
    a.) Frustrated directors/actors who have an extensive video cassettes or laser disc library.
    b.) Thwarted musicians who have...
        1.) an incredible sound system.
        2.) an extensive collection of obscure CDs or records (These "completists" have twelve different pressings of the same album for "historical" value.).
        3.) expensive or rare musical instruments they can't play well.
    c.) Failed authors with a large first-edition book collection.

If liberal, baits conservatives ("you hate government intervention with business but want tariffs and tax breaks.") if conservative, baits liberals ("you crusade for civil rights but live in an all-white neighborhood.").*

Never shares their emotions because the Brainiac vainly feels they're too complex ("Nobody knows the real me.").

Is brutally cynical but is also irrationally sentimental.

---

*World Of Fred Note: This particular political Brainiac is under the delusion that scoring points against their polemical foe is a way to convert people to their views; however, all it does is point out how both these types are hypocrites.

Pompous Brainiac culture views

Defends their ignorance of contemporary literature and music by saying, "I just stick to the classics."

Sees anyone who lives outside "The City" as culturally deprived, even though city-dwelling Brainiacs rarely visits the museum or attends the "theatre."

Avoids a "like" or "dislike" comment that might expose their ignorance about a film, piece of music, political idea, or painting. Instead, Brainiacs only say, "It's *interesting.*"

Uses two fingers of each hand to form quotes around words they want to stress in a conversation.

Dismisses any cutting edge art's significance by saying, "It's all shock value."

Supports their pigheadedness through the use of quoting famous people's similar views on the subject. ("Why won't I go to the party? Well as Samuel Johnson once said.....")

Puritanically believes all artists were at their best before they became a success. (The other option is dismissing a successful artist as insignificant because "they've become a "parody' or "caricature" of themselves.)

Says unfamiliar, archaic, and unnecessary vocabulary words.*

*****World Of Fred Note:** Brainiacs do this because they're out to lunch when it comes to passionately experiencing life through participation not observation. These mental patricians are clueless to new colloquialisms or slang (until they are discussed in a respected "Language" column). In an effort to conceal their ignorance to the world around them, Brainiacs retreat into their erudition to make you feel inferior.

Brainiac's look-down-at-the-world outlook

Thinks the holiday season is "too commercial."

Believes "no one reads anymore."

Acts like a world-weary traveller.

Maintains a new technology dehumanizes the thing it replaces. (For example, a Brainiac says, "CDs sanitize the old music recorded on albums.")

Disparagingly accuses anyone who likes mainstream art as being "middle class."*

Any time they are at a public event where the crowd is going nuts, the Brainiac doesn't become involved in the happening, instead they simply observe the people with an air of disbelief.

---

*World Of Fred Note: If a popular motion picture star's body of work is honored for its artistic merits, the Brainiac who pooh poohed the actor's commercialism becomes a convert and suddenly says they've learn to respect the artist. They say something like, "I'm *reassessing* Clint Eastwood's films."

Brainiac's look-down-at-the-world outlook (cont.)...

Admires a foreign country's culture more than their own and takes on the mannerism, i.e., Anglophiles, Francophiles. etc.

Takes the opposing view of anything that is popular.

Says everyone else...
- is unsophisticated for liking pop music, but...when the Brainiac listen to the same pop tunes they say, "It's music you love to hate."
- attends bad movies because they are stupid and lack taste, but...when a Brainiac goes to these films it's because the movies are "campy" or "so bad they're funny."
- makes spelling mistakes, but...Brainiacs make typos.
- pointlessly competes against others, but...the Brainiac "progresses at their own level."*
- uses drugs to "escape their lives," but...when the Brainiac takes drugs it's for "mind expansion."
- who buys a velvet painting of Elvis is a tacky idiot, but...when a Brainiac gets the same picture they rationalize it by saying the picture is "cool" or has a "hip tackiness."
- who laughs at fart jokes is a low brow into scatological humor, but...Brainiacs who laugh at farts are amused by "Rabelaisian" wit.

Is a mental and social retard about any subject outside their specialized area, but is condescending to others.

Mistakenly thinks their bratty child is precocious or "gifted."**

World Of Fred Note: Of course, this doesn't explain why most Brainiacs hate losing at *Trivial Pursuit* and chess, get aggravated when beaten on a *Jeopardy* answer, or irritated if someone figures out a crossword puzzle before them.

**Another World Of Fred Note:* Their child isn't any different than anyone else's progeny. The only difference? The Brainiac's child is around adults more, so, the youth speaks about different things to get their childish desires, such as money to buy toys. (Duh.)

Annoying synaptic Brainiac behavior

If someone points out a flaw in a Brainiac's specialized field of knowledge, the Brainiac derisively snorts, "Get a life."

Priggishly compares everything around them to the major city they're from; for example, "It's closed? Why, in New York you can get anything 24 hours a day."

Ends their description of something with a foreign phrase.

During a mystery or suspense movie, the Brainiac tries to show off their intelligence by loudly anticipating the...
- solution to the murder.
- next plot twist.
- surprise ending.

Baits people into arguments to watch them get angry or worked up (they call this "pushing buttons.").

Doesn't want anyone to see how predictable a Brainiac is, so, the Brainiac acts "spontaneous." For example, for no apparent reason, out-of-shape Brainiacs will bungy jump, parasail, fire walk, or sky dive.

Instead of simply saying take a "left" or a "right," the Brainiac says, "Go East at the intersection, then when you reach the light go North." (Or, gives a distance in kilometers not miles.)

Snootily says, "I don't watch television." or "I only watch a few shows and the news." (The implication is: you're a moron because you watched a popular show.)

Patronizingly corrects people's grammar or word choice.

Makes analogies using obscure references to Greek and Roman myths, religious figures, or history.

Thinks flirting is teasing people about their flaws.

Annoying synaptic Brainiac behavior (cont.)...

Uses their psychological knowledge for personal gain by manipulating people.

Ignores an "unaccredited" person's valid point of view.

When Brainiacs find out you haven't read a certain book, they say in a smug but aghast tone, "I can't believe you haven't read *(Fill in title)*! "

What Brainiacs do in the 'real world.'

19th-hole country club know-it-all offspring who inherited their parent's business and political point of view.

Public Board of Education members and teachers who want to reform the system but send their own children to private schools.

Opinionated tour guides of a famous person's estate, who punctuate their lecture with value judgments on the person's life, or say how the historical figure would "feel about today's world."

Snitty reference clerks who roll their eyes at your allegedly ignorant question but don't know the answer to it either.

Morning disc jockeys who hate their audience, disassociate themselves from coworkers, and believe "everyone is a moron" (which of course is why the DJ does so many fart and dick jokes).

Temperamental actors or actresses who perform in touring companies at community and dinner theaters.*

Philanthropists who live off their stock options (This type once tried to run a business but failed.).

---

*World Of Fred Note: The ones in "You're a Good Man Charlie Brown" are the most bitter in the group.

What Brainiacs do in the 'real world.' (cont.)...

Dissenting gadflies who attend town meetings, speak way too long on an issue, and lose whatever point they made by rambling, swearing, or making personal attacks on a board official.

Former government regulators who start-up their own consulting firms and find loopholes in laws they passed for the violators they once regulated.

Child prodigies who become sullen and undistinguished adults.

Substitute teachers who prove their superiority by brutally singling out adolescent students and ridicule their grammar usage or perceptions, such as a 12-year old's views on "Moby Dick."

Scholars only published by university presses--their books have more footnotes to the page than text--and who parlay their erudition into affairs with insecure graduate students.

Bitter I-use-to-be-a-reporter types who are lobbyists, public relation flacks, campaign strategists, advertising execs, or research assistants for alleged social and political commentators.

Corporate executives who "wanted to teach."

Millionaire professional athletes who have contempt for two-faced fans who cheer them for an accomplishment and within seconds boo the same athlete for a mistake.*

High-ranking military officials who botch up a policy or war maneuver but protect each other, blame an innocent soldiers, and drum them out to protect the "image of the corps."

*****World Of Fred Note:** It's not two-faced to boo and cheer the same person, unfortunately, it's the way of the world. Come on, anyone who has a boss knows they can be praised in the morning and yelled at in the afternoon for a screw-up. The world could be supportive, but if it was, you wouldn't be reading an insult book to deal with it.

What Brainiacs do in the 'real world.' (cont.)...

Peace Corps workers who return from undeveloped countries, get a well-paying job, and try to make you feel guilty for not questioning your high standard of living.*

Moral-reforming editorialists who say the "immorality" of a politician's life makes them unfit to hold office, but these scribbling sumptuaries don't believe their own immoral behavior jeopardizes their right to shape public opinion by judging the credibility of others.**

Humanity-award winning academics who are political/business interest think-tank pimps and cleverly misinterpret issues to rally public opinion in support of their employer's private agenda.

Non-profit organization fundraising executives who have six-figure salaries, only give ten percent of donations to the cause, but justify their graft because their job makes the world a better place.

Lionized poets/writers-in-residence who live on college campuses and endowment grants their whole careers, pen lifeless prose with implausible characters, and judge the false values in today's world.

Incompetent teachers with tenure.

Political appointees who have never been elected to any office but who initiate disastrous policies they're convinced the public needs.

---

*__World Of Fred Note:__ We're not entitled to enjoy a high standard of living. But, *they* are! Why? Because these Brainiacs supposedly attempted to "make a difference" by installing toilet facilities in Guam. Fine. But these missionaries never planned to remain in these deprived countries. All they did was purge their guilt (or passed a tapeworm they picked up).

**__Another World Of Fred Note:__ These same editors also insist any reporter's factual errors run in the corrections box to maintain the "newspaper's credibility," but if the factual error was the result of an editing mistake, they simply tell the reporter to write another story.

"Buzzwords, phrases, and sentences that you overhear Brainiacs loudly use in conversations"

- "I can't believe people *still* think like that."
- "...coming to terms with..."
- "...that presupposes that..."
- *(Justifies a bad movie that comments on politics or racism by saying.)* "It has a *message* that must be heard."
- "It's a sea change of public opinion."
- "Imagine if the roles were reversed."
- "I don't know how people can do things like that—it's *beyond* me."
- "It depends on which level of reality..."
- "Let me give you my *take* on that."
- "There is no in between with <u>*(Insert name of artist.)*</u> you either love or hate them.
- "Society conditions us to..."
- "...mutually exclusive..."
- "The basic concept behind..."
- "Morality is subjective..."
- "It takes a person with a certain *mentality* to do that."

Brainiac phrases and buzzwords (cont.)...

- "It's the system."
- "...brings in a certain element...."
- "...relate to..."
- "It depends on how you define *(Insert a word)*."
- "There are two types of people in this world..."
- "I enjoy *(Insert activity.)*, to get in touch with my body."
- "I'm not arguing, I'm being Devil's advocate."
- "I've never read him but I'm familiar with his work."
- "I see what they were *trying* to do with the film but I don't think the idea held up."
- "You don't want to do that, it'll be another Vietnam."
- "I've come full circle."
- "I object to the context that word was used."
- "...diametrically opposed..."
- *(Said by someone over thirty.)* "I haven't decided what I want to be when I grow up."
- "I disagreed with you completely, but I respect your position."
- "They looked like they were out of a Fellini movie..."
- "I'm not saying I don't want it in my back yard, I don't think it should be in anyone's back yard."*
- "It's a macrocosm of society."
- "Who's to define what normal?"
- "It's like *1984*."

In print, Brainiacs favor words like: hitherto, wherewithal, Dionysian, Zeitgeist, mise en scéne, Pyrrhic victory, Grand Guignol, fin de siècle, roman a clef, deus ex machina, Catch-22, phoenix from the ashes, archtypical, Dickensian, doppelgänger, epiphany, morning star, vouchsafe, strum and drang, hubris, crossing the Rubicon, Orwellian, Chesire-cat grin, dénouement, Roshomon, empirical, and using "former"-and-the-"later" prose combo.

---

*World Of Fred Note: Said by people who want to change the world as long as it doesn't affect their neighborhood, but alleviate their guilt or deny their hypocrisy by saying they "recognize the need" for low-income housing, nuclear power, a landfill, soup kitchen, or a roller rink.

**The worst type of Brainiac:
The cynical, wise-cracking reporter**

These street-wise reporters see themselves as above an event because these equal timers aren't part of one. Many are under the illusion their coveted access to the powerful and talented makes these correspondents equal in status and influence to the people they cover. They thrive in one-newspaper towns where these journalists are dedicated to protecting their source: the advertisers. These public-right-to-knowers pride themselves on their detached wit, short-hand cryptic analysis of a politician's motives, and their cheesy ability to get pictures of a deceased person from a grieving family. And what's worse, this reporter is impervious to criticism.* These scribbling losers are firmly convinced that if people dislike their reporting, it must mean they are doing their job well! Besides, these journalists have the last word, and if anyone is too critically vocal, they just don't quote those critics in their articles.

This delusionary breed of Brainiac firmly knows everything that's wrong with society and art. They deride the public, claiming their readership lacks the ability to interpret contemporary events without a journalist to guide them. Yet, in spite of all their alleged reportorial brilliance, these members of the press are lazy, drink too much, and fear working a straight eight-hour day. Most improve their salary by doctoring their gas-mileage/voucher slips. That's why these allegedly ethical scribes eagerly gobble up any freebies by taking press travel junkets, or writing reviews for free meals and entertainment. At press events, these underpaid Brainiacs are easy to spot. They're the ones drinking the most free booze and gorging on the chow. After they've enjoyed their host's hospitality, these stand-by-the-story reporters write nasty articles about the event, or ask rude questions. No one can buy these reporters, but it's acceptable to *feed* them.

Why insults work so well against Brainiacs

Brainiacs hate to be teased about their self-conscious behavior. They never laugh at themselves, but show their superiority by eagerly laughing at another's shortcomings. True, these supercilious frontal-lobe bullies are bemused at the "idea" of themselves, or at the "idea" of their presence in a situation. But, Brainiacs are the ones who have to perceive these things about themselves.

---

*World Of Fred Note: These reporter's are so proud of their ability to get both sides of an issue. They're unbiased. Anyone who has any point of view is suspect. In fact, if you believe you're right, they water down your point so it's lost. So, if someone says the earth is round, or orbits the sun, does the press assumes these are biased points and need an opposite point of view. Fred says, maybe sometimes a person doesn't just have a point of view, they're just right.

Insult technique: Brainiacs feel they are above everyone. When you point out their flawed logic, you're knocking the Brainiac from their disdainful balcony seat and down to the general admission level of everyone else, which the Brainiac considers a demotion. Like all losers, when faced with the reality of their behavior, and forced to acknowledge it, they decide to deny the truth by getting angry at you.

For example...

Situation:
Slamming A Judgmental Brainiac

Brainiac
You know me, I never over indulge like others. We went to The Four Seasons. Me, at that overpriced restaurant, a place I said I'd never be caught dead in! Anyway, the dinner was so decadent! The whole tab was on my friend's expense account. We pigged out on caviar, French entrees, champagne. We finished off the meal with a $150 glass of port. It's so ironic for a person like me to be doing these things, I mean can you imagine me *indulging* myself like that?

You With The Power Of *Insult And Live!*
How come it was the "dinner" that was decadent? Weren't you the one being decadent? Doesn't that go against all the things you stand for?

Brainiac
(Bristles)
Hey, at least I have a sense of humor about myself! At least, I was willing to admit it.

You With The Power Of *Insult And Live!*
Obviously, your brain has a dimmer switch.

Post-insult Outcome: You won! Cerebrally head-butting these frontal lobials immediately puts you on a superior footing above the Brainiac because you've proven their complex intellect is easily understood--and dismissed. So, the Brainiac must resentfully concede they're flawed, just like everyone else.

Hip Brainiacs are cultural elitists who look down on any form of "conventional" behavior. They have angst-ridden eyes. Most dress like impoverished immigrants caught in a dumpster explosion. The females have hairy armpits and legs, favor peasant dresses with black leotards; and, if they're attractive they try to look as ugly as possible. Hip Brainiacs are always boycotting some type of product. Most own a decal-covered Volkswagen car/bus, or some classic car that is falling apart, which they don't know how to fix. Hip losers lack a developed and mature ego shaped by life experiences so they favor art that deals with either orgasms, existential whining, or death.

Hip Brainiacs

Most Hip Brainiacs are in their twenties. This pimpled intelligentsia favors torn apparel (black, paisley, or tie-dye), as well as jeans, clown-like stretch pants, or baggy white painter's pants. Most wear ill-fitting hats, berets, or odd pieces of clothing, such as substituting cut-off pants legs, bandanas, or tee shirts for headgear. They shuffle in black military boots, sandals, or go about barefoot in ridiculous places to show they're natural and untamed. These sarcastic judgmentals are pale, glum, overeducated, unskilled, and out of shape. Their hair is unkempt and frayed with split ends. They choose knapsacks over luggage. Smoke clove cigarettes. Some constantly carry a musical instrument. This sect sloppily eats with their hands in restaurants. Have a form of incense burning near them. Form friendships based on shared dislikes. They repugnantly stare at the newspaper headlines in vending machines. These hipsters mind meld at coffee bistros, environmental workshops, dive bars, candlelight vigils, modern-dance classes, gallery openings (mainly abstract art), communes, die-ins, poetry readings, course registration, petition signings to protect the rights of annoying people, art-film theaters, any event requiring a student-activity card, blues festivals, crafts fairs, youth hostels, food co-ops, adult-education classes, recycling centers, bookstore cafes, pledge breaks for listener-supported stations, any disharmonious jam sessions, and reading as well as commenting upon the news in the Sunday paper at restaurant brunches.

After Hip Brainiacs graduate, most live in the town supported by college student revenues. They proudly chose an "alternative" lifestyle, which entails holding a part-time job and using their spare time to ski, surf, sail, etc. They look down on daily-bread pursuers. These hitchhiking road scholars pride themselves as being "different" for the way they dress or think compared to village folk. They don't want to "play the game" by dressing up, wearing uncomfortable shoes, working a solid 40-hour week, not speaking their mind, and laughing at the boss' jokes. Yet, these same nonconformists feel society's laws should be changed so Hip Brainiacs can receive all the mainstream's social and financial benefits without earning them through any personal sacrifice.

Hip Brainiacs are usually struggling musicians who work as CD-record store clerk and openly look down on "mainstream" music requests made by polite customers.

What Hip Brainiac do in the "real world"

Legal assistants who resent getting paid one-fourth of what the attorney charges to research a case.

Form improvisational groups that use references instead of punchlines and get angry if the audience doesn't "get it."

Surly arts and crafts dealers at handicrafts fairs.

Every other freelance writer/photographer/graphic artist.

Community college disc jockeys who have contempt for all music played by established labels.

In resort towns, Hip Brainiacs are...
- sidewalk artists (jugglers, street musicians, caricaturists, clowns, political theater troupes, mimes, paint tattoos or masks on children, and photographers who take pictures of you with tropical birds or beside one-dimensional cardboard cut-outs.)
- "crew" on tour boats.
- run a "kiosk."
- pedal taxi bicycles.
- edit restaurant and tour guide newspapers.

Activists in their thirties who only ride a bike, and carry a clipboard which contains political petitions to sign.*

Grant-subsidized performance artists.

Arrogant animal shelter employees who won't let you adopt an animal you originally brought into the shelter because they feel you wouldn't "properly" care for it.

---

*World Of Fred Note: The worst of this type prides themselves by pointing out that people who drive vehicles are "contributing to the death of the planet." Or, in the middle of conversation to promote their cause note your taxes go to fund death squads that kill nuns and peasants in foreign countries.

Hip Brainiacs hold service-oriented jobs but feel compelled to make the people they serve aware that the hipster is more intelligent than their customers.* Nearly, all their job areas have a tip jar nearby.

What Hip Brainiacs do in the "real world" (cont.)...

Comedy writers who glare at comics who get a huge laugh and snarl to anyone that will listen, "I wrote that!"**

---

*World of Fred Note: These avant-garde lobers spurn career-oriented jobs or trade-oriented college degrees. They make "just enough money to get by." Interestingly, when a Brainiac is doing one of these menial jobs and meets an artist who is financially and professionally successful, the Brainiac becomes defensive and says, "This isn't what I really do, this is something I just do part-time."

**Another World Of Fred Note: These writers or screenwriters are the most bitter of the bitter. They are furious their talents are used to make someone else popular. They brutally criticize everyone. They never face the real truth. They wasted their talent on someone else. Hey, when you're polishing someone else's star you can never be a marshal in your own town.

What Hip Brainiacs do in the "real world" (cont.)...

Left-wing journalists at local weeklies who are concerned about the common person's plight but are cultural elitists.*

Takes no-brainer jobs as...
- limo or taxi drivers
- sports or exercise instructors
- pizza delivery people
- survey takers
- office temps
- bank tellers
- waiters
- hotel night clerks
- health food store employees
- bike messengers/ or bike repair
- postal carriers
- orderlies
- clerks at comic book shops, used bookstores, video outlets, CD-record stores, or vintage clothing joints.
- photocopier employees
- handing out flyers or putting them under car windshield wipers
- theater ushers
- security guards (They like this job because they can read at work.)
- pool cleaning
- painting merchant windows with holiday scenes for special sales
- clerics who describe themselves as "administrative assistant"
- car-rental representatives

---

*World Of Fred Note: These conceited muckrakers churn out attitudinal-prose laden articles about workers, minorities, gays, or pieces criticizing the rich, businessmen, and conservatives. Yet, if you closely examine the paper, you'll notice most of the alleged "people's" weekly deals with "cool" happenings at local clubs, positive reviews of art films, profiles of angry musicians or impoverished artists "neglected by the establishment," as well as negative reviews of mainstream movies. The undertone is the pedestrian nature of the great majority doesn't appreciate refined aesthetics of an orgasmic, plotless, symbolic film.

Hip Brainiac culture-vulture habits

Reads books about alienation to meet other people.

Favors self-destructive artists of unfulfilled promise who die young.

Listens to "modern" music that lacks a beat or harmony; or has an upbeat melody with depressing or angry lyrics (which are usually unintelligible, slurred, and rhymed with a lot of words ending in "tion."

Laughs at porno films to conceal they are secretly aroused by a particular sex act.

If they disagree with an author, the Hip Brainiac writes sarcastic comments in the book's margins like "not true," "no way," or lists contrary facts.

Constantly brings up an obscure film, book, or work of art that has been "neglected" by everyone else but them.

Thinks you're not cool if you can't instinctively execute a pointlessly intricate handshake.

Distrusts pedantic critics, but is equally pompous about their knowledge of comic books, cartoons, slasher films, etc.

After an "art" film is over, the Hip Brainiac sits in their chair, thoughtfully stares at the screen, and allegedly mulls over the film's meaning (The truth: they didn't understand it.).

Hip Brainiac's detached social perspective

Never reads business news; in fact, a Hip Brainiac maintains knowledge of economics contaminates their spiritual growth.

Believes society "dehumanizes" people.

Hip Brainiac's detached social perspective (cont.)...

Scornfully says, "Anyone can make money." (Giving the impression they've chosen to be broke.)

Doesn't view humans as the next evolutionary step on the planet.

Bigotedly hyphenates people into cultural stereotypes; such as, "He's a Joe-Commuter-drinks-too-much-cheats-on-his-wife-tries-to-buy-kids-affection guy" (Variation: simplifying reality through hyphenation, such as saying the country is a "modern-corporate-industrial-military complex.")

Hip Brainiac political views

Claims they are "apolitical."

Never sees themselves as citizens of a country; instead, they are "strangers in a strange land."

Considers voting "choosing between the lesser of two evils."*

Believes everything is a conspiracy, from assassinations to gas prices to interest rates, as well as the origins of all wars.

Decrees there is no difference between a Republican or a Democrat, adding, "It doesn't matter who runs the country."

Thinks devoting any time to understanding politics will undermine their aesthetic appreciation of the arts.

Says most politicians are "out of touch with the real issues."

*****World Of Fred Note:** If the Hip Brainiac does vote, they always "make a statement" by casting their ballot for some ridiculous Third Party candidate who has no chance of winning.

Hip Brainiac personal habits and qualities

Keeps a personal journal/ sketchbook but lets everyone see it.

Loves to analyze your motivations. For example: "He dislikes you because there is something in you that he resents in himself."

Views responsibility as a "trap."

Thinks astrological signs define a personality.

Monopolizes tables in restaurants for hours by nibbling table munchies, sharing the cheapest food, or sipping coffee.

Is fascinated by the "dark underbelly" of society: disenfranchised individuals, self-exiles, and low lifes (Brainiacs also have a tendency speak ghetto slang and do inner-city dance gestures.).

Sees "being spacey" as their charming attribute.

Dances to music in free form movements. (They look like they're being dragged by an open parachute.)

Has an answer for everything.

Views the ego as a sign of insecurity and weakness, but feels self-effacing behavior represents courage.

Dwells on their untapped potential; for example, "I want to be a brain surgeon, but I want to spend the winter skiing."

Instead of developing a mature point of view, Hip Brainiacs enjoy shocking people with crude observations or sick humor.

In their room they have collages or mobiles.

Worst Hip Brainiac: The perpetual student

Perpetual students never know enough about anything to pursue a specific interest. They misinterpret reality because they only see everything around them in relation to their incomplete thesis. These self-containers view life as a class to audit forever. They're always "growing" as a person, but never develop any conviction to be one. They over analyze to the point of paralysis. They constantly switch majors and never attain a degree in any field.

These perpetuals fear the real world and desperately cling to the academic community. They aggressively hustle for education grants to escape reality. Most perpetual students grow well beyond typical college age and still say words like "off-campus living," "faculty member," "syllabus," "essay," and "tuition committee."

*World of Fred Note: Perpetual students are irritating political correcters who are against war, sexism, poverty, etc.--you know everything in the world everyone else is supposedly against. They're big on obvious bumper stickers, such as "Visualize peace," "You can't hug a child with nuclear arms," "Practice random kindness and senseless acts of beauty," and "Love your mother." (Meaning Earth.). Oooooooooh! Deep.

How to insult a Hip Brainiac

Hip Brainiacs are unable to point to any personal achievement that proves their socially or intellectually superior to anyone, so, they shut out reality and develop a psychological world where they convince themselves they are this pure spirit who is above everyone else, Like all losers, they never do anything for themselves. They always try to get other people to do it for them. In fact, they use their martyr-like disappointment in other people as the main excuse for never developing into a unique member of society.

These hipsters resent their social and economic station in life isn't as high as their opinion of themselves. Whatever the Hip Brainiac says, never respond to it. Just reflect it back on their reality. You need to do the patented World Of Fred one-two frontal lobotomy. First shot: insult them with a cerebral putdown. They're dazed, clinging to the ropes of their ego for support. Then, while they're partially stunned, hit them with your second punch: ridicule them for their socio-economic status on earth.

For example...

Situation:
Insulting a Hip Brainiac

*(The last train heading from The City to the suburbs. A **Hip Brainiac** is loudly talking to **Another Hip Brainiac**. They are sitting in a crowded train and disdainfully staring at the haggard commuters. The Hip Bainiacs are in their early twenties, slightly drunk, dressed in a tie-dyed shirts and ratty clothes. They are returning from a concert. An exhausted **Commuter With The Power To Insult And Live!** is sitting between the two. He is in a rumpled suit with his tie pulled down, drinking a beer.)*

Hip Brainiac
(To other Brainiac.)
Man, working 40 hours a week. Wearing a suit. Can you imagine taking this train *every* day?

Other Brainiac
But that's the trap of the American dream, everyone works hard with the belief that they'll earn enough to be able to buy back all the life they lost trying to achieve the dream. *(Look at all the commuters.)* How do they do it?

Commuter With The Power To *Insult And Live!*
(The first verbal punch.) I bet, if furballs were human they'd cough you up. *(Pauses. Then delivers the second verbal punch.)* You have an interesting theories, do you learn things like that by still living at home with your parents?

Post-insult Outcome: You win! The Hip Brainiacs were trying to get a reaction from you to validate their shallow and stereotypical view of your existence. Once again, by insulting the loser, you do a reversal. You didn't evaluate them by how these aloof frontal lobials view their state of existence. You slammed them by comparing their philosophy of life with how the Hip Brainiac makes a living in the "real world."

Snobs who feel morally superior to you:
Right-To-Your-Lifers

Right-To-Your-Lifers: 1.) A sanctimonious person who imposes their theory upon the world, but never allows the world into their theory. **2.)** Reformers who want to change the world but don't have the patience or personal time with the people in it. **3.)** Crusaders who believe they are trying to make the world a better place, which entitles them to engage in any immoral deed to get their message out. (After all, they've done so much for others, why should they be treated like them?) **4.)** An intellect who only listens to a point of view if it reinforces their own prejudices. **5.)** Anyone who turns an "issue" into a cause. **6.)** Spokesmen who fanatically believe they are the "voice" of a mysteriously inarticulate group.

Right-To-Your-Lifers are the most dangerous losers in this book. These glazed-eyed possessed pious paracletes believe they are always *morally* right. Now, whereas nearly all the losers in the World of Fred are selfish and don't care about other people, the Right-To-Your Lifer isn't content to just live their life according to their private code, these self-appointed mullahs want to impose their morality upon others. Instead of confronting the truth of their own lives, these rabid adherents try to exorcise their private demons in other people. Basically, Right-To-Your-Lifers get their jollies by suppressing you and *not* expressing themselves.

Arguing with these Right-To-Your-Lifers is a no-win situation. Try it. The topic can be anything, such as prayer in schools, abortion, gun-control, legalization of drugs, health-care, affirmative action, the designated hitter in baseball, gay rights, whether the Vietnam war was winnable, constitutional law, violence in children's programming on TV, low-income housing, the gold standard, censorship of books in the public library, pornography, equal rights, anything! Every discussion with these possessed judgmenicals never becomes an exchange of ideas.* These holier-in-the-head-than thous feel you're either for or against them.

For example...

Situation:
Why You Can't Win With A Right-To-Your Lifer Who Is Against Drunk Driving

Right-To-Your-Lifer Anti Drunk Driving Advocate
(Preaching to you.)
We need sobriety checkpoints set up along roads. That way the police can catch these drunk drivers who are responsible for *(Insert statistics here.)* highway deaths.

Neutral You
It's wrong to drink and drive. But, a person who just had two beers shouldn't have his life ruined. They're not a criminal!

Right-To-Your-Lifer Anti Drunk Driving Advocate
(Severely glares.)
Well, it's obvious which side you're on! *(Scornfully.)* I know what you *really* mean. You haven't been listening to a word I said.

*****World Of Fred Note:** One of the most irritating Right-To-Lifers is the reformed alcoholic/drug abuser who resolved the denial factor of their substance problem, but hasn't confronted the defective personality substance within themselves that is the source of their denial problem. So, instead of becoming a better person, these sober idiots replace their addiction with another one: a business career, religious beliefs, a sport, preaching against substance abuse, etc. Whatever their choice, they ruthlessly pursue it and crush anyone in their way.

**Bloviating health-food freaks:
Worst type of Right-To-Your Lifers***

Preachy Right-To-Your Lifer health-food freaks think nothing of chastising your poor eating habits by saying...
- "How you can eat that stuff?"
- *(If you're eating veal.)* "Do you know what they do to those animals?"
- "Don't you realize what caffeine does to you?"
- *(Points at your food.)* "That stuff will *kill* you!"

---

*World Of Fred Note: Like nearly every fanatical person, health-food freaks are hypocrites of their own philosophy. These brown-rice heads have unhealthy sweet tooth for rich desserts. Sure, they'll refuse any alleged carcinogenic foods with MSG, a high fat content, meat by-products, salt, or evil cholesterol. But, their knowledge of evil additives doesn't prevent these soy-burger brains from trying any pesticide-free hallucinogenic/addictive drug, or, after drinking tequila, eating the worm at the bottom of the bottle. Oddly, most healthies are pale, thin, sleepy, and sick all the time.

The best way to insult a Right-To-Your Lifer

Right-To-Your-Lifers have one major weakness: they can only exist in the presence of their enemy. An anti must get into a conflict with a pro.

The only way an anti meets a pro is at demonstration. The two passionately claim they want to "make other people aware of the issues." But, these ideologues never listen to the other side's views. They love yelling at each other. Really, have you ever seen any protester suddenly stop shouting, listen to their opposition, and respond, "You know, you got a point there," and change sides? No. Does the Right-To-Your-Lifer leave the demonstration because they've decided to moderate their position? No. Either they're both screaming at each other, or, one is screaming, while the other shakes their head in disbelief and stares through saintly eyes coated with glazed pity at their spiritually misguided foe, who "can't see the truth," or has "lost" their way.

Don't deal with Right-To-Lifer's ideas on an intellectual level. Never address their views. Remember, when in doubt, get personal. Expose them for the lost cause they really are!

For example...

Situation:
The Successful Way To Insult Right-To-Your Lifers

Right-To-Your Lifer Anti-Abortion Advocate
Abortion is murder. Life begins at conception.

You With The Power Of *Insult And Live!*
I bet your mother had an easy delivery with you because she ate a lot of bran.

Post-insult Outcome: You won! How? You didn't deal with their ideology. You forced the Right-To-Your Lifer to confront their personal limitations. The battle-damage assessment simply is: you reduce them from significance to a joke. Hey, if you can't change their mind, at least piss them off!

Snobs who see themselves as socially superior to everyone: Upper Crustie Wannabees, Powers That Be--Idiots, and Big Money Dwidheads

There definitely is an alleged superior class that snobbishly maintains their top-shelf life has a higher assessed market value than your low-end existence. This privileged and exclusive club of affluent effluenzas is comprised of tony Upper Crustie Wannabees and Big Money Dwidheads. This stuck-up select positions themselves apart from underclassers to show they're *socially* above everyone--especially, "the help."

Upper Crustie Wannabees: 1.) chi-chi social climbing yuppie scum. 2.) A patrician type who creates a fake background and puts a false front to the world because they want to give the impression to others that they're rich. 3.) Shallow twits who talks about their possessions more than their life. 4.) Anyone who has the money but lacks the influence of social position. 5.) A frustrated status seeker never accepted by the A-list social registry so they create their own social world.

Upper Crustie Wannabee tip-offs

Hates being called a "yuppie."

Dismisses anyone who dresses in a functional way as having "no class." (**Variation:** expensively overdresses for functional events, such as weather a dress-leather outfit on a cave tour, heels and an evening gown on a sailing excursion, etc.)

Gets involved with black-tie fundraisers to meet celebrities.

Has a doorbell or chimes that play a tune.

In any dispute about business, the Crustie takes management's side over labor ("After all, it's *their* investment.")

Puts more than two college decals on their car's rear window (which is the Wannabee's way to show they can afford to pay the high tuition at these schools).

Has a poorly done oil paintings of the family; or, a bust of themselves (which are prominently displayed in the house).

Buys expensive products to impress others.

Leaves "The City" to raise a family, overruns a small but quaint community (which is within commuting distance), then these upwardly-mobiling interlopers...
> a.) get politically active with other commuters, run for an elected office, and seize control of the town from the locals.
> b.) pass "quality-of-life" ordinances, which raise property values, forcing out lifetime residents and businesses.
> c.) revamp zoning ordinances to prevent anyone else from moving into their town and building a house.

Needlessly describes their possessions (For example, instead of saying, "I drove my car to my place to go skiing," the UC Wannabee says,"I drove my Rolls up to my two-story A-Frame ski lodge with a jacuzzi that overlooks the valley.")

Upper Crustie Wannabees lease expensive luxury cars, but give the impression they own them. No one like them, so, Wannabees become way too attached to their possessions which is why they are finicky over how every repair or finishing job is done to their car.

Irritating Upper Crustie Wannabee behavior

Name drops for no reason at all.

Joins a country club, then the Wannabee gets active on the board, and raises the entrance fees to "weed out" undesirables.

Preaches how you must at least be "making" your age in salary.

Interjects their foreign trips in casual conversations: "The streets are so dirty here, when I was in Paris...You know, in Spain at breakfast, they...

Signs first, middle, and last name; or, must be addressed by their full first name, you don't call them Mike, it's "Michael".

Arrogantly brags by saying, "You know, when I do something, I always go *first* class."

Sets their neighborhood apart from the town with a different name and have a separate post office.

Irritating Upper Crustie Wannabee behavior (cont.)...

Points to an object they own and asks, "You know how much this costs? *Guess.*"

Knowingly purchases a cheap house near an airport, raceway, a park, a well-used beach or popular nightspot, but then, once they live in the area try to upgrade it for their exclusive use by...
> a.) starting petition drives to remove the airport because it represents a "danger" to the residential community.
> b.) getting the town to reduce park hours due to "noise level."
> c.) posts resident-permit required parking signs near beach.

Boasts about going to the "best" restaurant, or owning the "best" car, the "best" vodka, etc., but they're not trying to share information with you, the Wannabee is bragging about their superior ability to chose the best in everything.

If you criticize a successful rich person's unethical rise or their lack of talent, an Upper Crustie says, "When you make as much money as them then you can criticize."*

Never pays bills.

---

*World Of Fred Note: Most people think financial success redeems an individual's shortcomings. For example, if you grow up with a ruthless competitive prick who cheats and steals, your parents will lecture to you with, "Don't you ever grow up like them." But, when that particular person becomes an adult and parlays those same immoral childhood traits into a highly successful business career, they become a role model. If you criticize this loser's ethics, the same people who condemned the jerk's repulsive childhood qualities, rise to the moron's defense by observing, "You can say what you want about (*Insert jerk's name.*), but they've done all right for themselves." In other words, money makes it okay. Look at it this way, a rude and demanding poor person is a "pain in the ass, but, if the person is rich, they're "eccentric"; or, if you're a guy who changes light bulbs for a living and win the lottery, all of a sudden, people ask for your opinion of world affairs.

Upper Crustie Variation:
Well-to-don't Wannabees dependent upon the Well-to-do's

Another gradation of the Upper Crustie Wannabee is the glorified torch-bearer whose living is completely dependent upon the patronage of the monied haves. These lackeys from central casteting deny their servant status by assuming the trappings and arrogant manners of their well-to-do clientele.*

Upper Crustie Wannabee's can also be paid-by-the-hour minions wine snobs who pour for you in tasting rooms.

*****World Of Fred Note:** There are even country club waiters who look down on other waiters because they serve the public.

Here is a dance card of lower-station courtiers who assume the haughty airs of their noble employers...

The Serf's Up! Short List

- Classy wedding arrangement and catering specialists.
- Imperious maître d's, concierges, negocients, auctioneers, sommeliers, butlers, nannies, bodyguards, limo drivers, hairdressers.
- Donnish college presidents.
- Ski, golf, tennis, or exercise instructors in resort towns who smugly note the tourists or day-trippers who aren't "in" by their style of dress and places they choose to eat.
- Très chic art gallery or museum trustees.
- Oh-so-proper weekly newspaper society columnists.
- Four-star restaurant chefs who cook special affairs.
- Artists who amuse their patron so they can stay rent free in an estate cottage, or come on weekends to the beach house during the summer.
- Snitty special events directors for wineries.
- Disdainful up-and-coming fashion or interior designers who flamboyantly screech their disapproval of everything.
- Brassy realtors who rent or sell exclusive houses.
- Pedigree dog or thoroughbred horse breeders (groomers included.).
- Regal headmasters at private schools.
- Ass-kissing toadies who fawningly write "as told to" biographies of famous celebrities.
- Journalists who pull their punches because they see themselves as equal peers to the powerful.
- Politicians who represent the financial interests of campaign contributors instead of their electorate.
- Anyone who works, represents, or serves an emir.
- Attorneys or accountants on retainer.
- Housesitters who live rent-free in a rich person's summer place in winter or in their winter home in summer.
- Sailors who take an Upper Crustie's yacht down to a tropical island so when the Crustie flies down, the boat will be there.
- Broker/investment bankers who "park" a rich person's stock, or handle their stock portfolio.

The worst type of Upper Crustie Wannabee: "I came up from nothing" doer

The "I came up from nothing" doer doesn't even enjoy what they have, so, they draw a perverse pleasure in showing off possessions the Wannabee won't share with anyone.

"I came up from nothing" Upper Crustie Wannabees came up the hard way. They're nasty and demanding and because they believe most people will back down or tolerate aggressiveness in exchange for money or influence. When a Wannabee fails in their rise, they discover the people the Upper Crustie used as steps in their ascent won't stop the Wannabee's fall down those same steps, so, they go into a major denial mode. Instead of seeing their relentless ambition turned people against them, Crusties label everyone who allegedly kissed their ass as "two-faced hypocrites" and vow "You won't have me to kick around anymore!"

These driven deal-addicted "players" ruthlessly use everyone around them. In fact, they'll brag about their business triumphs, "Show me a good loser. And I'll show you a loser." Everything they do is aimed at promoting their career and reducing everyone else's resume to a tombstone. They have no friends, just working relationships. These UC Wannabees are unhappily married and their children hate them. Why? Because the winning Wannabee devoted all their time to 100-hour work weeks and exotic business trips. During their rapacious because-it's-there ascent, the ambitious doer justifies their killer instinct by saying, "I'm just trying to make a buck." Once these clawing strivers become successful, they adorn themselves with tailored clothes, gold and expensive jewelry, drive a luxury car, and live in some ostentatious mansion. Most dump their spouse for a younger one and back their mate's career to attain status in other areas, such as fashion or the arts. Many try to counter their past reputation by reinventing themselves through philanthropic acts to gain social respectability. They buy their way onto influential boards and panels, or underwrite a museum's investments to become a trustee. Some make endowments to prestigious universities in exchange for honorary degrees.

Once "I came up from nothing" crustos attain their dream of making it, these achievers of noble berth become lonely and distrustful. But, once again, instead of acknowledging their well-grooved, self-aggrandizing behavior resulted in the lack of friends, the resentful fast tracker consoles themselves by poignantly lamenting it's "difficult" to meet or trust people because "everyone is after my money." These high-rolling doers baste themselves in self-pity by glumly saying, "It wasn't worth the climb." They see themselves as a trusting sap duped by a false dream of happiness. They're disillusioned. Their good intentions and personal sacrifices were betrayed. After all their hard work, this is the thanks they get. They're the victim! (Sob, sniff. Did someone cut an onion?) This particularly twisted achiever fetishly withholds their financial support from everyone--even their own family. Why? Because crispy Crusties want their offspring "to learn the value of a dollar." If Wannabees do bestow funds to their kids, it's never enough for financial independence. This way the Count of Monte Crusto makes the child dependent and degrades them by saying, "you've amounted to nothing," which is what they came *from*.

Even in death, the "I came from nothing" doer refuses to share...

The deceased Wannabee's last act of selfishness is leaving nothing to their "ungrateful" family because "building their own lives will provide them with greater joy than money." So the Crustie bequeaths their entire estate to a charitable foundation, museum, or college that names something after them. (Option: gives their mansion to an organization so everyone can see the standard of living the Wannabee Crustie enjoyed but never possess it; or leave everything to a pet.)

The best way to insult Upper Crustie Wannabees

A low-class insult depreciates an upscaling affluenza's net value by liquidating a Wannabee's inflated view of their prestigious social position. Insults are effective because you didn't give top-drawer Wannabees their market share of social respect. You show they aren't perceived by the public in the same elevated way they view themselves. Remember, the High-grade Loser doesn't care how others personally feel about them, but these high-profilers truly value what others think of the U.C. Wannabee's importance. *

For example...

Situation:
Getting The Upperhand On A Snob.

(Scene: *You With The Power Of Insult And Live!* are at a social gathering. You see a gentlemen who seems full of himself by his posture—stiff, slightly tilted up chin, a look of curiosity in his eyes, as if he's staring at creatures in a zoo. You approach the *Snob*.)

You With The Power Of *Insult And Live!*
(Extending your hand in a greeting.)
Hey, how you doing? Where are you from?

Snob
(Grudgingly takes your hand, winces, and haughtily says.)
I'm from (<u>Names affluent section of town.</u>)

You With The Power Of *Insult And Live!*
Oh, you are? Make yourself at home, snub someone.

Post-insult Outcome: You win on two levels! If the person you insult is a nice, they'll laugh. After all, there are successful people who are unaffected by status and don't like snoot heads either! If the high-ranking loser is deems your bon mot as a major faux paus, they'll stay away from you. Good. You'll only meet the more substantive people who truly matter.

---

*World Of Fred Note: A UC Wannabe's reputation is the mask they wear to rob others or to conceal sleazy mergers and acquisitions.

People who see themselves above the law: Powers-That-Be Idiots and Big Money Dwidheads

Powers That Be--Idiots: 1.) The establishment klatch who pass or enforce laws that apply to everyone but them; for example, judges who get out of speeding tickets; foreign diplomats with immunity who intentionally violate the law; or financial speculators who knowingly make bad loans to each other but use their political influence to get the government to bail them out. 2.) Leaders of society who feel people must only obey the rules that makes these self-anointed imperators rich or increases their power; for example, a local Planning Department, largely comprised of inefficient political appointees, who justify their jobs by making contractors endure needless building permit reviews, which delays the work and increases the costs of the project.

The "Short" List of the Powers That Be—Idiots.

The Powers That Be--Idiots are the few who ruin it for the many. They want you to work within the system--*their* system. These edict eructing societal magi are press barons, insider-trading brokers, planning-and-zoning satraps, education bureaucrats, conniving money-changing caliphs, utilities viziers, territorial concert promoters, arms-dealing sachems, draft-board consuls, bankers who charge you for a bad check someone wrote you, union representatives, war criminals viewed as elder statesmen, baseball clubowners, harbormasters, death merchants, university trustees, intelligence agency cabalas, board of directors with excessive compensation packages, political kingmakers, military tribunals, corporate chieftains, market-manipulating titans, hall monitors, power-tie lawgivers, and landlords who unjustly keep your security deposit. Oh, how these lucubrating luminaries know what's "best" for us (translation: screwing everyone to protect the status quo, i.e., them.). These posh potentate's pretentiously bask in the magisterial belief they have all the facts on any issue, and discount public opinion as "emotional, uniformed, and self indulgent."

Regardless of a PTB Idiot's elevated status, high-security clearance or proprietary info, their greedy ambition requires these plutocratic personages to publicly appear in the following ways...

- in court for cheating on their income tax.
- appearing at public hearings to propose a downtown "revitalization" plan for a shopping mall that would cripple small-town businesses.
- addressing a union meeting to justify why they didn't present a company contract offer to the membership for a vote (which would have ended a strike or prevented a plant closing.).
- sitting before a committee to get approval for their top-level political appointment (a process which they see as "degrading").
- at congressional hearings explaining why they never told their employees that they were working with cancer-causing chemicals.

PTB Idiots are insulated by an inner circle that excludes critics and encourages a train of kudoing kowtowers who pay tribute to success and power over character and ethics. That's why a

PTB Idiot's rare public appearance is the only available opening for most people to be insult them.

PTB Idiot insult technique: You must reduce the PTB Idiot's supposedly complex motives and theories down to what these top-tiered Tories' motives really are: a self-serving agenda to benefit their privileged group. Once the PTB Idiot's integrity is brought into question, the indignant autocrat is compelled to deflect your impudent criticism by implying you aren't intelligent enough to understand them. Why? Because you don't have exclusive access to classified information that gives the high-placed PTB Idiot their super-secret-smart-extra-power strength in the economy, local and world affairs. When this happens, and it will, deliver an unexpected Ruby-to-Oswald power shot right into the umpah-pontificating Sun King's gut.

For example...

Situation:
Power That Be--Idiot Government Bureaucrat Meets The Public

(*A **Government Bureaucrat** is addressing a Chamber of Commerce banquet. He's wearing a suit with cigarette ashes on its sleeves. He has a receding hairline, a few liver spots, steely eyes, a stern look and a pompous tone in his speech. A **Businessman With The Power Of Insult And Live!** whose finances have been hurt by the bureaucrat's policy is at the meeting.*)

Power That Be--Idiot Government Bureaucrat
(*Standing behind a podium.*)

This is a "bare bones budget. There isn't an ounce of fat on it. We must increase sales and gas taxes as well as user fees. We must cutback social services, recreational needs, and retirements benefits. We have to pull together to get this country moving again! (*Pauses.*) I'd like to open the floor for audience questions.

Businessman With The Power of *Insult And Live!*

I'm in business, and when I make a bad decision or a bad loan, I go out of business. But anytime the government screws up they just raise my taxes to pay for their mistakes. Your mistakes don't cost you anything, I pay for them. Hell, you're getting paid to stand there and listen to me. Why don't you have a blanket tax so we don't need lawyers? Why? Because you're a lawyer! You're so busy playing politics to please special interest groups you don't accomplish anything. I--

Power That Be--Idiot Government Bureaucrat
(Impatiently.)
Could you get to the specific question, please...

Businessman with the Power To *Insult and Live!*
You never make the real cuts! You legally mandate programs, fund them for a year, then pull out, and we wind up supporting them with local tax hikes. I want to see you make a cut that puts you out of work! Instead, you only cut services to libraries, youth programs, police and fire protection, sports in schools, and raise park entrance fees, camping fees, permit fees, and put in parking meters. While we're all struggling to make a living, raising kids, you're sitting around passing laws and having meetings we don't have the time to attend. You're not looking out for our interests. Isn't the whole purpose of this budget to self-perpetuate your existence instead of serve the public?

Power That Be--Idiot Government Bureaucrat
(Irritated.)
It's not that simple. You don't have the big picture. You obviously have your mind set. I can't talk to you. The issue is complicated, you must take other factors into account.

Businessman With The Power of *Insult And Live!*
On account of somewhere inside you there is a tapeworm wondering what he ate to pick you up?

Post-insult Outcome: You've won! By not showing any deference, you exposed the loser's theories and stripped him of his respectful aura. You've reconciled accounts. Called in their margins. You pinged their peerage pride, credibility, and their reputation. You demeaned the ruling poobah by rising to their level. Now, that's class!

The worst member of the Powers-That-Be--Idiots Club: The Big-Money Dwidhead

Big Money Dwidheads: 1.) The well-endowed haves who selfishly protect their established wealth, status, and privileges. **2.)** Trickle-down uponers who contribute nothing to society and earn more from unearned income than their own labor, but preach about the value of hard work. **3.)** Vested-interest elitists who believe in the rugged individualism, integrity, and the entrepreneurial spirit that founded the country, but in the name of competition in the free market place, form a trust, cartel, or monopoly to suppress, eliminate, or bankrupt individualism, originality, and--more importantly--destroy competition.

Those who dwell in The House Of Dwidhead know the right people who go to the right exclusive schools, belong to the right boards for hospitals, museums, ballet or opera houses. They attend the right social functions. And, sleep in the right beds. Or, marry the right people. But, taking this plebeian crosswalk doesn't prevent the genteel Dwid from being a loser. Just as a Low-grade loser's ignorance prevents them from acknowledging a blame, a Big Money Dwidhead uses their assets to deny the moral consequences of their High-grade loser actions. It's their deep-pocket cachet.

These moola mongers live the good life, they...

- Possess extensive wine cellars.
- Hire liveried servants to shine the family silver.
- Display childhood photographs of them beside a US. President or royalty.
- Ride in a chauffeur-driven limousine or a Rolls Royce Corniche (which they describe as their "car and driver").
- Travel first class or have a private jet.
- Eat in exquisite tie-and-jacket-only "eateries."
- Have winter ski chalets and summer beach mansions in different countries (they call these "cottages" or "houses".).
- Get drunk at fashion shows and art gallery openings.
- Reproduce a daughter who walks around the house in an equestrian outfit, or has periodic piano/cello recitals.
- Belong to an exclusive country/yacht club.
- Go fox hunting.
- Wear tailored clothes, gowns, raiments, etc.
- Attend private film premier screenings with movie stars.
- Own a luxury sky box in sports arena, or buy up all the best seats for an event to entertain their corporate clients.
- Amass rare art collections.*

Certainly, the ten percenters who control eight-six percent of the wealth are entitled to spend their mazuma the way they choose. But there's one thing this luxurious standard of living does to a loaded Dwid: they don't want to share! Despite the Big Money Dwidhead's civic pronouncements on how their financial success translates into a form of public service, and how these revenue generators create low-paying jobs, these alleged social benefactors know the bulk of wage-earning humanity intensely resents the blue-chipping Dwidhead for trickling down upon them. Regardless of how well-reasoned and complex a Dwid's political or economic views are to improve society, their bottom line is maintaining their respectable lifestyle at someone else's expense.

World Of Fred Note: This collection was the result of the Dwid using an art gallery dealer to scoop up valuable work for only a fraction of its potential worth from a trusting artist.

Big Money Dwidhead annoying behavior

Never tips.

Avoids any embarrassing public altercations through an attorney who...
- opposes any easements for public right-of-way through Dwidhead land.
- ties a Dwid's opponents up in court and bankrupts them with legal fees.
- handles all the estates bills (they rarely pay).*
- lobbies against land being used for a park when it could be slated for a commercial use.
- proposes the development of a marina and a hotel that would ruin a surf break or limit public-access to coastal or lake-front areas.
- raids corporations, guts them out, and loots the employee pension fund.
- irrationally demands wage or benefits concessions from the union in an effort to bust it.
- declares bankruptcy to shortchange creditors but still retains all the Dwid's assets.
- insists the town use taxpayer funds to build seawall to prevent erosion of their ocean-front property.
- sets up shell companies or launders money through foreign banks so the Dwid doesn't pay taxes.
- gets a slap-on-the-wrist fine for chemical dumping.

Maintains hard times are just a "state of mind."

Without permission, lands their private helicopter on other people's property or public lands.

Cheap over little things, such as returning deposit bottles, reusing items, or haggling over a few cents difference in price.

---

*World Of Fred Note: Most of the time, their lawyer avoids payment by ensuring the creditor's legal fees to collect the outstanding debt costs more than the actual bill. So, the creditor doesn't try to collect.

Big Money Dwidhead quirks

If they're not at social event, Dwids dress like bums.

Never carries cash because there is always someone who wants to impress the Dwid by picking up a check.

Big on swamis, channelers, past-life mystics, seances.

Does renovation work without obtaining proper permits.

Paranoid about security on their property (Most monied Dwids have way too many alarms, attack dogs, security guards, and automatic weapons.).

Distrusts anyone who knows them too well because the person could use that knowledge to exploit the Dwid.

Conceals the fact their established fortune came from a grandfather who was a robber baron; or through an embarrassing business, such as a rendering plant.

Dwid's wife runs a non-profit charity organization: she prides herself on her pushy ability to get donations or make volunteers work for nothing. (This proves to her that just because she has money doesn't mean she couldn't make money.)

Feels taxing the rich won't accomplish anything, but taxing the middle class will.

Never feels guilty about their disproportionate wealth because it would be a "greater sin to have the money and not enjoy it."

Is supposedly a "soft touch" but no one ever gets physically close enough to ask the Dwid for anything.

Rarely socializes with anyone outside their prep school, country club, or college grouping.

Big Money Dwidhead's scenic overlook views of reality

Is under the delusion they have good taste because everyone agrees with them.*

Thinks government should be run like a corporation.**

Believes it's pointless to tax business because industry only "passes the cost down to the consumer."

Is against the minimum wage.

Responds to critical charges about their financial dealings or unethical behavior, by indignantly snapping...
- "It's class envy."
- "They're jealous of my success."
- "No one said life would be *fair.*"
- "If you know so much, how come you're not rich?"
- "You're on private property. (*To an assistant.*) "Call security."
- "They're just fringe groups who are attacking me because they can't get accepted in mainstream society."
- "I was misquoted" or "My remarks were taken out of context." (*Then, shoves nearby news photographer.*)
- "I'd respond to that but I'm a gentleman/lady."
- (*If it's a phone call.*) "How'd you get this number?"

---

*__World Of Fred Note:__ The reason everyone agrees with the rich is to sell them an overpriced item. How else can you explain those horrendously ugly, expensive, and garish gowns worn by society matrons and dowagers? Or, their gaudy emerald necklaces and diamond rings?

**__Another World Of Fred Note:__ Dwidheads are firm believers in a free market system without any form of government intervention or taxation. They believe this system leads to progress and goodness. Yet, they also feel the same ineffective government should control freedom of speech and artistic expressions to "preserve the social fabric and values" of its citizens as well as prevent the nation from degenerating into a "permissive" society. In other words: trust business not democracy.

Big Money Dwidhead's scenic overlook views of reality (cont.)...

Feels they shouldn't be taxed because of what their business has "contributed to society."*

Opposes job quotas or any form of social welfare (with the exception of starting a relative out in their business, purchasing a house for their child, paying for their college, etc.).**

Sees themselves as different than people who are merely "rich" because the Dwid is from "established" money.

Firmly believes they're always being overcharged for bills because of their wealth.

See nothing wrong with hiring scabs to provoke union picket lines during a strike at the Dwid's plant or factory.

Wants to "give something back" to society by running for political office. ***

---

*World of Fred Note: These lucre lovers conceal they earn the bulk of their money through speculative financial dealings, not from business investments that create work for a labor force. Hey, at the drop of a polo mallet, these buy-American Dwids will shoot out a telex to shift their wealth to any foreign country whose currency gives an investment a higher return on interest rate.

**Another World Of Fred Note: If a blue-blood relative from the Dwid's family is hired to work for the Dwid's company, the person "learns the ropes" at the bottom in the mail room (but at a much higher salary than the average employee) and works their way up to be the Dwid's assistant within six months. This is called a "grooming" process.

***Yet Another World Of Fred Note: The Rich Dwidhead only runs for office because they lust for one more high: power. And what does this power do? Enable them to expand their financial holdings and control over people's lives. But, they deny these charges by claiming they are so rich they "can't be corrupted." (Have you ever met a greedy person who felt they had enough money?)

Why it's good to abuse rich Dwidheads

Big Money Dwidheads have a masochistic urge to be insulted. It's always considered "bad form" by a Dwid's colleagues to bring up a chap's failure or embarrassment, so, a Dwid's positively enthralled when someone degrades them. You see, every agoger around these old-line personages is so busy salaaming them and trying to kiss the Dwid's private-sector derrière to get something, the Dwid concludes your insult means you don't want anything from them. So, you must like them!

For example...

Situation:
Liquidating a Big Money Dwidhead

*(Scene: Country Club's 19th Hole. **You With The Power To Insult And Live!** are dining with several rich Dwidheads at their exclusive watering hole. The **Big Money Dwidhead** is shaking a dice cup because he is rolling to see who pays for the drinks.)*

Big Money Dwidhead
(Lifts up the dice cup.)
Gosh darn, I guess I poney up and sign for it. *(He signs the card.)* You know where that shrub is on 15? I was there on my second shot, hit the green and triple putt. *(Sips his drink.)* Delish! Lish! Lish. No one makes a bloody better than Rupert. *(Pause.)* Ah, I wonder what the other half is doing now on the *public* courses.

You With The Power Of *Insult And Live!*
It must have been rough for you, growing up as a kid, playing realtors and Indians.

Rich Dwidhead
(Laughing.)
Bungo! That line is a peach. *(Patting you on the back.)* You blighter, what brio! I must let Nigel hear that one, we use to crew at Yale with Cyril, Dicky, Chaz, and Tobias. You should have a go at those chaps. They nominated me for commodore. Let's repair to the pergola. *(Signalling for another round.)* Would you like another splash of cognac? It's scrummy. By the way, what are you doing for dinner? My grand-niece Kimberly is going to be here for Meegan's coming out party. She'd enjoy a bounder like you. *(Pause.)* What field of endeavor are you in?

Post-insult Outcome: Pip, pip. You've "arrived"! You didn't kiss the Old-World Dwid's buttocks. Your hostile-takeover slam will leverage you into the high-yielder's trust. Insults give you a high return. He'll offer to back your financial ventures, introduce you to a more influential social circle, fill you in on merger acquisition tips, or underwrite your career advancement.

Insult and Live! by Fred Reiss

Basic insults for elitist snotheads who *think* they are superior to you

I bet there's a tapeworm inside you wondering what he ate to pick you up.

Are you just being kept alive until they can find a brain donor for your body?

Did someone have a seance and summon you into this room?

Are you angry because Jodi Foster hasn't been answering your letters?

Listening to you talk about yourself is like watching a dialysis machine back up.

Did you get the proper permits to turn your skull into a hazardous waste site?

I'm sorry I reduced you to a cultural stereotype, but it's only because you don't have any depth.

It's strange how your mind stopped growing at age two, but your body continues to grow around it.

You have an open mind. Unfortunately, it's just been exposed to the air too long.

You're a fine wine, you should be in a cellar for fifty years.

Yes, there are leaders and followers, and you're the one who cleans up after the parade.

You know, on a planet of autistic people, you'd be a slow learner.

Basic insults for elitist snotheads who *think* they are superior to you (cont.)...

I only know you superficially, but I feel that's enough.

This is a dream come true being introduced to you, I've always wanted to meet a spore from *Star Trek*.

After hearing what you just said, I think your gene pool only had a shallow section.

With a brain like yours, you can qualify to park in handicapped zones.

You obviously have the brains of JFK—well, what was left of them, anyway.

I'm glad you're here, because you make everyone else here feel so much better about their own lives.

You'd be a good cross reference for mediocrity.

If they had a bounty on *Spam*, you'd be an endangered species.

If you're here, evolution has a reverse gear.

You ought to join MENSA, then there'd be a curve and we could all get in.

Most brain matter is gray, yours is dark meat.

If I was a surfer, I don't think I'd ever get tubed on your brain wave.

At your last job, were you replaced by a delivery boy with a better car?

Basic insults for elitist snotheads who *think* they are superior to you (cont.)...

So, I guess you can get brain damage from eating white paste in childhood.

I'm sorry, but you've used up your PSAT credit line.

It's too bad the earth cooled, you'd have friends.

Looking at you, I feel somewhere a banana slug is having an out-of-body experience.

I bet, if furballs were human they'd cough you up.

When you were born, they didn't break the mold, they scraped it off you.

You're what happens when sea monkeys get out of the tank.

When your family took home movies, did you have to audition?

You're *(Insert Brainiac's full name here)*, I looked that up in "All Of God's Creatures", and you weren't in the index.

You know, Geoffrey Dalmer would take a bite out of you and lose interest.

Say, if Stephen King stops typing, do you disappear?

Hey, can I call you what everyone else calls you? The defendant.

Why do I feel that something inside of you died and your body doesn't know about it yet.

Basic insults for elitist snotheads who *think* they are superior to you (cont.)...

Why do I have the feeling that David Lynch is directing our conversation?

How'd you get here? Is someone nearby experimenting with genetic bacteria?

When people say things could be worse, do they point at you a lot?

A Right-to-Lifer would look at you and say, "Well, maybe."

That's an incredibly inaccurate statement, until now, I thought all the former members of the Warren Commission were dead.

I think your body is rejecting your personality.

Did Jane Goodall work with you as a child?

For you, a stool sample is a trail.

I'd like to teach you hang gliding: with a noose.

You're what happens when the sphincter controls the man.

It's tragic, I see your white blood cells have died and the bacteria has taken over.

When I was a kid, you're what I thought was hiding under the bed.

There are right-brained people, left-brained people, and you, a no-brained people.

Basic insults for elitist snotheads who *think* they are superior to you (cont.)...

Do dolphins look at you to see what they've evolved from?

Getting an intelligent response from you is like trying to get an aspirin from a Christian Scientist.

Yeah, you read classic novels, you bought *War and Peace* so you could color in the o's.

You've come out of your shell, and it's too bad, because I thought the shell was the most attractive part of your body.

What's it like to play an adult version of keep away your whole life?

You're an item, marked down, but still an item.

I bet, if you experience personal growth, it will be a tumor.

Were you the first human being cloned from plankton?

Lepers thought they were kept together so they wouldn't get what you have.

Did a wart just stand there and you grew underneath it?

You read me like a book--slowly.

You've proven God doesn't believe in a filtering process.

You'd make a suicide machine pull the plug on itself.

Dianetics wouldn't even help you.

Did your pet turtle try to flush you down the toilet?

Basic insults for elitist snotheads who *think* they are superior to you (cont.)...

Relax, think of me as someone you can relate to, like your court-appointed psychologist.

You shouldn't have left your bubble, you've become infected again.

It takes all kinds to make the world. Where are you building yours?

After you were born, God created Satan for spin control.

You're proof you can have children through false labor.

Looking at you I can see that you don't need a skin surface for a cyst to grow.

It's nice to see someone who has polished dysfunctional behavior into an art form.

Bitter because the morlocks stole your time machine?

You went to college? I didn't know they had Nazi war criminal scholarship fund.

I usually don't like to stereotype people, but you just don't have any depth.

As a child in day care, were you abused by kennel help?

Karma doesn't even want to come back to you.

Some people are two faced, they're nice to you in one place but not another, but I'd be rude to you here and rude *everywhere* I went.

Basic insults for elitist snotheads who *think* they are superior to you (cont.)...

Well, after seeing you I know Planned Parenthood isn't doing its job.

Since you're here, I assume genetic researchers don't pack their trash.

You're probably a dolphin-attack victim.

Why weren't you recalled by God for character defects?

When you were born from a c-section, it was a nice way of telling you that your mother left you in the bleachers.

I think you're further proof that God doesn't replace divots.

You're what happens to devil babies when they grow up.

Are *Exxon* crews still cleaning up your afterbirth?

With your charm, you'd get death threats from Leo Buscalia.

Nintendo wouldn't even play with you.

Did Clive Barker copyright your birth certificate?

Are you in a Hardy Boy mystery "Man without a Clue"?

The only thing that separates you from the apes is a cage. How did you get out?

Is your birth certificate being used as a position paper by the pro-choice movement?

Basic insults for elitist snotheads who *think* they are superior to you (cont.)...

So you never got over you're disappointment at not being the Christ child?

I guess it's possible to stop growing as a person.

If they injected you into penicillin, it would turn back into moldy bread.

I bet your imaginary playmate left you for another kid.

When a Jehovah's Witness has a nightmare, I bet it's you knocking on *their* door.

It's too bad orphanages don't use repo men.

Do great white shark go into cages to study you?

Jez, sometimes I wish the eco-system wasn't for everyone.

I hope your birth certificate has an expiration date.

Odd, you've experience conception, but life still hasn't begun.

I see improvements to the environment have brought lower life forms back into the area.

As a kid, you did stuff that separated you from the other children, you asked to play with them and they said no.

I bet moonies wouldn't want you in their group.

In tourist areas cardboard figures stand next to you to have *their* pictures taken.

Basic insults for elitist snotheads who *think* they are superior to you (cont.)...

Are you waiting for Hannible Lecter to come out with a cookbook?

There's a novel inside you, and I hope it's being digested.

I think you started out as a lab experiment. Did you grow from a tiny potato suspended in a glass of water with toothpicks?

I can't figure out if you're a control sample or a stool sample.

Some people want to go back to the womb, you want to go back to the petrie dish.

No offense, but I wouldn't use the high dive in your gene pool.

If someone is building a slow learner they could use you for parts.

You're off by a fraction: 9/10.

Excuse me, but can you try to construct a *point* around this conversation?

When you were a kid, were you the test-case in the ban against lawn darts?

Why are you still here? Am I giving off static electricity to attract lint?

You're a case study waiting to happen.

Basic insults for elitist snotheads who *think* they are superior to you (cont.)...

You have to hold the record for the farthest a toadfish has crawled on the shore.

On the bumper of your car is there a "Larouche 88" sticker?

I hope when you're called back to your maker—*Walmart*.

Did they pull you off life-support to save the machine's life?

It's sad looking at you, because it proves the immune system is gone and the germ survived.

Talking to you makes me feel like I reached level eight in *Donkey Kong*.

After you were born, did your mother want her womb's security deposit back?

You'd constipate a prune.

I'm trying to figure what Noah took two of, so that you got here.

Were you handing out paychecks on the grassy knoll?

To God, you'd be called a first draft.

I guess there is such a thing as birth by injection.

Your life is an open book—and all the pages have been colored in.

Basic insults for elitist snotheads who *think* they are superior to you (cont.)...

Animal Advocates would classify you as bait.

If you lived in Arizona, people would leave it for their health.

You've protected the child inside you, now we have to get rid of the adult outside you.

I bet if I covered you with *Preparation H* you'd shrink.

Hard to believe they removed you but couldn't save the prostate.

After talking to you, it's so refreshing to meet someone who has one point of view, do you know a lot of Klansmen?

Your brain is a live yogurt culture.

Freddy Kreuger doesn't go to sleep because he's afraid he'll dream about you.

Why don't you like me? Are you just having an allergic reaction to an open mind?

Yes, what is the price of human life, no one can really tell, but you're making it a blue light special.

If you're self-centered, you're filled with sap.

Weren't you on the wing of that plane in *The Twilight Zone?*

I bet the United Way is trying is starting a funding drive to prevent you.

Basic insults for elitist snotheads who *think* they are superior to you (cont.)...

If I hit you with a stick, would a pinata would come out.

The last time you saw a foreign film was when you wiped your teeth.

Nice making you acquaintance, it's a pleasure to meet an actual creature from the Cthulu Mythos.

Downwardly mobiling insults for yuppie scum and monied snobs

You're such a yuppie woman, when you get pregnant, you won't go into labor, you're going into management.

You guys are so conservative, you don't get circumcisions, you get button downs.

What's slumming to you? Playing tennis on a public court?

As a kid, did you have *insider* trading cards?

What's the last book you read that affected you? Let me guess, was it *Man Without a Country...Club* ?

Hey guy, what's that bulge in your pants? Your father's *Visa* card?

You're so upwardly mobile, you don't have to ménage a trois anymore, you network.

Your wife isn't with child, she's with client.

Downwardly mobiling insults for yuppie scum and monied snobs (cont.)...

How'd you break your leg, falling off the corporate ladder?

Well, I see you have a new upwardly mobile polo shirt, it has the alligator on it, but it's eating a blue-collar worker.

You two probably have a time-share condom.

(To a group.) Like the sweaters and the pants, you guys look like the student council on skid row.

Miss, I'm going to call you the "C" word: "career" woman.

I know you're not a yuppie, you were into being shallow and materialistic long before it was fashionable.

Come on, sure you're a yuppie, you look like you were breast fed by caterers.

It must be tough when your life peaks after being Chess Club captain.

I know how to hurt you, I'll promote someone above you.

Well, this is probably the farthest you've traveled without a caddie.

When you get drunk, do you tattoo a business card to your chest?

What did you play as kids? Realtors and Indians?

What's a major decision for you? Playing the nine iron off your back foot?

Downwardly mobiling insults for yuppie scum and monied snobs (cont.)...

What do you call hookers? Leverage buyouts?

Enjoy yourself, exploit an employee.

You'd never be missing as a child, you'd just be held in escrow for two years.

What are you doing here? I guess no one is watching the desk at the racquetball spa.

You think *Executive Suite* is a symphony.

How'd did you two meet, member-guest tournament?

What's science fiction to you? A Democratic Senate and Congress?

If all you guys sit here long enough, you'll be able to turn into a brunch.

Why did you marry each other, need the dental plan?

When you corporate guys go to a party and put on some music, do you form a line and commute around the room?

I'm not saying you're privileged, but when the other kids played army, I bet you got a deferment.

Look at you guys, you look like yuppie salt and pepper shakers.

What brings you here? A cappuccino spill?

Your cells don't multiply, they subdivide.

Downwardly mobiling insults for yuppie scum and monied snobs (cont.)...

You're a yuppie! Hey, if you were Superman you'd wear a red sweater tied around your neck.

You were born to the purple, I bet you had a stretch-pedal limo with a chauffeur.

When you guys play charades at a party, do you act out your resumes?

If the corporate world destroyed itself, you'd be mutants.

Yes, I bet you think the Third World is a *Star Trek* episode.

How do you live on the edge? Drink a French Bordeaux that wasn't reviewed in the *Wine Spectator*?

I guess you two guys are into kinky sex, like what could that be? Investment stocks and bondage?

You probably think handicapped parking is for anyone who shoots over 90.

Why are your around? Guess the mixed doubles group lost their court tonight.

How would you catch her cheating on you? If she started sending out her resume?

Gez, you're working for a living? I guess you're living on the edge until the trust fund kicks in.

Must have been a risk coming to a place without valet parking.

Downwardly mobiling insults for yuppie scum and monied snobs (cont.)...

You people don't reproduce, you promote within.

(To a group.) You guys on your way to the Kennedy audition?

You're so conservative, you have a nine-to-five o'clock shadow.

When you break up with a guy Miss, do you give them two weeks notice with severance?

I bet you think white nouveau is the person who moved next door.

You didn't have an umbilical cord, you had a cable hook-up

When you resist arrest, do the police subdue you with a *Choate* hold?

You don't put paper down on the toilet, you put a spreadsheet.

Don't you have to go home and melt some brie?

As a kid did you and your dad play hide the birthright?

I know why you ride an overpriced road bike, it's because you're use to paying a lot of money for anything you put between your legs.

You probably think they should put pictures of missing children on bottles of Cabernet Sauvignon.

Blasting Blitzed Boozer Losers and Substance Abusers

Assorted sampler of annoying substance abusers we've all been victimized by...

- Off-duty cops.
- Bar flies.
- Post-game softball players.
- Celebrants at birthdays, keg bashes, town festivals, trade shows, Christmas parties, conventions and company picnics, graduation or prom nights, and reunions.
- Girls/guy's night out groups.
- Free-form dancing burnouts at music festivals.
- Carousers who feel some moral obligation to stay at your house until dawn to "kill the keg."
- High school athletes having their first beer.
- Commuters in the train bar car who hate their jobs.
- Homeless panhandlers.
- Every other inebriate at 25-cent draft night.
- Stoned-out people at midnight movies or rock concerts.
- Hecklers in nightclubs.
- Restaurant help drinking for free at another bar.
- Hungover mechanics who improperly repair your car.
- Anyone on a business trip with company expense accounts who act like they own the joint.
- Obnoxious fans in the stands.
- Military personnel on leave.
- Indignant intellectuals loudly discussing their politics in a bohemian bar.
- Jealous or vindictive relatives at wedding receptions.
- Bar-hopping college kids back for the holidays, or partying down at resort towns for Spring breaks.
- Every other person who is in their twenties.
- Prigs at vertical tastings at wineries.
- Surfboard shapers who take your advance payment, get drunk, and don't get your board done for months.
- Yuppies in microbrewries.
- Stag parties in strip joints.
- Regulars at their watering hole who are rude to strangers.
- Bikers at county fairs.

Purpose of this section: Teaches you the proper ways to verbally cut off Boozer Losers and Substance Abusers.

Boozer Losers and Substance Abusers

Potential twelve-steppers verbally or physically attack anyone who has a better future than them. Actually, let's make that anyone who has a future. These space cases hate you for living beyond their limitations. They vehemently deny self-destructive impulses ruined their lives. Instead, these burnouts unjustly blame others for burdening the loser with emotional problems that drove them to heavily abuse booze and drugs. Blasted abusers aren't "feeling any pain" because they cause it.

Boozer Losers or druggies are essentially interchangeable because a substance abuser's state of mind appears to come from another planet, time zone, sub-zero IQ quotient, or parallel universe.

For example...

Situation:
Dealing With a Pothead

(Scene: college dormitory. A group of stoners are passing a bong pipe around and watching the movie "Dumbo" on TV. You enter the room and realize everyone is so wasted it's impossible to have a normal conversation.)

Pothead
(Exhaling bong hit he's held in his lungs.)
Man, you know, there are a lot of elephants in this film. *(Pause.)* Those guys must have been on something to make a movie like this—

You With The Power To *Insult And Live!*
Are you just bummed out because you dropped acid and you're only seeing one color?

Pothead
(Exhaling pot smoke held in his lungs for 40 seconds.)
Hey, this guy's a trip.

Post-insult Outcome: You won! These stoners are too wasted to have any pride. They're not offended. You entertained them.

Approach shots to down boozer losers:
The three mood shifts of lost last callers for alcohol

While the stoners are basically mellow and risk-free in terms of physical confrontation, Boozer Losers recycle three emotional shifts from their limited playlist. That's why it's important to know the exact emotional moment to pop the putdown.

Here are the three attention-seeking stages of drunkenness in the Bar World of Fred...

Stage 1.
Boozer Loser gets sentimental

State of mind: Very happy.

Insult status: The most fertile happy-hour stage to insult a drunk. This bar-stool sample is affectionate, sentimental, and says embarrassing revelations ("I love you, I really love you."). They make prolonged eye contact, and offer to buy you a drink.

Warning: If you reject the boozer loser's physical advances, turn down a drink, or neglect to return their compliment, the blubbering boozer stumbles into **Stage Two**.

Stage Two:
Boozer Loser starts crying in their beer

State of mind: Reflective.

Insult status: Still a good stage for an insult, because a well-timed verbal jab prevents the boozer from taking their troubles too seriously. In this slightly sullen and soused stage, the brooding drunk indulges in self-pity by muttering "I'm all alone"..."It's all bullshit"..."I'm sorry."

Warning: If you refrain from insulting them, this stage-two drunk staggers to the red-alert level of drunkenness: **Stage Three**.

Stage Three
Boozer Loser becomes nobody's friend

State of Mind: Volatile organic compound.

Insult status: Don't even think about it! In this highly combustible stage a drunk's self-hatred is distilled into a boiler-making rage at life. These stewing drunks have a hard and flat stare. They tighten their fists and grunt challenging questions. Never make prolonged eye contact with these borderliners. Don't touch them. Never disagree! Go with their energy not against it. The liquor's cyclical effects will chemically returns the drunk to the manageable **Stage One,** where you can safely insult the wasted boozer.

Warning: Don't insult! Boozer losers drink to escape themselves. A slam ruins the escape. It forces the loser to soberly see they're responsible for their failures. They shift into denial by lashing out at the person who makes them see this truth. They'll attack you with a beer bottle, gnaw off your ear, punch you, throw a drink, or suck your eye from its socket and bite it off at the optic nerve.

Why insults work on Boozer Losers and substance abusers

The worst mistake you can make is to treat an impaired Boozer Loser like a sober and responsible person. If you lecture this drunk about their rude behavior, the Boozer Loser becomes indignant. If you ignore them, the drunk resents your superior attitude. That's why an insult is the solution to this dilemma. An insult doesn't treat a whacked-out-of-their-skull loser as a mature adult. Let's face it, if the Boozer Loser wanted to act responsible they wouldn't be wasted! When you insult a substance abuser, you're acknowledging their condition. They respect that.

For example...

Situation
Insulting A "Nobody Loves Me" Boozer Loser
(You With The Power Of Insult And Live! sitting next to a blubbering stage-two drunk.)

"Nobody Loves Me" Boozer Loser
(Staring at a glass they've broken.)
I'm sorry, I'm sorry.

You With The Power of *Insult To Live!*
I see AA lost another member.

"Nobody Loves Me" Boozer Loser
(Snickering.)
You been there too, huh? *(Pause.)* Buddy, what are you drinking?

Post-insult Outcome: You won! Your well-placed insult avoided the emotional factors that drove the person to escape through substances. This acknowledgment makes a drunk feel as if they've found a real "buddy."

Boozer Loser's physically offensive moves

Blows smoke in your face.

Throws up near you, or on your car.

Talks to you through teeth covered with pieces of cocktail peanuts, pork rind specks, orange remnants from goldfish crackers, popcorn kernels, or deviled eggs.

Breathes a foul odor upon you.

Leaves their soiled underwear or pants in your shrubs.

Spills their drinks.

Turns and belches in your face.

Pulls down their pants.

Exhibitionistically urinates.

Speaks and obliviously spits food fragments on you.

Puts their cigarette out in your drink or food.

Drunks enjoy loudly swearing in front of children at sporting events, especially in the bleachers at ballgames.

Inconsiderate Boozer Loser public acts

Carelessly shoots off low-flying fireworks in crowded areas.

Scrambles for a ball that lands near their seats at a professional game, knocking down children or strangers.

Maliciously tangles people's fishing lines on charter boats.

Boogies on a crowded dance floor with a drink in one hand and a cigarette in the other; spilling liquor and burning everyone else.

Inconsiderate Boozer Loser public acts (cont.)...

Drunks ruin a concert for you by...
- blocking your view by standing or dancing in front of your seat (Putting a girlfriend on their shoulders is optional.).
- shoving their way through the crowd without saying 'excuse me" to get to the front of the stage.
- running naked to the stage.
- loudly singing so you can only hear the drunk's out-of-tune voice and not the singer.
- slam dancing around you and steps on your feet; or (If drunk has long or beaded hair.), dances and spins their head around, twirling their long hair in your face.
- leaving garbage everywhere.

Drunkenly drives their speedboats or jet skis into "bathers-only" areas. (Another addled antic is driving close to anglers in rowboats or sailboats, nearly capsizing the crafts.)*.

Fires guns in the air on Independence Day or New Year's Eve.

From a high area, throws bottles, full cups of beer, or drives golf balls at anyone or anything below them.

Hogs all the free munchies put out for happy hour.

Ways Boozer Losers violate others property rights

Urinates in doorways or people's yards.

Cowtipping.

Turning over tombstones.

---

*World Of Fred Note: These drunks base their selfish aquatic acts on the belief that the "ocean is for everyone, nobody owns it."

Ways Boozer Losers violate others property rights (cont.)...

Leaves empties wherever they finished them.

Breaks apart park benches or wooden fences for firewood.

Puts liquor bottles on the tips of tree branches.

In restaurant/bar bathrooms, the Boozer Loser...
- rips off toilet stall doors in a bar's bathroom.
- shoves tissue rolls in the toilet to clog it.
- punches holes in walls.
- writes obscene or racist graffiti on stall walls.
- pukes in urinals or sinks.
- urinates on walls, sinks, or all over toilet seats.
- breaks mirrors.
- throws cherry bombs down toilets.
- pulls out the towel rack.

Forgets about lit cigarettes they leave on window sills.

Throws bottles from moving cars.

Sits in your bar seat and refuses to give it back.

Takes your drink.

Steals beer mugs, life-size liquor-promotion cardboard cutouts, a leather jacket left on a bar stool, or waitress' tips.*

Tries to damage your Halloween costume.

In a bar, when told by the proprietor the drunk can't leave with their drink, the boozer swears and leaves with it.

***World Of Fred Note:** If you caught the drunk in the act of trying to rip you off, the Boozer Loser covers for themselves by saying, "I thought it was my friend's!"

Annoying Boozer Loser behavioral habits

Takes a 30-second joke, stretches it into a four minute story, and screws up the punch line.

Tries to stick you with the tab.

Repeats the same story over and over again.

Makes nasty and partially true accusations about your flaws.

Tries to get you to bet them a drink in a boring bar game, such as finding a certain figure in a dollar bill, word puzzles, etc.

Annoying Boozer Loser behavioral habits (cont.)...

Rudely signals for service by snapping their fingers or sharply whistling at the wait staff.

Cruelly and loudly calls others "fat" or "ugly."

Verbally abuses the nightclub's disc jockey for not playing their requests.

Gets angry at the bill because they "didn't drink that much." (After they're forced to pay the bill, the drunk self-righteously refuses to leave a tip, and loudly vows never to come back.)

When an offended person challenges them to a fight, the drunk falsely bellows, "Hey, better not, I'm a black belt."

Thinks it's fun to play some dangerous game of "chicken" or a William Tell stunt.

Makes generous drunken offers they never honor when sober.

Buys you a drink so you have to listen to them talk about themselves for an hour.

Constantly talks about new drinks they invented. (For example, "I found when you mix tequila and Jello together...")

Monotonously goes on and on about their hangovers or describes how sick they were the night before.

Is only comfortable if you're drunk or drinking at the same pace with them.

Gets indignant when they're "cut off" at the bar.

Always turning you on to some sweet or fruity shot and describe it as "going down easy but they hit you real hard."

Annoying Boozer Loser behavioral habits (cont.)...

When thrown out of a bar, yells they'll sue.

When slightly drunk, gives you their car keys because they don't think they should drive, then when wasted hours later, get belligerent if you don't give their keys back.

Starts food fights.

Won't allow you to play on the bar's open shuffleboard, pool table, or dart board, unless you play them first.

Boozer Loser car moves

Knocks down or takes mailboxes.

Runs over animals.

Drives in the wrong direction, but vehemently insists they are heading the right way.

Leaves tire tracks on playing fields or a homeowner's lawn.

Collides into a parked car and drives off.

Survives a car crash that injures or kills others.

If you're driving, Boozer Loser attempts to seize the wheel, hits the accelerator, or loudly criticizes your driving.

Believes they drive better wasted than others drive sober.

Swerves into the opposite lane because they are reaching for another beer in the nearby cooler, fumbling for a roach in the ashtray, or patting the floor for a music disc.

Justifies drunk driving because off-duty cops do it too.

Boozer Loser wit

Drunk losers order a drink with someone their own age, but usually make a crack that implies their buddy is older and looks in worse shape than the loser.

Boozer Loser quips

"I know it's not my fart because I like the smell."

"Another day older, another Bud*wiser*."

(To a companion as a toast.) "I knew you when you were nothing and you're *still* nothing."

"I don't like to go out on St. Patrick's Day or New Year's Eve—it's amateur night."

"I'd rather have a bottle in front of me, than a frontal lobotomy."

(After you give the drunk something.) "Thank you very *little*."

Drunk Loser quips (cont.)...

"I've got to take a leak so bad my back teeth are floating."

"Anyone can piss on the floor, it takes a real man to shit on the ceiling."

(*To the opposite sex.*) "If I told you that you had a beautiful body would you hold it against me?"

"Liquor, sure I'll lick her."

(*Explains why they drink.*) "It's a dirty job, but somebody's got to do it."

"I'm feeling single and seeing double."

"They all get prettier at closing time."

(*When asked "What have you been up to?" Loser says.*) "No good."

"Sure drinking kills your brains cells, but just the weak ones."

(*When asked, "Where are you going?"*) "Crazy, wanna come?"

(*Toast.*) "Here's to you and here's to me, and if disagree—well, fuck you!"

"Never go 'straight,' go forward."

(*Rubbing thumb and forefinger together as you tell a hard luck tale.*) "This is me playing the world's smallest violin."

"They say three out of ten people are alcoholics so that makes me a minority group."

(*If the phone rings.*) "If that's for me, I'm not here."

Insults for slurring substance abusers

Are you doing your remedial phonics drill?

I bet it's hard to speak with a hemorrhoid in your throat.

Whatever you said can pass for a for phlegm.

I didn't know there were any *Challenger* survivors.

Are you still thawing out from a game of freeze tag?

Just having a difficult time speaking because your batteries are running down?

I'll speak to you in a language you'll understand: *(Hit your throat to produce a vibrating vocal effect.)* "People of earth."

Hey, here's a quick tip, don't try to learn a second language until you master the vowels from the first one.

You just reminded me, I have to stop by the video store, I have *Awakenings* on reserve.

That didn't make much sense, are you picking up an old show through a satellite dish?

Why are you slurring? Still stunned from running into that bug zapper?

Was going after your buddy in the septic tank the last thing you remember?

I didn't understand that, I don't have a "Klingon-to-Alcoholic" dictionary.

Say, were you bitten by *Old Yeller* years ago?

Insults for slurring substance abusers (cont.)...

I'm sorry, I was looking around you to see if there was a chute on your back that didn't open.

I never heard Satan sing acappella.

If I played your remark backwards I'd get, "This person is an idiot."

Are you trying to lip sync a stroke?

Are you speaking or forming words by flapping your armpits?

I never met a born-again dyslexic.

Take your time in answering my question, I know it's a long way back from a coma.

Obviously, you're still recovering from the effects of Captain Kirk's phaser blast.

Why don't you get a producer to mix that sound because I think I'm only getting one channel.

It's nice to meet the first bungy-cord breech victim.

Years ago, did you challenge Dylan Thomas to a shooter contest?

Now I know the sound *Thunderbird* makes when it ferments.

If that's the liquor talking, your scotch is dyslexic.

Who were you last bar hopping with? River Phoenix?

Insults for slurring substance abusers (cont.)...

You have a speech impediment—your brain.

Why do you speak like that? Did you French kiss Geoffrey Dalmer?

Do you think cutting down on cocaine means just doing dotted lines?

I bet you use to drink Charles Bukowski under the table.

Is Betty Ford sending you dunning notices?

In *Lost Weekend,* did you do all the stunt drinking?

It must be frustrating, being an alcoholic trapped within a drug-addict's body.

What's the name of your drinking buddy? Let me guess. Is it low self-esteem?

Keep drinking. Because if you sober up, you'll look at your life, and only start drinking again.

It's nice to meet secret agent--orange

I've always wanted to meet the bitter Fifth Beatle.

Insults to use on a drunk's delayed response time, poor reflexes, and physical uncoordination

I see data retrieval isn't one of your strengths.

Do you get frequent flyer mileage for acid trips?

I guess crack can cause brain damage when taken through the umbilical cord.

You know, I don't think you're drunk, you're just stupid.

It must be quite an accomplishment to push the envelop of a mental lapse.

Are you trying to get into character for "The Tony Conigliaro Story"?

This proves drugs lead to harder things—those things for you are reading and writing.

Do you think you have job security because there is no drug testing at *Jiffy Lube?*

How did your brain get through customs?

If the body is a temple, yours is a crack house.

Your pupils are fine, but your body is dilating.

In your case, alcoholism isn't heredity, you've just carved your own niche out.

Did you suffer some form of damage because you weren't wearing...
- your protective suit at the nuclear power plant?
- the monoxide mask at the toll plaza?

Insults to use on a drunk's delayed response time, poor reflexes, and physical uncoordination (cont.)...

For you a drug problem is converting pounds of cocaine into its metric weight.

I bet even the voices in your head would rather talk to each other than you.

When they tried to embalm you, did you just wake up?

I know this is difficult for you, I guess your flashback must be experiencing a sudden attack of the present.

Relax, do what you usually do in a room of people, say, "My name is (*Fill in name.*) and I'm an alcoholic.

So, let me guess, in semi-pro ball you intentionally got hit by pitches more than once?

It's been wonderful sharing a mental lapse with you.

It's funny how alcohol can take a person who is insecure, shy, and make them even more boring.

I guess, after you, the auto accident researchers decided to switch from humans to test dummies.

Hey, no one here is in your encounter group, we don't want to understand your insecurities.

You don't have to leave, I can just wait for the alcohol to evaporate and you'll disappear.

When I listen to you, I feel like I'm getting the *Disney Channel* on acid.

Insults to use on a drunk's delayed response time, poor reflexes, and physical uncoordination (cont.)...

When you see reality, do get an audio?

If I could read your lips, they'd say "open other end."

Is that your mouth or an exit wound?

Don't you have to get back for your bed check at the detox center?

I know you're having a difficulty expressing yourself, it's hard for you to relate to people who aren't on the same type of medication.

You're so wasted, I think we'll see you outside trying to jump-start your car by licking the ignition.

There are party animals, you're just a party vegetable.

You're wasted. I mean Keith Richards would look at you and say, "I've never been that fucked up, ever."

For you conspicuous consumption is drinking in public without a bag around the bottle.

How did you get here? Were you were thrown free from the blast and you're trying to get help?

Hey everybody, let's form a human wave and try to wash this person out of the room.

You know, coming from you, that's not much of anything.

What's it like to meet the same person on the way down?

> **Insults to use on a drunk's delayed response time, poor reflexes, and physical uncoordination (cont.)...**

Are you Charles Manson's imaginary playmate?

Were you a fourth grade science project that didn't work out?

It's hard to believe Ygor grabbed another deformed brain.

I'm afraid to say anything contradictory to you, because I hear it's really dangerous to wake a sleepwalker.

You wouldn't be this way if you bleached your needles.

Have you ever considered renting out your mind for use as a planetarium?

Why do I feel like I'm talking to a space shuttle remnant?

If you're here, they must have established direct flights between Earth and Uranus.

Eraserhead looks at you and says, "And I thought I was weird!"

Driving people *to* drink doesn't mean you're a designated driver.

When you step out of character, do you have to scrap off your shoes?

I think, you're a gaseous mass waiting to turn into a planet.

I've never met a living sundry before.

Say were you a stunt double in *Rain Man*?

Cutting Down Vanity Heads and Ugly Dinks

Insulting a person's physical looks:
Beauty is what's within you. Sure, it's a universal truth, but people don't believe it. Let Fred illustrate, Cyrano De Bergerac had noble soul but was considered an ugly person because he had a nose the size of a large meatball-and-onion grinder. But, when this legendary symbol of romance cruised for a babe, did he look for an eagle-beaked woofer with a beautiful personality? No! Cyrano fell in love with a noble soul that also had a lotta bucks, high-social ranking, a perfect nose, firm bazooms, and a real tight butt you could crack an egg on.

Purpose of this section: Identifies Vanity Heads or Ugly Dinks and teaches you how to deftly insult their style of dress and physical looks.

A brief precautionary preface on insulting anyone's looks

It's unconscionable to insult a person's actual face value. After all, biological shortcomings aren't caused by a selfish personality. How can anyone help being short, having skinny legs, cracked or missing teeth, crossed eyes, thinning hair, a severe case of acne, scars, an odd birthmark, wrinkles, hives, liver spots, fungal growths, unwanted facial hair, etc.? That's why it's cruel and indefensible to ridicule these physical characteristics. But, in the World Of Fred, there are ways *around* it!

Let us proceed...

Insulting a person's style of dress

No one can declare what's fashionable or stylish. But, if someone intentionally overdresses for an event, such as wearing high heels on a camping trip or dresses in dark clothes to a beach party, they need to be put in line with the program. The moment just calls for a slam. You don't think so? Come on, let's get real, if a fat guy wears a black-and-yellow striped shirt that makes them look like a bumblebee, they must be insulted.

Check it out, there are dysfunctional fashion plates dressed for a casting call in a movie no one plans to make (Most of these people can be seen waiting for the bus.). All these oddly attired disenfranchisers have one major thing in common: they actually believed they looked good when they left their home; or, what's even more unfortunate for them, thought it was the appropriate way to appear before a circuit-court judge.

For example...

Losers in search of style points

Bra-less older women in ridiculously revealing dresses, halter tops, or two-piece swimwear.

Bimbos who wear undergarments outside their clothing.

Jabba-The-Hut shaped guys who wear...
- jeans that reveal fault-line quality butt crack.
- pants way below their natural waistline.
- a bikini-bottom tiger-striped bathing suit.
- a small shirt revealing a bulging gut or underwear.

Girls with skinny legs who wear short skirts.

Suburban cowboys who haven't ridden a horse or put in a fence, but walk into bars wearing a cowboy hat, a western shirt, bolo tie, and cowboy boots (usually with the jeans tucked *into* the boots.)

Bogus dudes who dress like surfers but don't surf.

High-water types who wear pants that are too short (Their bottoms reach five inches above the ankles.).

Guys wearing shorts without underwear, so, their testicles hang out when they sit down.

Aging jocks who dress like they're still in their twenties.

Hipsters who wear sunglasses at night.

Jump-on-the-bandwagon fans who attend a party dressed in the full regalia of the hottest professional sports team.

Ding dongs who wear all dark clothing on hot and sunny days.

Aerobic housewives in Danskins that show too much cellulite.

Losers in search of style points (cont.)...

Anyone who....
- puts their tee shirt or baseball hat on backwards.
- misbuttons their shirt.
- shows a half open fly.
- has rings or pearl studs in their nose, tongue, navek, or too many in their ears.
- wears a dress shirt but underneath it you can see a tee shirt with writing on it.
- still has a dry cleaning or price tag on their outfit.
- a white suit in winter (hell, a white suit anywhere.).
- strolls about in a thong bathing suit.
- wears camouflage clothing and is not in the armed services, attempting to rescue hostages from terrorists, part of a SWAT team, or hunting.
- dresses in all green with a yellow tie.
- wears a felt hat in summer and a straw hat in winter.
- walks about in sandals with socks.
- has a partially shaved head.
- dyes hair red, green, or blue (most have a partially shaved head too.)*
- intentionally wears oversized clothing and doesn't lace their sneakers.
- tattooes their head, neck, or butt (which you can see when they wear white sweatpants.).

Balding men who have a long braided tail of hair sticking out from the back of their scalp.

Men or women who think they look like the latest sex object and wear the same hairstyle or dress like them.

Highly undeveloped male geeks dressed in tight-fitting garb designed for muscular men. (This type is big on Spandex clothing when they ride ridiculously over-priced bikes.)

---

*World Of Fred Note: 99.9 percent of the time, anyone with a tie-dyed pattern baldness look works in record/CD stores and is in a band.

The worst loser in search of style points:
Upper-middle class white people with dreadlocks who sport Rastafarian garb and speak like Jamaican, mon.

Clothing insults: the best way to go.

Ridiculing a person's style of dress is the safest and most versatile insult attack because...

- you're not insulting anything they can't change.
- without getting personal, you ridicule what a loser thinks makes them look cool, appealing, and individualistic.
- you don't have to dislike the person to insult them.
- you can slam friends to affectionately "bust stones."

> **The only reason to insult a person's looks**
>
> Never insult someone's physical looks unless they insult your looks or someone else's first.

For example...

    People who try on your glasses and disparage your eyesight: The most common offense made by Vanity Heads is comparing their eyesight to yours. They grab your glasses without permission, put them on, and belittle you, as if your hereditary eyesight was preventable. After humiliating you and extolling their vision, the Vanity Head returns your glasses (with slightly bent frames).

Vanity Head: 1.) Someone who derives their self-esteem through their physical superiority over others.

Vanity Heads
People who are beautiful on the outside but ugly on the inside

Without provocation or justification, these well-endowed Vanity Heads cruelly ridicule someone's race or physical shortcomings, such as height, weight, skin complexion, baldness, or age.

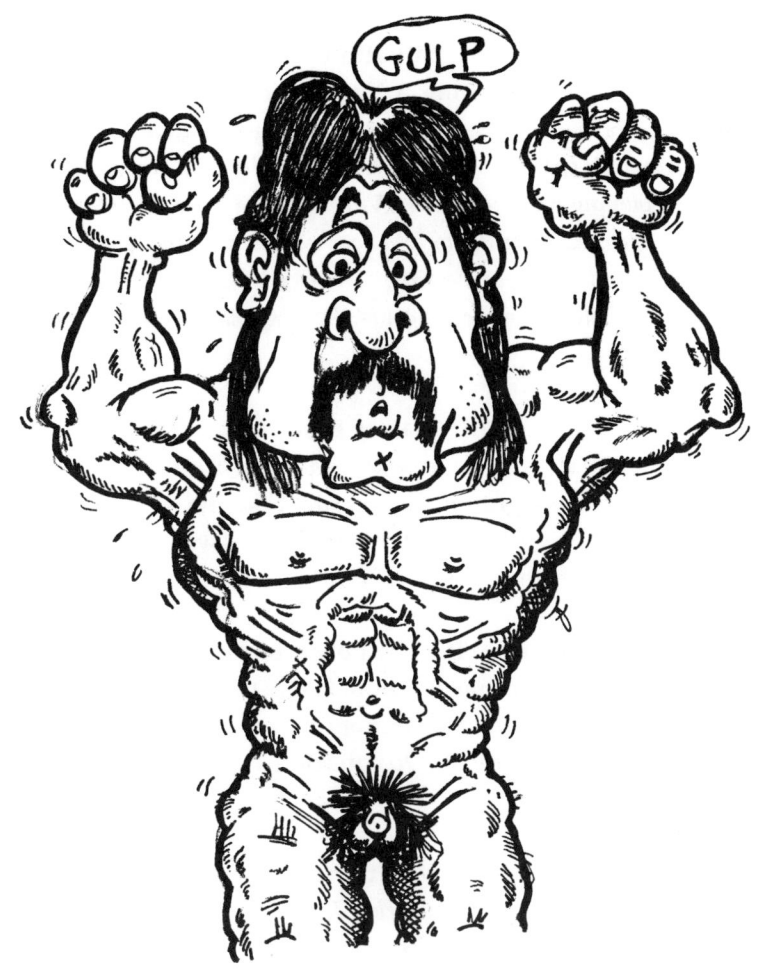

Big muscles but teeny weenie
Every vain person is arrogantly proud about their one dominant and perfectly shaped physical characteristic, but they are also completely attuned to their one particular physical shortcoming.

Vanity Head Insult Technique: Remember the basic loser vulnerability: their strength is also their weakness. The way to uncover this specific weakness is targeting the body flaw the Vanity Head is desperately trying to conceal.

For example...

Situation
Insulting A Vanity Head

*(Scene: juice and beer bar in a health spa. **Overweight Guy With The Power Of Insult And Live!** is standing by the water cooler. He has been playing racquetball. **Mr. Vanity Head** struts to the bar. He has just emerged from the weight room. He is wearing a sleeveless sweatshirt and shorts, along with a stomach belt. But, he's trying to conceal his balding by keeping his thinning hair in place with a headband.)*

Mr. Vanity Head
(Sharply slaps his hand on the Overweight guy's gut.)
Putting a little weight on there, huh? Like the love handles. *(Squeezes the man's biceps.)* You obviously don't work out. *(Pause.)* I use to weigh as much as you, but then I got *tired* of it.

Overweight Guy With The Power of *Insult And Live!*
I'm not buffed to the max like you, Fabio. *(Pause. This gives the insult more punch because the victim isn't expecting it.)* But, that hair! What did you do to it? Do you comb it like that to hide the blowhole?

Mr. Vanity Head
(Infuriated.)
Hey back off! *(Stomps away.)*

Post-insult Outcome: You won! You laced that spiraling insult through his defenses and scored a solid hit into the Vanity Head's sensitive area. Do your victory dance. Why did you win? Once again, it all fits into the denial transference principle: the loser is so in love with themselves, when someone rudely treats them the same way they treat others, it forces them to admit their flaws. They can't. The Vanity Head short circuits and storms off. Sure, the Vanity Head will dislike you. Complain about you. Belittle you. But, he won't pick on you again, will he?

Ugly Dink: 1.) A physically flawed loser jealous of anyone's good looks. **2.)** A loser who firmly believes an appealing person feels more attractive then them.

Ugly Dinks criticize attractive people for being vain about their appearance, but furtively revel within one particular aspect of their own appearance. For example, a fat person who admires their luxuriant hair, yet doesn't see their huge butt.

Ugly Dinks:
People who are ugly on the outside and the inside

An Ugly Dink is a Vanity Head turned inside out. Ugly Dinks refuse to admit their personality repels people. These envious uglies transfer their denial by refusing to see it's character not looks that makes a person popular.

Ugly Dink insult technique: Never attack the Dink's most glaring physical flaw, instead, tear apart the Ugly Dink's most attractive asset (This way you avoid seeming cruel.).

Most common unattractive dink:
Antagonistic man with a short-guy complex

Guys with a short-guy complex are over aggressive, predictably argumentative, and take jobs to push other people around. They compensate for their height by wearing 3-inch platform heels. Short-complexes walk with their arms out to take up more space. They take a combative dislike to anyone who is tall, easy-going, and has a sense of humor.

Here's how to insult someone's physical shortcomings without being cruel...

Situation:
How To Attack An Ugly Dink

*(Scene: Basketball court during an adult league game. A **Tall Guy With The Power of Insult And Live!** is driving to the hoop. **Man With Short-Guy Complex** is guarding him. The short guy is overly buffed, and reeks of cologne. He intentionally scratches the Tall Guy's arm while reaching for the ball. Then and out of frustration, tries to trip him. Referee calls a foul.)*

Man With Short-Guy Complex
(Furious.)
I can't believe you're calling a foul on that! I hardly touched him. The tall geek was pushing me around.

Tall Guy With The Power Of *Insult And Live!*
You're calling me a tall geek? I know with your build you'd never be a geek. Come on, with that build you couldn't be a bouncer at a bulimic bar.

Post-insult Outcome: You won! Why? You weren't cruel because you didn't flout the short guy's height. You did a reversal. You went after the Ugly Dink's build and exposed his vanity.

The lowest loser life form:
anyone who ridicules physically handicapped people

The cruelest losers openly treat handicapped people as "half a person." This low-life loser deserves to be insulted more than anyone else in this book. They are the truly handicapped. They don't see the beauty within a person because this loser has none in themselves. Their crippled spirit is unable to love.

Remember, losers adore themselves, they hate the thought of a stroke or accident that could physically disable them. They avoid funerals, never visit terminally-ill relatives or friends in the hospital, and refuse to listen to any description of someone's physical suffering. They deny their fear of mortality by seeking refuge within the alleged permanence of their youth, physical strength, or looks. They callously strike out at injured, retarded, maimed, brain damaged, disfigured, or aging people.

Insult technique: The only way to handle these low-lifers is to loudly point out their cruelty and insult them in front of the largest group possible.

For example...

Situation:
How A Wheelchair-bound Person Can Insult Low-life Losers Who Are Cruel to the Handicapped

(Scene: a supermarket. **Loser** *is hurriedly wheeling a shopping cart. A* **Wheelchair-bound Insult And Live! Person** *is shopping and is reaching for an item.)*

Loser
(Intentionally hitting the wheelchair with their shopping cart.)
Move.

Wheelchair-bound Insult And Live! Person
(Yells at Loser who doesn't turn around.)
It takes a lot to hit a person like me! *(Pause. People are looking at the scene.)* I wish they gave me this electric chair for killing you!

Post-insult Outcome: You won! You pointed out the loser's handicap and your superiority to them. If you can, follow the loser pushing the shopping cart around, and tailgate!

Insult and Live! by Fred Reiss

Insults for a Male Loser's looks

Oh yeah, you think you're a muscle man. Come on, you couldn't lift weights until *Nintendo* comes out with a game.

Nice tight body, I guess that's advantage to having a weight room in prison.

Were you the last goalie in the NHL not to a wear mask?

I think a blind woman waking up next to you would feel your face and say, "Oh, God, was I drunk last night."

Either you're buffed, or *Platex* has come out with a push-up men's bra.

What a stud! Did *American Gladiators* have a layoff?

You'd be considered an attractive man on any cell block.

For you, dressing for success means buying a new black lunchbox.

Nice build, you look like...
- a Ninja turtle without its shell.
- a lesbian without estrogen.
- a polyp with a neck.
- a penile implant with a toupee.
- a Chippendale's dancer with water retention.

Sir, why don't you gain weight, buy loud clothes, take up golf, and give up?

Nice face, have you thought of getting laser removal?

That's a real neat suit, matching tie, pants. Did you just come back from an altar boy banquet?

Insults for a Male Loser's looks (cont.)...

You're a "big"...
- When you work out on an abdominizer do you cause aftershocks?
- When you back up, do you beep?
- Is someone inside you working the levers?
- I've never met a pituitary gland on auto-pilot.
- Did a bolt of lightning hit the render plant's dumpster and you got up and walked away?
- A designer doesn't let out your clothes, he redistricts them.

Did you get cosmetic surgery to have the bolts removed from your neck?

Is that a chain through your wallet, or a pull-start?

Nice tight pants, I guess that's one of the advantages to buying men's pants with a boy's crotch.

Great outfit...
- If you're working in a pit crew.
- You a polka instructor?
- Do you get a free clipboard with it?
- Did they throw in a thermos with the shirt?
- Lost the organ, the monkey, but kept the work clothes?
- I didn't know a paternity suit came with a vest.
- You must be a golfer—your clothes don't match.

Do you work with computers? Or did Nerds R Us have a close-out sale?

Wow, nice look: the open shirt, the gold chain. Obviously there was a bargain at the Disco Is Dead factory outlet.

Insults for a Male Loser's looks (cont.)...

Insults to direct at guys in cowboy hats...
- Waiting for the rest of the posse, are we?
- Is there a *Village People* reunion?
- Yeah, cowboy, you wouldn't like my shoes, they don't have shit on them.
- Just killing time until you "Pah" shows up with the dump truck?
- Still chasing the dream they call rodeo?
- Are you one of the *Hee Haw* travelling All Stars?

Insults for adults wearing baseball uniforms in public...
- Isn't it a drag when you're the only one who shows up for your 15th Little League reunion?
- Bummed out because there's no one to flip baseball cards with?
- Real impressive getup, if you're nine.

Insulting a Female Loser's looks

Miss, you're definitely a nine, if I had three drinks.

Is that a birthmark on your forehead? Or, is that where your boyfriend's rests his beer?

You're a ten, on a transvestite scale, but still a ten.

If I felt you up, would it be a true or falsie test?

Why don't you shave your legs? Or are you a centaur in drag?

When you walk into a room, heads turn--*away* from you.

Insulting a Female Loser's looks (cont.)...

You'd be attractive, if men like waking up next to a woman who looks like Paul Scorvino.

Did your gynecologist get confused and put your ears in the stirrups?

Nice figure, but I guess bulimia isn't for everybody.

Like your make-over, who gives you cosmetics tips, battered women?

Look at it this way, the best thing about water retention is you're never thirsty.

Like your ankle bracelet, did it come with a kickstand?

Showing a lot of cleavage. It's attractive. Why don't you just lay on your back and be a bike rack?

Wow! I didn't know Stevie Nicks had activewear.

I like the fishnet stockings, you even have tuna and dolphins trapped in there.

I've never seen skin-tight pants with cellulite on them.

(If showing a lot of leg.) Like the *Pac Man* panties.

How do you decide if a dress fits you? Do you have a man come in the fitting room and pull it over your head?

Like the bracelet, incredible what they're doing with wrist leashes.

Couldn't get any floppy clown shoes to match the purse?

Insulting a Female Loser's looks (cont.)

Jez, that's odd, you waxed your chin, but kept the mustache.

Miss, have you ever thought of hanging plants from your armpit hair?

Is that a purse or...
- a canteen?
- a large case for your diaphragm?
- are you delivering mail today?
- do they make female condoms with straps?

Your jewelry is top drawer—from a tackle box

That's a marvelous necklace, I love what they're doing with chewable candies.

Loser hair cut-ups

Nice way to style your hair, love that weed whacker trim.

Like the hair, couldn't get the sides cut any shorter because the lawn mower would take off your ears?

Do you do that to your hair intentionally, or were you attacked by vandals?

Even guys in the armed service laugh at that "do."

That's the most hair I've seen on a mole.

Great perm. Do you have a schitzu dog growing out of your head?

Nice mustache, how do you get your nose hairs to do that?

Loser hair cut-ups (cont.)...

Scarecrows usually stand in the cornrows, they don't stand under them.

Nice Mohawk, do you work during the day as a driving tee at a golf range?

How'd you get the beard, did the Velcro come off your inflatable doll?

Come on, you're not a natural blonde, let's face it, the one thing you have in common with Kunta Kinte is *black* roots.

Nice haircut...
- I like the haircut, didn't realize *Supercuts* had a drive-thru window.
- Tough when those first-grade yearbook photo crewcuts don't grow back.
- Odd way to comb it, did you come out of a fire and they tried to push your scalp back?
- Is that styling gel in your hair, or were you sitting in front of Pee Wee at the theater?
- Like the long hair, I see *Guns N' Roses* has a lay-away plan.
- It's wild, looks like someone shot a bird sitting on your head.
- Do you have to maintain your hair that short to keep your job as a security guard?
- If you want to look like an unwatered lawn.
- You look like a vibrator with a part.

Unisexual Loser appearance insults (lines that be used for either sex, or if you're unsure of a person's sex.)

You look like you just punched your way out of a microwave popcorn bag.

With that face, do you startle burn victims?

You know, if fungus were in style you'd be hip.

If you were a plastic surgeon, you'd still be working on your self portrait.

I have wear to glasses to see, you don't, but you have no depth perception, so it evens out.

Is that your complexion, or are those the chemicals you work with in the lab?

I've never met someone with a vaccination mark on their face.

Like the tie-dye, you in between *Grateful Dead* shows?

Ooooooh, love the nose ring. It's really a great look, if you want to look like a hand grenade.

Do you dress that dull all the time, or are you heading out to an assessor convention?

Like the flannel shirt and the bluejeans and workboots. Somewhere there's a lesbian without clothing.

That's the first suit I've ever seen made from carpet remnants.

Insult and Live! by Fred Reiss

Unisexual Loser appearance insults (lines that be used for either sex, or if you're unsure of a person's sex.) (cont.)...

Like the tie, is the shirt a clip-on?

Is that a rental costume or do you live in *(Insert name of a local hick town)*?

Cool threads, hard to part with that old band uniform?

Is that a bolo tie? Or, you just couldn't cut the umbilical cord?

Are you test marketing Michael Jackson's outfits?

I see, your fashion consciousness is still in a coma.

Look at all this color coordination. It's like "The Night of the Living Macy's Display Case."

Nice military uniform. The Army, "Be all you can be." You've peaked.

Boy, I want to get a reggae knit cap like that. I just want to look like a human cat toy.

Are those your real clothes, or are you just wearing that stuff because you're doing your laundry next door?

Nice cologne, flea dip?

I like the necklace, I think the leash clip is what makes it.

Really like that red blazer, when do you get the *Century 21* patch to go with it?

Unisexual Loser appearance insults (lines that be used for either sex, or if you're unsure of a person's sex.) (cont.)...

Is that birthmark from the doctor pulling you out, or pushing you back in?

Nice shirt...
- Guess the rest of the bowling team couldn't make it.
- Didn't realize *Domino's* had Springwear.
- It's nice that dropcloths are in style.
- Just get out of a game of paintball?

Nice earring, were you tagged by the humane society and released?

Is that a bracelet or one of the electronic parole monitors?

That a tattoo? Or did someone write "wash me" on your arm?

Did you make that face as a child and it stayed that way?

Is that an ankle tattoo? Or, is that a mud line from last year's flood?

You have an interesting look, I've never seen a paramecium without the aid of a microscope.

Looking at you is enlightening. It's like seeing a flea magnified 1,000 times.

Are you two twins? Or bad sequels?

You have an athletic build--of a six year old.

Sharp look, a combination blazer and self restraint suit.

Unisexual Loser appearance insults (lines that be used for either sex, or if you're unsure of a person's sex.) (cont.)...

Bulimics have in one thing in common: your picture over their toilet.

You have one of those faces that says, "Admits to six more slayings, bringing total up to sixty."

Nice outfit...
- Goodwill Industry wouldn't accept that clothing.
- I like the back-to-the-sea look.
- Did you get it after working five years as a crossing guard?
- I didn't know *Green Acres* had a gift shop?
- *(Dressed in all white.)* Did someone call for a medic?
- Let me guess? Court appearance?
- Hey, does the vest double as a reversible life jacket?
- An attractive look, if you're on a roller derby team.
- Did the police evidence room have a garage sale?
- I didn't know vocational schools had a dress code.
- Didn't know *Burger King* had a new uniform.
- You must be the fashion consultant to the homeless.
- How do you shop, cruising for an unraided drop-off bins?
- Did you have to notify next of kin before you can wear it?
- So, years ago, I guess undertakers didn't bury people in their clothes.
- You have a job interview for a bike messenger spot?
- Did you get first-place in the many-uses-of-weather-stripping contest?
- Obviously, you're cross dressing until you decide to go ahead with the sex-change operation.
- When does the rental run out on those clothes?
- You can stand next to a "Dip" sign and validate it.

Handicap-access insults wheelchair-bound people can use to sideswipe losers in wheelchairs

Don't push it, or I'll let the air out of your tires.

I'd like to buy you a drink, don't worry, I won't make you crawl for it.

It's incredible how someone can overcome a physical handicap, but still be burdened with a personality such as yours.

I see you were the only one to survive the accident.

So, *Ironside*, are you on your way to solve a crime?

I bet you're really glad you wore your motorcycle crash helmet?

---

*World Of Fred Note: Just as the world has handicapped access, Fred adheres to the same principle. In the spirit of insulting everyone on a politically correct level, He has written these lines for wheelchair-bound people to use against others in wheelchairs.

Handicap-access insults wheelchair-bound people can use to sideswipe losers in wheelchairs (cont.)...

Say, I'd like to take a guess at what you did? Mine sweeper?

Wow, I didn't know Stephen Hawkins had an untalented brother.

Does your wheelchair run on gas or is your colostomy bag full?

Why are you here? Are they remaking *Born On The Fourth Of July*?

I didn't know they gave purple hearts to people who contracted diabetes?

Nice uniform, is there a photo shoot for *Special Olympics* baseball cards?

After meeting you, I don't feel too bad about taking up those two blue parking spaces.

Insults wheelchair-bound people can use against insensitive losers who have perfectly functioning bodies but poorly tuned minds*

I wish they gave me this electric chair for killing you.

After meeting you, I have a good mind to just get out of this chair and beat the shit out of you.

You know, you better run, I drive without insurance.

The only way I'd ever be handicapped is if I were related to you.

If I'm physically challenged, then you're physically offensive.

What are you looking at? What do you think I am? The opening scene for *Sunrise At Campobello?*

Your face would improve with tire tracks.

After I'm through with you, you'll have *real* skid marks on your underwear.

If you don't move, you'll go from human being to speed bump.

Bitter because I tagged you out in the *Special Olympics?*

Have you ever been hit in the face with a bag of urine?

*****World Of Fred Note:** Fred dedicates this section to the late Benjamin Stewert, a wonderfully funny comedian who performed in a wheelchair, and had an aggressively sick mind. His heart walked upright.

Heckling Hack Comedians

Hack Comedian (also known as a "road comic"): 1.) A comedian who uses old jokes, insults, or stolen material. 2.) A comedian who juggles, does magic, uses props, plays guitar or an organ, sings rap songs, and uses all those talents to do stock premises, stolen material, as well as jokes that are ethnic or penis-oriented. (For example, a typical song parody by a Hack: change "Since I was a young boy, I played the silver ball" from The Who's 'Pinball Wizard' to "Since I was a young boy, I played with my own balls."

Purpose: Helps identify Hack Comedians and teaches you how to heckle these generic comics with their own "stock material."*

Why you must insult Hack Comedians

Hack Comedians deserve to be insulted because these generic performers earn their living by insulting you with material that's not even theirs.

For example...

Situation:
Getting insulted by a Hack Comedian

(Scene: You're sitting in the front row of the Ha Ha's Comedy Club. A Hack Comedian is bombing on the stage. **You Without The Power To Insult And Live!** *are quiet and polite, want to be entertained, but don't find this opening-act comedian very funny. You paid to see the headliner, Fred Reiss, whose book you purchased and loved.)*

Hack Comedian
This bum is walking around the town, drinking booze, and throwing up. And he was the mayor! *(No one laughs. The Hack points at you.)* So, what do you do for a living?

You Without The Power Of *Insult And Live!*
(Not wanting to be part of the act.)
Nothing.

Hack Comedian
So how do you know when you're done!

*****World Of Fred Note:** The term "stock material" connotes the use of old jokes or tired premises for routines, for example: the differences between dogs and cats, men who don't put down the toilet seat, women who apply make-up while driving, men who comb over their bald spots, how white people can't dance, etc. "Stock" material is so widely used it's considered by professionals as public domain.

You must discover the heckler within you to insult Hack Comedians

Insult technique: "So how do you know when you're done?" is a stock adlib used by thousands of Hack Comedians. Like all losers, the Hack's strength is their weakness. You see, if the Hack is getting their lines from stock material, what's to prevent you from using the same material to heckle them? If the Hack points out to the crowd you're saying a stock insult, the comic has to confess they were going to use the same line.* So, true to the loser coda, the Hack avoids confronting the truth by getting angry at their accuser.

---

*World Of Fred Note: Hacks are notorious joke thieves, but justify the theft by claiming they "tell the joke better." Most Hacks become whacky morning disc jockeys, where they use material they've stolen from other comedians, or steal material by paying a joke service (whose authors stole material from other comedians.).

Let's replay the scene...

Take Two:
Revenge of The Heckler

Hack Comedian
So, what do you do for a living?

You With the Power Of *Insult And Live!*
(Not wanting to be part of the act.)
Nothing.

Hack Comedian
So how do you know when you're done! *(This remark gets a huge laugh.)* Nice shirt, some—

You With The Power Of *Insult And Live!*
I like your shirt too, somewhere there's a Pinto without seat covers! *(You get a laugh. The Hack is stunned. Hit them again with another line.)* Hey, don't quit your day job. *(Audience laughs again.)*

Hack Comedian
(Furious.)
Hey, no one paid to see you! So, shut the fuck up! I'm trying to do comedy here, asshole!

Post-insult Outcome: You won! You forced the Hack Comedian to actually be funny instead of using a line they've stolen, and because losers don't have a sense of humor, the comedian lost it. The audience will side with you over the comic. No one likes a funny man who can't laugh at themselves.

**Warning:
If you heckle a comic make sure it's a Hack Comedian.**

It's wrong to heckle a comedian. Before you insult a performer it's very important to be certain they are a Hack Comedian. The only way you can identify a Hack is by their use of stock material ad-libs, and squelch lines. Since the average comedy consumer doesn't know the difference between stock jokes and original material, the World Of Fred is going to provide you with an example of a typical Hack Comedian's stage act, including ad-libs, and insults.

What is going to follow is a facsimile of a typical Hack Comedian's performance. After you have experienced it, you'll be able to easily tell the difference between a Hack Comedian and an original performer who deserves your respect.

Ready, it's show time...

Hack Comedian Act
"An Evening at Ha Ha's Comedy Club"

(*Scene: Evening. We are in Ha Ha's comedy club in a hypothetical town of Newark, which is a medium-sized city near a farm town called Livermore. It's a smoke-filled nightclub. Nearly everyone in the audience has gotten into the club on a free pass. Rock music blares from the speakers. The music stops. The room lights dim. The spot lights come up on a small stage We see a microphone in a stand, beside it, a bar stool. Behind the stage is brick wall with "Ha Ha's" painted on it.* **The Clubowner**, *an overweight and balding man in his late thirties steps on the stage.)*

Clubowner
(*Touching the microphone.*)
Testes, testes one two. (*Stops touching the microphone.*) Mike Test, Mike Test, phone call. Mike Test. (*Takes out a note.*) Will the gentlemen who owns a beat up Pinto in the parking lot, please remove it, you're embarrassing the club. Ladies and gentlemen, are you ready for comedy! *(The crowd goes "Yeaaah" or barks.)* Well, your first act this evening at Ha Ha's, a very funny man who plays all around the country. Ladies and gentlemen, a big hand for your opening act! *(Exits stage.)*

(*The* **Hack Comedian** *hits the stage. He is holding a beer, which he puts on the stool. He is wearing a blazer, a tee shirt with a comedy club's name on it, bluejeans, and sneakers. He takes the mike from the stand.*)

Step 1.
Introductory Hack Comedian Remarks

Hack Comedian
Thank you. How about a hand for Bobby Dodge, your club owner. Bobby and I are good friends and male lovers. Just kidding, we're *not* good friends. Hey don't laugh sir, he's more

woman than you'll ever need. Oh boy, it's nice to be in Newark. It's great to be playing at my favorite club. *(Pauses. Looks behind him on the wall for the club's name. Finds it. Turns back to the crowd.)* Ha Ha's... I could have been playing Las Vegas tonight. I got a call from my agent about a gig there. But, I said, "No, I'd rather be in Newark." Yes, Newark, the gateway to Livermore. I was in Livermore last night, yeah nice town.

Audience Member
(From the back of the room.)
Boo!

Hack Comedian
You from Livermore, sir? Then, I'll talk real slow. *(Pause.)* You're really from Livermore, wow! *(Looking about the stage.)* So this must seem like Vegas to you. Livermore. Make you feel at home. *(Does a sheep baaaing sound and acts like he's humping it.)* Yes, Livermore, where cowpoke is a verb! *(Audience laughs.)* Okay, so we've established the level of the crowd. You're a sick group, and I like it. Well, it's great to be here in Newark. This is a nice town, when they finish it. I love the college near this place, after you graduate they let you keep the tools. What else is going on? Hey, Livermore has to be better than the South. Really, it's nice to play to people with *teeth* for a change. And dense. They have the "Dukes of Hazzard" on PBS. In the South there are guys named Bubba who are their own father and mother and sister and brother--you don't have a choice, it's the law. Everybody looks like extras in 'Deliverance'. I'm talking about a place where the zip code is E-I-E-I-0. The South where "shitload" is a unit of measurement. Folks, you can't make this stuff up. *(Pause.)* But you don't make fun of the South down there. *(Imitates a Southern voice.)* "Boy, that's not funny." *(Makes the sound of a shotgun being loaded and cocked. The Hack pauses. He surveys the room.)* Here I am doing comedy in the cellar of a restaurant just outside Livermore, my career is really on fire.

Part 2.
Warming up the room

Hack Comedian
(Talking to audience members.)
I see a table of all guys together. What is this a computer date mix-up? Or are you guys from San Francisco? *(Goes to a table that's talking.)* Hey, did I give you guys permission to break up into small discussion groups? Let me guess your names? Your name is Bob and his is Neil, are those your names or is that what you do?
(Goes to the next table.)

Look at this, one guy with three women. I think it's a safe bet to ask how much cocaine you're carrying. *(The audience laughs. Hack says to the laughers.)* At least we know who the dealers are in the crowd. *(Back to the same table again.)* Come on, one guy three women, either you're carrying drugs or you're hung like a horse. And since you're white I think we know what the answer is! Pow!
(Goes to another table. A guy sitting all alone.)

You seem normal sir, but I'd feel a lot better if you look at me without keeping both your hands under the table. Hey, I'm sorry. Waitress, bring this table a drink and charge it to that guy over there. *(Points to a guy he previously talked to. Pauses. Sips beer.)* So where you from, sir?

Audience Member
Here.

Hack Comedian
Can you be a little more vague, sir? Are these questions too hard? Say, did you go to school on the small bus? You two guys should heckle me at the same time so I can get stereo assholes. I'm kidding, you're a big guy. Big. I mean when you lay on the beach do Greenpeace workers try to push you back into the ocean? *(Pause.)* Sir, are you in show business?

Audience Member
No.

Hack Comedian
Then get your feet off the fucking stage! By the way sir, nice to see you back in men's clothes again. *(Pause.)* Any Mormons here? *(Silence.)* Funny, I saw their bikes parked out in front. You know what I'd like to do, find out where a Jehovah's Witness lives, go to their door, and wake them up at seven in the morning! *(Looks over at another table. Reaches over and takes a dollar off it.)* Jez, you shouldn't leave the money lying around like that. *(Goes to another table.)* Where you from? *(There is a long pause. Comedian makes the sound of a buzzer like it's a quiz show game.)* Wrong answer. Try again. You know, the questions get harder when we enter the bonus round. So where you from?

Audience Member
Australia.

Hack Comedian
Australia? So, I guess you'll be spending the night instead of driving back home. You're from Australia? I can see why you'd want to come to Newark for vacation. Yeah, you're going through the map, "Let's see honey, shall we go to Paris, London, Venice? I tell you what, let's go to Newark!"

Audience Member
(Another drunk yells something no one can understand.)
Allageealllaaah

Hack Comedian
You want to throw a vowel in there, sir? Just yell out any incoherent shit. *(Gestures to the drunk but appeals to the crowd.)* Yes, ladies and gentlemen, another alcoholic who should have remained Anonymous. *(Pause.)* I'm kidding, it's nice to see the same brain cell shared by two guys. *(Takes a sip of beer.)* What do you say we just start a wave? *(The audience does the wave.)* All right, that was good. Now, let's have all the women show their

cleavage. *(Pats his pockets.)* Really, let's relax and get to know each other. Everyone turn to their neighbor and grab that person's crotch. *(Pause.)* Anyone have a cigarette? *(Gets one from the audience and pulls out a pack from his pocket and puts he cigarette into it.)* Thank you. Five more and I'll have a full pack. *(He looks around and finds a table that looks like a first date.)* This is a nice couple over here. Lovely couple. Are you dating or just using each other? Or is she you're social worker, sir?

The Guy In The Couple
It's a first date.

Hack Comedian
It is! Why don't you give the girl a little kiss right now? *(They kiss.)* Now go for a little titty. *(Goes over to another female.)* So, you seem young. Go to school?

The Woman From The Couple
Yes, Livermore Community College.

Hack Comedian
What do you need to enter that school? A number-two pencil? *(Pause.)* What the hell, my parents sent me to school for eight years to become an architect. Now, I'm a comedian in Newerk, I bet they're proud. *(Quickly goes over to another table and grabs a dollar bill.)* I just told them not to do that you should have listened. *(Pauses.)* You guys are a nice crowd. Last night these people kept on yelling, "You suck get off the stage!" Finally, I had to say, "Mom, Dad, please." *(Moves to another table.)* Where are you from?

Audience Member
Australia!

Hack Comedian
(Goes over to the Australian guy.)
Hey, I think I found you a ride home. *(Goes to another woman.)* Excuse me Miss, I'm getting an echo, please keep your legs crossed. You heard me lady. And don't bother me. I don't jump

on the bed when you're working. *(Pause.)* Excuse me, my throat's dry. Can I take a little sip of your water? *(Reaches over, takes the glass, and sips.)* Really, don't mind the cold sore. It's going away. *(Pause. Lowers mike stand to crotch level.)* Want to hear a little ventriloquism? *(Goes to another woman.)* Miss, you look a little German. You sure you're don't have a little German in you?

Audience Member
No, I don't have a little German in me.

Hack Comedian
Would you like some? *(Pause.)* Take a chill pill lady, you look like you're only twenty-five--in dog years. *(Pause.)* Angry because a house fell on your sister?

Unknown Female Audience Member
(The woman starts shouting.)
You're not funny.

Hack Comedian
(To an oooohing audience.)
Hey, relax. I'm a professional. I can handle this situation. I have a wide repertoire of witty putdown lines to choose from. *(Flips off the person.)* Fuck you! *(Pause.)* Hey lady, don't bother me. I don't go to where you work and slap the dick out of your mouth. You know Miss, if we had seventeen more of you, we could make a golf course. But folks...*(Takes another sip of beer.)* You're a good group, let's all join hands and start singing "Kumbaya"? *(Points to a guy who is returning from the bathroom.)* You're trailing paper. *(Goes to a couple.)* So what do you do for a living, sir? *(The man doesn't respond.)* Sir, I'm...*(Points to himself.)* ... speaking...*(Points to his mouth.)* ...to... *(Points to the heckler.)* ...you...*(Does a masturbatory gesture.)*

Wife
(Answering for the husband)
He's a loser.

Hack
(To the husband.)
Incredible how you're able to throw your voice into this woman without her sitting on your lap. You know, if I leave you alone you heckle yourself. *(Says to the guy.)* So, sir, you're a loser. I guess you're not going to get laid tonight. *(Pause.)* Thanks for sharing.

Step 3.
The act

Hack Comedian
I was watching television and I saw this ad for the Marines. How's that for a segue, folks? Anyway, this Marine ad said, "We do more by nine o' clock in the morning than you do all day." Is this suppose to make me want to join? *(Laughter.)* Oh, yeah. Sign me up. You know what I'm saying here, people? You can't make this stuff up! *(To a woman who has a high squealing laugh.)* Hey, lady. You sitting on your keys? *(Does homosexual voice.)* "Marines. We're looking for a few good men." *(Pause. Back in his normal voice.)* How many people think I do that voice a little too well? I was talking to some guy during one of my shows and he says, "You a fag?" And I said, "Why don't you and your wife bend over and we'll see which one I fuck first." *(Pause.)* Folks, I'm straight. There's something about homosexuality I have a hard time swallowing, you know. *(Bends over.)* Hey, where I come from this is an exit not an entrance. I've been in San Francisco, I dropped my car keys, no way was I going to bend over and pick them up. I'm kicking my keys all the way back to New Jersey. *(Crowd groans.)* Oh come on! You'll be telling it at work tomorrow. And you'll be telling it wrong: "So this guy says can I help you and he fucks his wife in the ass." And I'm not gay. In fact, the other day I got my first blowjob. I didn't like the taste. By the way, I know that I've said the word

"fuck" a few times, and for those who might be offended by the word, I'd just want you to know I say it with a "ph." *(Pause.)* I'd like to do a quick impression, you like impressions? You do, well then go ahead a do one, sir. No, here's my impression of every sorority girl I've ever known. *(Hack takes a sip of the beer and spits foam out of his mouth and says in an angry woman's voice.)* "You said you were going to tell me when you were close." *(Pause.)* Oh yeah, like I'm the only one. It's crazy, folks. Everyone's talking about safe sex. I believe in wearing a condom. In fact, I'm wearing one right now. *(To an audience member.)* You ever seen the writing at the bottom of the condom?

Audience Member
No.

Hack Comedian
Well, maybe you haven't rolled it down far enough! Pow, badda-bing! Guys, they have condoms now that are ribbed "for her pleasure." I'm selfish. I wear mine inside out. *(Pause.)* Is it just me, or do you think every car that has a ski rack should have a sign on it: "Not a cop!"? Let me tell you a little about myself. I live alone. Surprise! I'm actually going on a diet, I'm trying to get back down to my original weight: six pounds, three ounces. Badada bing, folks. *(To the waitress.)* Can I have a tequila please? *(Back to the crowd.)* It's important to drink folks, remember, the more you drink the funnier this shit gets. See, cause I'm not one of those studs. You ever see these macho weight-lifting guys? And really, after making their muscles larger, all it does it make their dick look smaller! *(Pause.)* My father walked in and caught me masturbating. He said, "Son, you keep doing that and you'll go blind." I said, "Dad, I'm over here." You know, they pay people to donate sperm. When I think of all the money I've let slip through my fingers. My sister came home and found my father stirring his beer with her vibrator. She said, "What are you doing?" He said, "Just having a drink with my future son-in-law." Let me tell you about myself, how's that for a segue? My neighborhood was rough. How tough? Anytime you stared at someone and they took it personally, "Hey, yo! You got a problem. I got your problem right here!" And these are the

girls! *(Pause.)* "Gilligan's Island," explain this show to me. They got a guy called The Professor who can make a radio out of coconuts, but he can't fix a hole in a goddamn boat! *(Pause.)* The bank told me my account was overdrawn, I asked, "How could that happen? I still have plenty of checks."

Audience Member
(Yells out.)
You suck!

Hack Comedian
Yeah, and you swallow. *(Pauses. Returns to his act.)* I'd like to give you people an update on my life, I'm dating now, thank you very much. And I'm really excited about it. Because—well, I'm married. I'm kidding, I just broke up with my girlfriend. *(Pause. Audience give a mock sympathetic "oooooooh.)* Yeah, she wanted to get personal. She wanted to know my name. I like saying that joke. The guys on dates want to laugh, but they'll wait to see if the woman laughs before they do. Because they know if they laugh and the woman doesn't, they're not going to get any! *(Sips beer.)* Man, it's crazy. I just look at the world in a weird way, you know. Like, they say cocaine is killing all these athletes. I've learn my lesson, I've given up sports. I don't like cocaine anyway, I just like its smell. *(Pauses. Takes sip of beer.)* You ever read the instructions on shampoo? I know it's weird, but this is my job, think up weird shit during the say and tell it to you guys. The instructions say "Lather. Rinse. Repeat." My question is: when do you know when to stop? *(Pause.)* First, before I go any further, I want to say women are smarter than men. *(Usually gets applause from the women.)* But come on, yesterday, I saw this ad for a vinegar and oil douche, are you with me on this ladies? I guess it's nice to have a douche that can double as a salad dressing. You know, I have a tattoo that says, "Mom" on my butt. But when I bend over it says, "Wow." *(Takes another sip of beer.)* You know what the great thing about Alzheimer's disease is? You're always get to meet new people every day. *(To a female.)* Watch out lady or I'll have Ted Kennedy drive you home. *(There are boos.)* Oh yeah, boo me, like I killed the broad at Chappaquiddick. Fuck me with a sharp stick.

(Pause.) I don't need this gig folks, I have a paper route. *(To another female.)* So Miss, how long have you been married to this guy? I'm sorry, that's too personal a question. How much do you weigh?

Woman In The Audience
We've been married four months.

Hack Comedian
And they said it wouldn't last...*(To the woman.)* Aren't men stupid? I mean we're dumb and always wrong. *(This remark gets applause by women in the audience.)* I said that because it makes women like me and I want to get laid.

Part 4.
The big finish

Hack Comedian
Okay, I have to go. But I want to leave you folks with a take-home joke you can say tomorrow. First do you want clean or dirty?*(Audience yells, "Dirty!")* Okay, the teacher tells the class I want a story with a moral. The boy gets in front of the class and says, "I was carrying some milk, and it spilled, and I cried. And the moral is don't cry over spilled milk." Another guy says, "My father was in Vietnam and he had a gun, and a machete, and a bottle of Jack Daniels. The Viet Cong came over the wire. My Dad mowed down forty of them with his gun, then chopped up the other twenty with the machete." The teacher says, "What's the moral of the story?" The kid says, "The moral is don't fuck with my old man if he's been drinking." *(Takes another sip of beer.)* I want to tell you guys, you've really been...an audience. And we've had crowds all week and you guys have been one of them. I'm kidding. Well folks, I have to go. I have another gig *(Checks watch)* in March. *(Pause.)* How about a hand for our waitresses? *(Audience applauds.)* They're carrying my children. All of them. I'm kinda proud of that. And please, remember to tip them. Oh hell, just push them over. No, really, they survive on your tips. And remember drugs cost just as much for them as they do for you. Hey, they're $30 short of a gram and they

share with the comedians. *(Waitress brings up the tequila shot. Hack downs it.)* And remember folks, if you've been drinking and you're going to be driving, when you leave this club, drive real fast! Oh, by the way, this week I just signed a contract with HBO. *(Audience will usually applaud.)* Thank you. I get to see two movies each month. *(Pause.)* You know a lot of performers say, "You're such a lovely audience I'd like to take you home with me." You guys have been good, but if I catch any of you guys in my house, I'll beat the crap out of you. Thanks again for supporting comedy. For those of you that want to see me again, next week I'll be playing a bus terminal in Livermore! You guys have been fun. Good night and God bless you.

Other ways to spot a Hack: fake adlibs

Hacks attempt to give the impression they are making spontaneously witty comments on various situations that predictably happen throughout a comedy show.

Here is a list of various situations and the Hack's predictable response:

If an audience member arrives late, a Hack says...

"We all just took off our clothes and got naked when you were gone, now it's you're turn."

"Tell you what you missed." *(Then repeats a medley of the last six jokes.)*

"You're late, you are the period of this room."

"You're late. The show already started. We're going to chip in and buy you something, like a fucking watch."

As a person heads to the bathroom, the Hack Comedian says...*

"Relax it might be gas."

"Hey, the small ones fill up real quick don't they?"

"Anyone who thinks they're gay please report to the bathroom immediately."

(*Stares at them.*) "You're going to the bathroom?" (*Folds arms.*) "We'll wait."

"Why are you going to the bathroom without your friends, just don't want to share what's in the vial?"

(*To Guys.*) "You going to show each other your dicks?"

(*To Women.*) "Where you going? Shopping?"

(*After the person has left.*) "Let's go to the video camera hidden in the bathroom to see what they're doing."

*****World Of Fred Note:** Here's an optional routine...After the person has left the room, the Hack finds out their name. He says to the crowd: "Let's goof on them. When they return, I'm going to say, 'And that was in the car.' And you people are going to start laughing and stand up and applaud me like it's the funniest thing you ever heard." The person comes back, the Comedian says, "And that was in the car." Everyone laughs and gives him a standing ovation. The Hack says to the person, "See what you missed."

Anytime a waitress or patron loudly drops or rattles glass, the Hack Comedian says...

"Just put that anywhere."

"Don't you hate those hard contacts?"

"What is this, a Jewish wedding?"

"Nice to know Thumbelina could make it."

If a joke bombs, the Hack Comedian says...

"Thanks for sharing my pain."

"Some I just do for me."

(To the one person laughing) "Sir, you want to run around the room and make it seem like a crowd."

"You'll get that one on the way home from the club."

"When you guys get silent as a group, you really do a good job."

"You're not laughing, but somewhere in a comedy club in a parallel universe people are pissing in their pants."

(When someone hisses.) "Are you hissing? Or, is your date losing air?"

"That wasn't a joke, it was a cry for help."

(Makes a whooshing air sound and passes a flat hand above the head.) "I guess that one went over you."

If a joke bombs, the Hack Comedian says (cont.)...

"I never knew dead people could sit up."

"I feel like I'm staring at trout." (*Stares. Opens and closes mouth like a fish.)*

(Taps microphone.) "Is this thing on?"

(Flips the people off.) "Fuck you people, that's funny".

"Remember, I can piss on you from here."

"It's so quiet in here, I can hear a pinhead drop."

How Hack Comedian uses the microphone stand as a prop, or make comments about it during their act...

(Holds the stand and moves it across the stage like it's a metal detector.) "Beep, beep beep."

(Turns the stand upside down, and spins its round base.) "I'm a desperate man. I'll flood this place."

"Quick impression." *(Points to the thin mike stand.)* "Karen Carpenter." *(Crowd boos because the star died from anorexia.)*

(Angles microphone in stand like it's a handle, lifts the upper portion of the stand like it's a dynamite plunger.) "I told you I'm desperate. I'll blow this place up!"

(Limply dangles the microphone down to their knees and holds onto the cord. Says to table of men.) "Look familiar, boys?" *(To women, but said in an apologetic male voice.)* 'Honey, this has never happened to me before.'"

(Dangles the microphone from its stand so it resembles a pole and line.) "Let's go fishing for assholes."

Insult and Live! by Fred Reiss

Insult and Live! by Fred Reiss

Insult and Live! by Fred Reiss

Insults used by all Hack Comedians

When I want to hear from an asshole, I'll fart.

(To a drunk.) What did you say? I don't speak quaalude.

Is that your head or did your neck throw up?

If your IQ gets to 60, sell.

I do my act like you have sex--*alone.*

Watch out or after the show, I'll let the air out of your date.

When you masturbate do you like to be on the top or the bottom?

If your dick was a big as your mouth, you'd have a date tonight, sir.

Did your dog leave you for another leg?

How old were you when you found out your mother and father were related?

You're so ugly that when you cry the tears don't go down your face, they go over the back of your head.

After you got a drink of water, did you hurt yourself bumping your head on the toilet seat?

When you got a divorce, did you ask, "Can we still be cousins?"

You're so small you have to stick your thumb up your butt to get your dick to pop out.

I can't believe they club seals and let people like you live.

Insults used by all Hack Comedians (cont.)...

Save your breath pal, you'll need it to blow up your date.

I see the detox center has an outpatient program.

I'd like to meet your parents so I can get the blueprints to build my own asshole.

The last piece of ass you got is when your finger went through the toilet paper.

If I want any shit, I'll just squeeze your head.

Why don't you wear a condom over your head so you can be a *real* dick.

You're so small, you don't go for length, you fold it in half and go for width.

If your mother swallowed, I wouldn't have to deal with you.

You're what you get when cousins marry.

When you go to a mind reader, do you get 50 percent off?

Here's an example of a fetus not getting enough oxygen.

(To an older person.) Proof only the good die young.

With a personality like that you must save a lot of money on birth control.

You're one drink away from being brain dead, and I'd like to buy you that drink.

When I go hunting for assholes, can I use you as a decoy?

Insults used by all Hack Comedians (cont.)...

I get *paid* for being an asshole, what's your excuse?

It's hard to believe that out of three million sperm you were the quickest.

Sir, I'd call you a cocksucker, but I hear you're trying to quit.

Are you in the Army? No? You told someone to cut your hair like that?

If I want any lip from you, I'll pull it off my zipper.

Hey, I don't interrupt you at work when you say, "Do you want fries with that?"

Think you're such a smart ass, sit on some ice cream and tell me what flavor it is.

When have sex, do you hit your head on the coffin lid?

After you take a drink of water, do you hit your head on the toilet lid?

(To someone extending a middle finger.) Is that your IQ or penis size?

To understand you I need an English-to-Butthead dictionary.

Losers you should *never* Insult

Warning!

Insulting certain losers in denial can result in personal injury, loss of limb, or life. A key giveaway is a flat affect look in the eyes: a blank stare that doesn't register any focus. This look is accompanied by a rant against the world. The person isn't speaking to you, they are speaking to their pain. If you become part of the discussion, they see you as their pain, and physically attack you. Disturbed losers think they're disturbed because people keep unjustly telling them they're "crazy." People who try to bring the dejected, gun-wielding maniac back to reality make this mistake, so, they unfortunately get shot for telling the gun-wielding maniac, "You're crazy!" If the loser were sane they wouldn't be wielding a weapon.*

---

*__World Of Fred Note:__. That's why if a whacko threatens someone at gunpoint and the person goofs and calls the loser a nut, the person becomes--in the whacko's mind--the physical embodiment of all the loser's mental problems. You know what happens then? Bang! Bang! Bang! You go from valid census figure to a death toll.

Losers you should never insult

Inner-city youths

Simian-shelf types who smack themselves and grunt, "Stupid!"

Conan-like men bearing cell-made tattoos who loudly vow, "There's no prison that'll keep me locked up."

Adherents who know "God's plan" or talk about an "Avenging Angel."

Goons with heavily scabbed knuckles who believe hitting people is a way to express a point of view.

Recently fired civil servants.

Loners who keep to themselves, are quiet, and never bother anybody.

Slightly disoriented people with institutional ID bands on their slash-scarred wrists.

Tire-iron toting bums who wait at traffic lights, approach your stopped car, wipe a dirty rag across the windshield, and demand cash for smearing it.

A cellmate in the drunk tank who calls you "cupcakes" or "sweetmeat."

Mass-transit passengers who glare at you for no apparent reason.

Hunters who shoot their weapons near residential areas.

Banana Republic generals who throw a coup and declare a "state of siege" until the military can restore law and order.

Losers you should never insult (cont.)...

Religious adherents who claim you are an "infidel."

Coworkers who you accidentally catch smoking PCP during their breaks.

Intensely disoriented males who hang around jogging trails at dusk.

Huge da-kine Hawaiians floating on surf boards who give you stinkeye at their home break.

Shotgun-carrying ex-husbands who enter a county office and rail against the unfair burden of their child-support payments.

Messianic mothers obsessed with getting their teenage daughter on the cheerleading squad.

Belligerent police officials with a heavily scuffed night stick.

Smelly and poorly dressed people who hang by the magazines and newspapers in the public library reading rooms.

Panic-stricken people who have diarrhea and are desperately looking for a public toilet.

Last-call boozers who stagger in roadhouse parking lots, have caked white powder on their nostril rims, and carry a pool cue.

Every other person in a bus terminal.

Fanatical old ladies dressed in baseball uniforms who sit in the bleachers at a major league game.

Anyone dressed as Jesus Christ.

Teenage guerrilla foot patrols in the jungle near a border.

Losers you should never insult (cont.)...

Strangers who hang out in housing project stairwells.

Rude mob hitmen sitting tableside by the stage.

Anyone who seems to be reaching for a concealed weapon.

Machete-swinging tribesmen walking through the aisles of commuter trains in Third World country.

Strung-out wackos who claim you are one of the inner voices speaking to them.

Returning veterans frozen in mid flashback.

Drunk roofers who just finished working on a hot summer day.

Overly emotional people who have no one in their lives but just experienced the death of their favorite pet.

Bat-wielding racial supremacists.

Anyone over twenty-five years of age who is still obsessed with their childhood dreams and walk around with a well-thumbed and heavily underlined copy of *Catcher In The Rye*.

Rude relatives of local organized crime figures.

Turkish prison guards.

The Final Solution

No matter how guilty a loser is, they always see themselves as the victim.

Purpose: Ends the book with a final solution to the world's problems.

The Final Solution

The most common drawback all losers share is lying to themselves about their true natures. They are secret identities without super heroes. Lying to yourself is where all our problems start. Anytime we lose our direction in life it's because we've veered from the wavelength that feeds our passions and nurtures our strengths. Occasionally, we've all been guilty of it. It's when we exchange the risks to chase our dream for the safety of financial or emotional security that kills our dream.* It's when we take a job that's against our principles. It's when we say "I love you" and don't mean it. It's when we pull back from taking a professional gamble. It's when we go along to get along. It's when we cling to our habits and possessions instead of going out of our way to help stragglers. We become a disoriented animal caught in a trap of its own making who can't distinguish the pain they feel from their imprisonment apart from the compassionate assistance of a stranger trying to free them. We impulsively lash out at anyone and everything. We constantly criticize and judge people's motives. We become dependent instead of independent. We can fight the world but not ourselves. We can't face the person we really are inside. That's the a reflection we avoid through any diversion such as booze, drugs, promiscuity. We just can't face that reflection of ourselves because all we ever see in the mirror is the traitor who conspired with the enemy. We become losers in denial.

The enemy isn't other people. It's ourselves.

---

*World Of Fred Note: Sometimes we have no choice. We can't afford to pursue our path due to responsibilities we have to others, such as an illness in the family, or the welfare of our children. Still, if a we avoid a reconciliation with that challenging path, we start to hate ourselves, look bored at our jobs, and dislike the people around us. You have to say goodbye to the enemy within before you can say hello to the world.

The Loser's self-imposed life sentence: Solitary confinement without parole

No matter how frustrated you are with a loser, you can never hate a jerk more than they hate themselves. These Me-Myself-And-I misfits only see their criminal motives in other people. These morons don't possess a conscience, their world gets smaller and smaller each day. That's why losers watch their back all the time. Whatever offense these remorseless jerkoids get away with is one more crime they suspect other people will attempt to do to them.

Haven't you noticed that...

- moochers are quick to point out other moochers?
- name droppers are quick to identify other name droppers?
- cheaters are quick to spot other cheaters?
- users quick to detect users?
- phonies quick to see through phonies?
- etc.?

Isolated social theorists self-righteously posit we should be aware of the emotional and economic factors that screwed up the poor deprived loser so badly this victim of society can't distinguish between right and wrong. Get it? We're responsible because losers never had the same advantages we had. It's our fault!

Now, let's try to cash that theory with a reality check. It bounces. Losers consciously develop an intricate screening system of self-deception and highly complex subterfuges to manipulate any sign of human compassion as an opportunity to exploit a situation to the loser's advantage. They use being a victim as a guise to be an aggressor, blame someone else for the crime, and continue on to their next offense. After all, the loser reasons, we drove them to the act, and someone besides themselves has to pay for their behavior. But, just because a loser hasn't conscience doesn't mean they don't know the difference between right and wrong.

If a loser doesn't know right from wrong, then why do...

- murderers hide the body of their victims?
- shoplifters look around the store before they steal?
- child-abusive parents refuse to take their injured kids to hospitals for medical treatment?
- corrupt bureaucrats shred documents?

Really, if the loser's bent logic can't distinguish right from wrong, then why conceal the deed? *

These tenured social diagnostics cite us part of the problem which perpetuates the growth of more losers. We're told losers are

---

World Of Fred Note: The obvious exception to this theory is an insane person. But most of the time, if a loser can tell left from right, they can tell right from wrong. They're selectively dysfunction. Let's take a slightly extreme example: most murderers and sickos have day jobs. But do they offer their coworkers the flesh of one of their victims at lunch? No. So, they do know there are moments in life when they have to properly function. It gives them the opportunity to strike. A loser knows what's right and wrong. They just don't *feel* they're wrong.

a symptom of a disease in us. Everything could be solved if we became conscious of the loser's underlying motivations and try to reach them. Yeah, right. These social profs can pass themselves off as compassionate humanists because these problem solvers don't have to live among the losers they study.

Losers expect us to understand every detail of their lives, but they don't even bother to understand us. How come they don't realize we haven't been privileged enough to have the same *dis*advantages they had? Who cares if a loser rationalizes their crimes and cruel behavior and rude acts because the victim represented something within the loser they didn't like? Or, because the loser was abused as a child? Or, because of an unresolved conflict with the loser's mother? Or, because the loser grew up poor and was deprived of things others had? Or, because their father never gave them support? All losers give out highly articulate excuses for their faults, but can't find any reason to be an *improved* person. The real issue is change can only come from within a person, they have to confront their personal shortcomings and atone, and if they don't, they're coming after us!

Losers don't have underlying motivations. They have motives. Who cares if we're aware of the loser's psychological problem, the problem should be aware of itself. Our only choice is to duck their bullet, run for cover, install a security system, find a weapon, put up the shark netting, call the police, check the batteries in the stun gun, hit the fire alarm, change the motorcade route, or *insult* them!

Losers hate themselves so they hate you. It's that simple. Why not verbally slam them? If they're not going to like you, they might as well really not like you. Insult them. Force them to see themselves for what they are. Stick their nose deep in it! Insult them. Make them miserable and angry and resentful. Insult them. Let them scream and rage about you. Make them a victim of themselves. Insult them. Let them cry injustice and threaten the jury. Let them rattle their cage. Insult them. Give them a one-way ticket back to their personal hell. It's the only way to make your inner life a happier and more peaceful place in the World Of Fred.

How Losers will deny their similarity
to the Jerks described in this Book

The Ultimate Denial
Rejecting The World Of Fred
or Fred

Denial. The Big D. Even losers who know better, when confronted with their flaws, aptly deflect being identified in the World of Fred's by...

    a.) attacking Fred's personal life.*
    b.) belittling Fred's economic status.**
    c.) dismissing Fred's mental abilities, such as saying there is "some truth" to what Fred said, but that his Fredness lacked depth because he reduced people to stereotypes.
    d.) criticizing Fred's own shortcomings, or sexual performance.***
    e.) heckling him on stage during his show.
    f.) questioning his surfing abilities.****

Let Fred say this, Fred is more than a person, He is a being, a state of mind, a presence. You are Fred and Fred is you. When you are attacking him, you are attacking yourself. In order to illustrate this point, Fred has tried to anticipate how the losers in this book will react to their depictions.

For example, to see how losers in denial respond to seeing themselves in this tome, check out the opposite page...

---

*World Of Fred Note: Valid
**Another World Of Fred Note: Extremely valid.
***Yet Another World Of Fred Note: Go ahead if it makes you feel any better.
****You're kidding, Yet Even Another World Of Fred Note: Hey, make fun of Fred as a man, demean him as an economic unit, scoff at his sexual prowess, criticized his comedy, but leave His surfing out of this!

Insult and Live! by Fred Reiss

About the Illustrator

Ron Winnick has been drawing ever since he can remember being able to hold a pencil. (Just a pencil?--**Fred note.**) He has always drawn cartoons as a way to entertain others and as a personal form of relaxation and meditation (This sounds heavy, but he grew up in Santa Cruz--**Fred note.**) He has a BA degree in radio and television production and worked for ten years in TV broadcasting, where his graphics and cartoons were featured on the nightly news. Ron currently works as a computer artist/animator for a large publisher of children's education software. He resides in Campbell, California He has a wife, Susan, and two small sons, Spencer and Morgan. He and Fred are currently on speaking terms and socialize, but as they both succeed in life, the friendship will become estranged and bitter.

About the author

Fred Reiss is an insult comedian who goes on the stage with a scoreboard. The premise is: he gets a point when he insults the audience and the crowd gets a point when they insult him. He is author of *How To Abuse And Insult Everyone*. His Fredness has appeared on Fox Television's *Comic Strip Live!* He hosted "Ask Fred," a popular insult-call talk show on San Jose's KSJO 92.3 FM, the number one rock station in the San Francisco Bay area. After being treated for testicular cancer, Fred decided to do what He does best: insult people. He has worked as a journalist, and held a variety of other dead-end jobs. He attended Antioch College and studied American Literature and Theatre. He lives in Northern California where he surfs a longboard.

If you wish to order a copy of *Insult And Live!* signed by His Fredness, send $14.95 (Add two dollars for shipping and handling) to:

Fred Reiss
P. O. Box 3523
Santa Cruz, Ca. 95062

Also, Fred offers a *Fred's Pocketbook Of Insults,* a tiny booklet of insults you can carry in your pocket or purse. The price is $2.00 each, or get five booklets for $5 (both booklet prices include shipping).